Children's Perspectives on Domestic Violence

Audrey Mullender

Gill Hague

Umme Imam

Liz Kelly

Ellen Malos

Linda Regan

SAGE Publications
London • Thousand Oaks • New Delhi

SAGE Publications Ltd
6 Bonhill Street
London EC2A 4PU

SAGE Publications Inc.
2455 Teller Road
Thousand Oaks, California 91320

SSAGE Publications India Pvt Ltd
B-42, Panchsheel Enclave
Post Box 4109
New Delhi 110 017

British Library Cataloguing in Publication data

A catalogue record for this book is available from
the British Library

ISBN 0 7619 7105 X
ISBN 0 7619 7106 8 (pbk)

Library of Congress Control Number: 2002103334

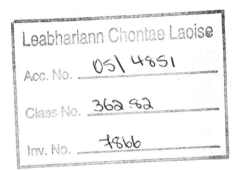
Typeset by C&M Digitals (P) Ltd., Chennai, India
Printed and bound in Great Britain by Athenaeum Press, Gateshead

Contents

About the Authors

Audrey Mullender is Professor of Social Work at the University of Warwick where she chairs both the School of Health and Social Studies and the Faculty of Social Studies and directs the Centre for the Study of Safety and Well-being (SWELL). She has over twenty years' experience of teaching social work, prior to which her background was in the statutory social services. She is the immediate past Editor of the *British Journal of Social Work* and has herself produced well over a hundred publications in the social work field, including more than a dozen books. Notable amongst these are: *Children Living with Domestic Violence: Putting Men's Abuse of Women on the Child Care Agenda* (edited jointly with Rebecca Morley and published in 1994 by Whiting and Birch) and *Rethinking Domestic Violence: The Social Work and Probation Response* (published in 1996 by Routledge). Her research has spanned women's issues in domestic violence and responses to perpetrators as well as services for children. In 2000, she was elected to the Academy of Learned Societies for the Social Sciences and she is a member of the Sociology, History, Anthropology and Resources College (SHARe) of the ESRC.

Gill Hague is the Joint Co-ordinator of, and a Senior Research Fellow in, the Domestic Violence Research Group of the School for Policy Studies at the University of Bristol. This group conducts national and international studies of domestic violence and offers wide-ranging consultancy, teaching and training on the issue, working broadly alongside the major practitioner organisations in the field and Women's Aid in particular. She holds professional qualifications in social work and in pre-school education, as well as a doctorate in social policy. She has worked on violence against women issues for nearly 30 years as an activist and has specialized in the issue as an academic since 1990. Overall, she has 20 years' experience as a social worker and has worked in academic teaching and research since the 1980s. She has written extensively on violence against women, as well as on other subjects, and, with Ellen Malos, is recognised as an authority on multi-agency work and domestic violence. Her publications include the popular overview book with Ellen Malos, *Domestic Violence: Action for Change* (second edition, Cheltenham: New Clarion Press, 1998) and many widely-read reports, papers and government briefing notes on the inter-agency approach. She has also written on the views and voices of abused women, and on children's issues, historical perspectives, international responses and housing issues, all in specific relation to domestic violence. Recent collaborative work (some with other authors of this book) includes research for the British Council, the ESRC, the Joseph Rowntree Foundation and the Home Office.

Umme Farvah Imam is Head of Community and Youth Work Studies at the University of Durham, specializing in issues concerned with race and gender. Born and educated in India, she was formerly employed at Roshni, Asian Women's Association, Newcastle upon Tyne, and was a co-founder of Panah, the black women's refuge there. She has been active for over a decade on wider issues of preventing and responding to the abuse of women and children in the black and Asian communities. She is one of a tiny number of minority ethnic women in Britain combining this particular professional and community involvement with related academic research interests focusing on domestic violence, particularly its impact on children and young people. She is currently drawing on British and South Asian literature to conceptualize the impact of abuse in the lives of young Asian women, and is forging links with academics and women's organizations in India for future research activity on this topic. Her publications include 'Asian children and domestic violence' in Mullender, A. and Morley, R. (eds) *Children Living with Domestic Violence* (London: Whiting and Birch, 1994) and 'Training Black Women in Newcastle upon Tyne' in *Training European Women: A Study of NOW Projects in Four European Cities* (NOW joint Evaluation Project, Newcastle upon Tyne, 1995). She was co-editor of the 'Black Perspectives' issue of *Youth and Policy* (49: 1995). She has presented at national and international conferences on her range of interests, including in a workshop at the major conference on children living with woman abuse that was held in London, Ontario, in June 1997.

Liz Kelly is Professor of Sexualised Violence and Director of the Child and Woman Abuse Studies Unit at London Metropolitan University. She has worked in the field of violence against women and children for almost 30 years. She jointly undertook the key British work on the prevalence of sexual abuse in childhood. Prior to, and alongside her academic role, she has been active in establishing and working in local services including refuges and rape crisis centres, and in local, regional and national campaign groups. In the early 1970s she worked with children in a refuge in East Anglia. Her internationally respected groundbreaking work on women's experiences of male violence was published as *Surviving Sexual Violence* (Cambridge: Polity Press, 1988) and is known in the USA through a chapter of a standard text of the same year: 'How women define their experiences of violence' in Yllö, K. and Bogard, M. *Feminist Perspectives on Wife Abuse* (Newbury Park, CA: Sage). She is also one of the key thinkers who has made the connections between woman abuse and child abuse, challenging family dysfunction theories, and setting a clear research agenda for further work in this field in her chapter in Mullender and Morley's 1994 book *Children Living with Domestic Violence*. Her theorizing continues to broach new territory, dealing currently with topics such as abuse in lesbian relationships, trafficking in women, the public focus on the term 'paedophile', and the issues surrounding 'victim' and 'survivor' as long-term core identities. She chaired the expert group established by the Council of Europe to formulate a plan of action to be adopted as official policy. She also increasingly provides expert testimony in court and advises the media in her areas of interest. She was awarded the CBE in 2000 for services combatting violence against women and children.

Ellen Malos is a Senior Lecturer in the Domestic Violence Research Group of the School for Policy Studies at the University of Bristol. Her work spans interests in child care, domestic violence and gender studies. Funded work has resulted in research reports, conference papers, chapters and articles on custodianship, family violence, and an edited book *The Politics of Housework* (1980, revised in 1995 for New Clarion Press, Cheltenham). She has undertaken policy research work with funding from the Joseph Rowntree Foundation, the Department of Health, the Lord Chancellor's Department and the Economic and Social Research Council. Currently, she is co-ordinating a four-university collaborative evaluation of the domestic violence multi-service interventions in the Home Office Crime Reduction Programme.

Linda Regan is currently a senior research officer at the Child and Woman Abuse Studies Unit, London Metropolitan University, where she has been based for over 10 years. During that time she has been involved in over 30 research and evaluation projects, presented at numerous national and international conferences and delivered training to participants in both the voluntary and statutory sector at home and overseas. Linda is a member of several advisory boards and is a trustee of the Emma Humphreys Memorial Prize.

Acknowledgements

We should like to acknowledge the invaluable work of Wendy Dear, Cassie Hague and Christina Pantazis in Bristol, and particularly the extensive efforts of Sheila Burton in London and Parveen Akhtar in Durham, at various stages of the research on which this book is based. We should also like to thank all the schools and their pupils who were involved in Phase I of the project, the agencies who helped to locate a sample for Phase II, and, most especially, all the children, young people, their mothers and key professionals who gave unstintingly of their time to be interviewed. Thangam Debbonaire, former National Children's Officer of the Women's Aid Federation of England, kindly provided consultancy during the early stages of the research team's work. Whilst, as authors, we naturally take responsibility for any errors that may have crept in, we are delighted to have shared a commitment to completing this important project with all those who helped us undertake it.

1 Children in Their Own Issue: A Shift of Approach

INTRODUCTION

No precise figures are available as to how many children in the UK live with domestic violence.[1] We do know, however, that there are many and that they are everywhere because this can be extrapolated from studies of the number of women who experience abuse. Mooney (1994), for example, had self-reports from approaching one in three women, across all social and ethnic groupings, that they had experienced violence worse than being pushed, grabbed or shaken at some point in their adult lives. Since her study was designed to take a representative sample of the general population of women, we may assume that many of those interviewed had children living with them at the time the domestic violence occurred. Certainly, the British Crime Survey in 1996 found that half the women who reported experiencing domestic violence in the previous year were living with children under 16, and that having children in the household was associated with an increased risk of assault (Mirrlees-Black, 1999).

There is now a widespread recognition that children living in households where their mothers are abused by partners or ex-partners experience considerable distress (Jaffe et al., 1990) and frequently display adverse reactions (Wolfe et al., 1986). Yet, though some practitioners and policy makers now go as far as regarding this as a form of indirect abuse, mainstream services are still failing to give the most appropriate help (McGee, 2000; Mullender and Morley, 1994; Peled et al., 1995). This book will suggest that part of the problem is that the children and young people themselves – those who live with domestic violence going on around them – are not being listened to and that their own understandings of their situation are overlooked, as are the ways in which they attempt to deal with it. There is a wider issue, too, about educating the public, at all ages and beginning in schools, about domestic violence and what can be done about it.

Professionals and policy makers in a range of public and voluntary sector agencies do now recognize that they should be responding to children who live with violence but are often confused as to what to do (Abrahams, 1994; McWilliams and McKiernan, 1993). There is a tendency to encompass domestic violence as just another child protection issue (Humphreys, 2000a; Parkinson and Humphreys, 1998), without acknowledging the complex interactions between women's safety and children's well-being (Kelly, 1994b). Although there is a clear overlap between direct child abuse and domestic violence (see summaries in Morley and Mullender, 1994, and in Hester et al., 2000), focusing too narrowly on safeguarding children without a raised awareness of the potential for partnership with the non-abusing parent and for tackling the perpetrator's behaviour can lead to dangerously ineffectual responses both for women and children. Women are left in fear of their lives, opportunities are missed to keep children safe, and dangerous men are avoided (Farmer and Owen, 1995, pp. 223–6; Hester and Pearson, 1998; Humphreys, 2000a). Women's services, especially Women's Aid, with its 30-year history of working with children accompanying their mothers into refuges, have developed a more integrated approach (Ball, 1990; Debbonaire, 1994; Hague et al., 1996). However, it is not always accorded the respect it deserves by those responsible for policy and practice in the statutory sector so that, once again, the safety of women and children is not maximized.

When the academic and professional debate first started in this field, children were conceptualized in conference titles and training events as 'passive victims' or 'silent witnesses'. The present authors' earlier work (Hague et al., 1996; Kelly, 1994a; Mullender et al., 1998) showed, on the contrary, that children who live with domestic violence have their own coping strategies and their own perspectives on what happens to them. Each child reacts as an individual. There is no one pattern of responses and no syndrome to sum up the impact of their experiences (Morley and Mullender, 1994). This realization led to a conviction that research in this field must involve children directly, as well as those who care for and work with them. It also means that, as users of services, children require interventions tailored to their levels of understanding, their age and stage of development, their particular viewpoint, and their specific circumstances. There are dangers in adults making assumptions about children's needs, rather than basing policy and practice on evidence from child-centred research.

The earlier work by the present authors further suggested that, over time, most children are able to talk about their experiences and that their views could inform a more coherent interagency response. Very little research to date has been designed with the intention of hearing the voices of children and young people about domestic violence, either in general terms or concerning how those who have lived with it cope with and make sense of their experiences. The present team (Hague et al., 1996; Kelly, 1994a; Mullender et al., 1998) had already revealed the potential for this within previous carefully designed and sensitive studies. There is an urgent need to know more about children's experiences as they perceive them, the impact these have, how children make sense of them, the responses they receive from various agencies, and whether there is any fit between what children feel they need and what they get. Readiness to incorporate messages from research on this topic is indicated by the rash of publishing on domestic violence, for example in relation to social work (Mullender, 1996; Pryke and Thomas, 1998; Thomas and Lebacq, 2000) and health (Bewley et al., 1997; Mezey, 1997; SNAP, 1997; BMA, 1998), and by levels of activity in reviewing policy and practice (e.g. Mullender and Humphreys, 1998; Humphreys and Mullender, 2000).

The primary objectives of the major research study reported in this book were, in the first phase, to learn about children's general understandings and perceptions of domestic violence and, in the second phase, more specifically, to learn from children who have lived with domestic violence what they consider would be the most helpful forms of response. This latter point includes building on children's agency in the situation and not treating them as passive victims. In order to meet these aims, a multi-methodological, multi-stage approach was employed which will be outlined in detail in the next chapter. Particular care was taken to include ethnically diverse voices and to consider the gender implications of girls' and boys' responses about men's and women's behaviour.

The remainder of this chapter will explore why it seemed important – and potentially possible – to conduct such research, and what knowledge we were building on, including from our own earlier work.

CHILDHOOD STUDIES

Academic interest in childhood and in 'the child' has gone under the generic title of the 'sociology of childhood' (perhaps misleadingly, since sociology does not have the longest tradition here and is only one of many disciplines involved) or 'childhood studies' (James et al., 1998). Broadly, it may be seen as part of a challenge to researchers' accounts of 'the other' (including from standpoint and post-modern approaches), in this case of perceptions of children and of concepts of childhood constructed by adult observers. We now understand that adult representations and interpretations of children's lives might say more about the observer than the observed and, to avoid this, it has come to be seen as essential to convey children's own accounts at first hand – to include their voices. France et al. (2000) see this also as a feature of 'grounded theory' (Glaser and Strauss, 1967); that is, as theory emerging from the data so that, rather than preconceptualizing children's lives, we are able to build our understandings on hearing from children and young people themselves about what the issues are for them and how they make sense of what they are experiencing. In fact, the implications go wider than grounded theory, having relevance for every research methodology and method, both within quantitative (Hill, 1997a; Scott, 2000) and qualitative (Hill, 1997a; Mauthner, 1997) traditions, with an increasingly participatory role for children themselves, right through to acting as their own researchers (Alderson, 2000).

Such a paradigm shift has not been easy to make. Adults have been accustomed to regarding children as growing up into the adult world – being educated and socialized so as to be assimilated into (adult) society – which carries the connotation that children *qua* children are incomplete, that they are becoming rather than being (Qvortrup, 1994). They are somehow seen as not yet competent, not integrated into adult concerns and understandings, purely because of their stage of biological and social development. Developmental psychology, always one of the strongest influences on child care policy and practice, for example, is grounded in this kind of deficit model of childhood (Butler and Williamson, 1994) and all the earliest work on children and domestic violence falls within this tradition, as does most of the related research that continues in North America. Children are thereby marginalized as a source of information about their own lives, and too readily ignored in the design and delivery of policy and practice responses.

But other approaches are possible. Childhood is now understood as socially constructed (Archard, 1993; Ariès, 1979; Jenks, 1982) since children are regarded in different ways by adults according to historical, social and cultural context and are expected to behave accordingly. For example, children are still expected to remain innocent yet, nowadays, to learn to protect themselves from abuse (being taught in school about stranger danger, less often about the potential dangers at home). Childhood is also a context in which part of everyone's life is lived, in whatever era or cultural group they are born. All the big issues of contemporary existence and of social science – the role of the State, shifting morality, the state of welfare, the (de)construction of the family – can be looked at from and in relation to the perspective of childhood; all these matters impinge on children and children have their own attitudes towards them. Children who live with violence, for instance, form views about why it occurs, whose fault it is, and whether anyone from outside should intervene.

Children search for their own meanings and understandings in what happens to them and they act accordingly. Thus childhood is not simply socially constructed within a culturally relative context or biologically determined through processes of child development; children also have agency within it: 'childhood is a negotiated process where children are active in constructing their own social worlds, and reflecting upon and understanding its meaning and significance to their own personal lives' (France et al., 2000, p. 151). This may seem an odd claim to make in introducing a study about a phenomenon – domestic violence – where both the children and their non-abusing parent are held under the power and control of the perpetrator (Pence and Paymar, 1996), sometimes virtually to the point of being imprisoned in their own home. The findings from the study reported here will show, however, the many ways in which children do form their own views and take their own actions in order to survive in such an adverse situation. Chapter 5 will explore in some detail the coping strategies they adopt. This raises new issues for parents and professionals about explaining to children what is happening when their mothers are being abused and involving them in decisions about what will happen in their lives as a result. It connects with some quite deep-seated questions as to whether children are ontologically different from adults and whether or not adults have a ' "natural" right to exert power over children' (Qvortrup, 1994, p. 3). We are used to seeing adults as the more important social actors and as acting in the best interests of children, nowhere more so than in child care policy and practice. Some of the conclusions of this book will challenge whether adults always make the right assumptions about children and their needs in situations where there is violence, and will call for a radical rethink.

CHILDREN'S RIGHTS

Rights for children have received both philosophical (Archard, 1993) and more policy-focused attention in the literature (Franklin, 1995). After many years of the children's rights movement in various countries of the world, children do now have limited individual rights. These are enshrined most notably in the 1989 UN Convention on the Rights of the Child, ratified in the UK in 1991. In particular, children have the right, under Article 12 of the Convention, to express their views in all matters affecting them. Children also have a right to have their wishes and feelings taken into account by local authorities and courts who are making decisions about them under the Children Act 1989.

When it comes to domestic violence, however, questions have begun to be posed as to whether the current enunciation of children's rights is sufficiently sophisticated to encompass the complexities of living with abuse (Kelly and Mullender, 2000). In relation to the UN Convention, there is no doubt that children require protection by the state from all forms of abuse, exploitation and neglect (Articles 19 and 34) and to have their survival and development ensured (Article 6) by policy and practice responses that operate in their best interests (Article 3). How this is best achieved can, however, become a vexed question where there is one abusing and one non-abusing parent and the Convention offers no clarification in these circumstances. It encompasses, for example, both parents providing guidance (Article 5), maintaining contact (Article 9), being protected from interference with privacy, family and home (Article 16) and sharing primary responsibility for bringing up children (Article 18), all without acknowledging that there is a difference in every one of these regards between a parent who is posing a threat and one who is seeking to protect. An abusive parent may well not have the child's interests at heart and may be using parental guidance to instil ideas of male dominance, for example, or seeking post-separation contact so as to regain the opportunity to abuse and intimidate (Hester and Radford, 1996; Women's Aid Federation of England, 1997; Radford et al., 1999). Exposure to the perpetrator may be damaging or dangerous for the child as well as the woman. In other words, issues of parental contact, care and guidance are not equal or neutral where the situation involves violence and abuse. Similarly, an abusive man kidnapping his child does not in any way equate with an abused woman fleeing with the child to safety, yet Article 11 (the state's obligation to try to prevent and remedy the kidnapping or retention abroad by a parent or third party) makes no apparent distinction between abduction and protection. The child's mother could be accused of kidnapping the child and preventing her or him from having contact with the other parent if the situation is not seen in gendered terms or analysed in relation to the power, control and abuse that drive its dynamics. The UN Convention does not recognize that two parents may not have a shared view of good parenting and that, in many contexts, they are not 'equal' either in the home or before the law. Its apparent neutrality in encompassing both parents is therefore actually working to reinforce and collude with their inherent inequality. As a consequence, we would argue that children's rights cannot be fully pursued unless women's rights are also taken on board in any situation where both are being threatened. Indeed, we would go further and argue that the UN's consideration of children's rights should be meshed in with its work on women's rights, notably through the Convention on the Elimination of All Forms of Discrimination Against Women (CEDAW) (an optional protocol which has not to date been signed by the UK).

This dilemma concerning an abusing and a non-abusing parent also occurs under the Children Act 1989 if the state, in the shape of social workers, does not distinguish between the culpability of the two. A common manifestation of this is an accusation against an abused woman of 'failure to protect' her children, even when she is in fear of her own life and typically without offering her any help to preserve her own safety so that she can better care for her children (see Humphreys, 2000a, for a fuller discussion). Often, this is a thinly veiled attempt to persuade the woman to leave her abuser, with little understanding that she may be in intensified danger if she does so (Wilson and Daly, 1992). A third of women killed by male partners and ex-partners are already living apart (Edwards, 1989) from men who appear to work on the premise 'If I can't have you, no one will'. Overall, then, the debate about children's rights needs to be gendered and to take on board the risks of abuse both of children and their mothers.

RESEARCHING WITH CHILDREN

The direct corollary of the theoretical and legal developments outlined above, in recognizing the social agency and voice of children, is that research should focus centrally upon them, accepting that their 'social relationships and cultures are worthy of study in their own right' (James and Prout, 1997, p. 4). Is researching children different from researching adults? This may depend on whether we regard children as uniquely vulnerable and in need of protection (Morrow and Richards, 1996), which would tend to place them in a passive and ultimately silenced position. France et al. (2000) argue that grounding research in the views and experiences of those being researched, in this case children, is the same practice as with adults but that, within this, it is necessary to respect difference. The key issues, they argue – teasing out the practical issues which flow from adopting a different ontological position – may be the age difference between the researched and the researcher, together with the way the latter is perceived, the need to develop methods most likely to help children and young people express themselves, and the particular dynamics of consent and confidentiality. The latter were of even greater concern to the present authors, given the sensitivity of the topic we were exploring (that of abuse), and will be dealt with at some length in the next chapter.

What has to change if we are serious about researching *with* children rather than conducting research *about* children? Research with children – and the theory and resultant policy and practice it generates – will only be rounded and useful if it is based upon:

- taking children seriously
- seeking to understand children as people in their own right
- acknowledging children as social actors in the social contexts of their own lives
- acknowledging children as playing a role in society as a whole

- conceptualizing children as having their own life arenas, their own concept and use of time, and their own activities, which are not ... merely colonized by adult society for its own purposes and interests.

(Based on Qvortrup et al., 1994)

According to Mayall (1996), placing children at the centre of our research requires three methodological shifts. It means regarding children as competent and reflexive in reporting on their own experiences, giving them a voice and taking seriously what they say, and working for children rather than on them in ways that may lead to the betterment of their social worlds. All three of these aims applied to our own project and to a growing body of work that preceded us in other fields of enquiry.

THE ETHICS OF RESEARCHING WITH CHILDREN

Until recently in this country, children were not thought to be capable of judgement or of bearing reliable witness to their own experience. Adults also thought they knew best and set the boundaries of what they were prepared to ask or hear from children (Qvortrup, 1994). The challenge posed by according children more respect as research subjects is to rethink our approach to ethics along the same lines. If children have agency in their lives, then this applies to the choices we construe as ethical dilemmas in social research. And to construct a separate ethics for research with children might be to stereotype them as somehow less competent if they are seen as needing adults to intervene with special protective measures. But are there limitations on treating children exactly like adults where research ethics are concerned? Are there any areas in which we *should* treat children and young people differently from adults, or are there only areas in which, though they may have arisen in the context of debates about children, ethical dilemmas would in fact be posed whoever the research subjects happened to be? Mayall (1994) sees the problems that some regard as inherent in gathering data from children – that children may fantasize or try to please the interviewer, that they are too inexperienced to comment, that they only repeat what adults have told them – as being also present in work with adults and hence not valid objections to researching with children or, we might add, necessitating a separate ethical code. The same is true of research questions that are imposed on the subject rather than being framed out of their own experience, and of negative images employed by researchers that do not serve the wider interests of the group being researched. Any group that is relatively lacking in power and influence can find itself subject to these forms of exclusion and marginalization.

CONSENT

More than we might initially suppose, then, is common to adult and child research subjects. Particular ethical questions in research with children do arise, however. Notable among them is the issue of whose consent should be sought to involve the child in research. Should this be the parent (or anyone *in loco parentis*) or the child or both? And, if the parent or carer is approached, does this only cover access to the child, so that the child can still be separately asked whether they want to take part, or does it amount to a proxy consent to conduct the interview (Mahon et al., 1996)? If we do by-pass parents, we need to consider whether the outcome is solely to accord young people greater autonomy or whether we are also depriving them of their parents' protection – the 'respect vs. protect' debate (Alderson, 1995).

The area in which this question has been most fully considered is that of young people's right to give consent to medical treatment. Priscilla Alderson outlines the now somewhat confused state of the legislation in England and Wales. The concept of 'Gillick competence' – the idea that young people achieve, over time, a level of understanding at which they can make their own choices (as set down in the House of Lords ruling on the Gillick case; see Alderson, 1995) – has been followed by apparently contradictory case law. Alderson encourages us to consider whether the approach taken in the Gillick judgement establishes a framework for best practice in obtaining research consent from children and young people. She states the additional caveat that research is rarely in an individual's immediate interests, as medical treatment could be argued to be, and should therefore carry even less risk of harm to the subject than intervention for reasons of treatment or care in case it is later challenged. The overall outcome of all the legal cogitation is a need for every professional to judge whether a child or young person is competent to consent on his or her own behalf.

Alderson's complex discussion has been summarized by Ward (1997: 20) as boiling down to whether a child is able to make 'informed, wise and voluntary decisions'. These three concepts of understanding, wisdom and freedom are certainly equally relevant to research studies in which children are asked to participate; they mean that we have a responsibility to explain the study and its implications as fully as we possibly can, to decide whether or not the child is able to act in his or her own best interests, and to give her or him every opportunity to exercise a free choice over whether or not to participate in some or all of the exercise. Alderson (1995) offers a checklist of points to consider about children's consent in order to make this a more fully informed and freely chosen process. For example, children may need time to think about whether or not to agree to be interviewed, together with reassurance that a refusal would not be held against them in any way. Also, the child may or may not want a parent to be present, depending on whether they are nervous of being alone with a stranger or keen to get their own ideas across in privacy. Context may also be crucial. Compliance may replace consent in school, for example, if children see the research as just another piece of work they are given to do in class (Morrow and Richards, 1996; Costley, 2000) and ways may need to be found to give them at least a real choice of opting out (see Chapter 2). On the other hand, it could be argued that school is one of children's familiar places and that where research into abuse in the family is concerned it has the advantage of being somewhere safely away from the perpetrator.

CHILD PROTECTION AND RESEARCH ETHICS

Where children have already had adverse experiences that may have been distressing or damaging – which has traditionally been true of the majority of children who have interested researchers (Alderson, 1995) and is certainly true of those we interviewed – there could arguably be a greater need for protection from potentially exploitative researchers (Morrow and Richards, 1996). It is not clear, though, that this would be fundamentally different from researching vulnerable adults except, again, for the role of the parent or carer in being consulted. The same could even be said of children's lack of knowledge and experience and their political marginalization in that not all adults are equally sophisticated in these regards (Lansdown, 1994). There is always a risk of exploitation and potential harm caused by any insensitive or unscrupulous research.

On the other hand, it has been argued that parents, carers or researchers who exclude children from research 'in their best interests' may do harm of a different kind, leaving children silenced as opposed to unprotected (Alderson, 1995): 'too tight ethical guidelines might be used to shut the door on what young people have to tell us' (researcher cited in Alderson, 1995, p. 43). Perhaps it is unethical to overprotect children from research, not only because this excludes them (Alderson, 1995), but also because we will then end up intervening in their lives in ways which adults have established to be best, without understanding how children and young people themselves perceive or experience these well-intentioned but perhaps misguided efforts.

Nevertheless, there may be particular concerns. Morrow and Richards (1996) refer to the adult duty to protect children from harm so that if, for example, there is a disclosure of risk or actual abuse, most researchers would regard themselves as obliged to report this through child protection channels (or, better, to have the child or a parent or carer report it, with the researcher supporting them in an appropriate way), and consequently would only ever offer children limited confidentiality at the outset of the research. Morrow and Richards discuss the balance between the loss of trust (and potentially access) if such a report is made, against the loss of credibility if nothing is done. Butler and Williamson (1994) departed from this norm and operated from a basis of negotiating with the child what to do should such an eventuality arise, exactly as one would do with a vulnerable adult, as opposed to someone in the status category of 'child'. In other words, they offered young people complete rather than limited confidentiality. Few have been brave enough to follow their lead without caveats (see Mahon et al., 1996; Thomas and O'Kane, 1998).

At the end of the day, the ethics of research with children may boil down to not underestimating them while, at the same time, ensuring that they come to no harm (Morrow and Richards, 1996). (Alderson's respect/protect idea – see above.)

CHILD-CENTRED ETHICS: METHODS PROCESS AND THEORY

Even though most ethical considerations may be common to adults and children, or at least overlap substantially, it can equally well be argued that there are residual elements throughout research design and process that can exclude or exploit children if age-appropriateness is not observed. These therefore have ethical implications. Morrow and Richards (1996) suggest that they include the following: avoiding adult-framed questions and implied answers; taking time to develop trust, especially as children are not used to being asked their opinions; involving children and young people far more in the research process; and triangulation of methods to avoid bias in such a marginalized population (where they may not fully trust us and we may not fully hear them). The present authors hoped, for example, that triangulating data between individual and group interviews would increase the chances of children sharing fuller information with us; we also built trust over time and left diaries for the children to complete in their own time and in privacy (*op. cit.* and see Chapter 2, this volume). Hood et al. (1996) add 'getting the context right' to this list: we need to consider, for example, where children will feel most easily able to talk and who they will feel comfortable talking to (see Chapter 6, this volume, on the enormous difference it made when Asian children could talk to Asian researchers from a basis of shared understanding). A child's willingness to be open and honest with the researcher has, of course, an impact on the overall validity of the research (Mahon et al., 1996). Berry Mayall (1994), who has done as much as anyone to equalize the treatment of children and adults in research, still sees the ensuing analysis and resultant theorizing as having to be conducted by adults, on the grounds of greater knowledge, albeit at the risk of reintroducing a conflict of perspective and interests. There is a literature, though, that would push even at these boundaries, where specialist knowledge might be needed to 'crunch the numbers' but not necessarily to make sense of what they can tell us (see Dullea and Mullender, 1999, for a summary). There are also ethical aspects of dissemination (Morrow and Richards, 1996). Since children are largely powerless to challenge media hype and distortion, particular caution may need to be exercised both with the sense made of data they have shared and with the way findings are presented.

Finally, at the broadest possible level, there are ethical implications in the model of childhood that is being applied. If children are seen as 'mature moral agents' (Alderson, 1995, p. 5), then relevant considerations include not just the research methods adopted but also the reporting of children's own words, a portrayal of positive images of childhood, and the impact of the research both on these children and on children more generally. Taking this contextualization still further, if the socio-political or policy/practice environment is ignored (Alderson, 1995), and the subjects are studied as if they lived in a vacuum, then individualistic analyses will result that tend to 'blame the victim' (Ryan, 1971). In domestic violence research, for example, most researchers would make a link between gender stereotyping and violence against women; most would also regard this as having policy and practice implications in relation to tackling perpetrators' behaviour rather than re-victimizing women and children. It is important not to lose sight of these wider issues when researching with the children involved, for example by not applying narrowly child protectionist models that focus on intervening with mothers and their children to the exclusion of confronting dangerous men.

CREATING NEW KNOWLEDGE WITH CHILDREN

Once researchers began to conduct studies involving children directly, and the ethical dilemmas began to be resolved, work flourished in a number of areas. Notable recent examples include studies in the field of health (e.g. Alderson and Montgomery, 1996, on health care choices; France et al., 2000, on children's beliefs about health) and children's experiences of disability (Beresford, 1997; Davis et al., 2000; Morris, 1998; Ward, 1997). Children's opinions have been sought on social issues as wide-ranging as the family (Morrow, 1998), parenting (National Family and Parenting Institute, 2000), physical punishment (Willow and Hyder, 1998), current anxieties about harm and risk (Butler and Williamson, 1994), their broader concerns for the future (The Young Researchers, 1998; NCH Action for Children, undated) and their general social attitudes (Roberts and Sachdev, 1996; Ghate and Daniels, 1997). These publications further reveal that all the major child care charities have involved their own or academic researchers in eliciting children and young people's views. The major social science research funders have also devoted whole research programmes to children and to youth, with a particular focus on children's and young people's own perspectives. We know, then, that we are seeing an important trend.

Children and young people have recently been consulted on the services available to them on a scale ranging from a single residential respite care service for learning disabled children (Marchant, Jones, Julyan and Giles, 1999; Marchant, Jones and Martyn, 1999), through to the totality of council services in Newham (Students from Sarah Bonnell and Brampton Manor Schools, 1997). In the welfare field, feedback has encompassed most elements of what children and young people experience. It has ranged from eliciting their views on professional intervention following child sexual abuse (NCH Action for Children in partnership with the Newcomen Centre and the Bloomfield Clinic at Guy's Hospital, 1994; Westcott and Davies, 1996), in child protection cases more generally (Barford, 1993) and regarding involvement in child protection conferences (Shemmings, 1996), through being 'looked after' in the public care (Baldry and Kemmis, 1998) and involved in decisions during that experience (Thomas and O'Kane, 2000), to adoption (Thomas and Beckford, 1999). In relation to child and family social work more broadly, Hill (1997b) has published a research synthesis of over 70 publications featuring children's perspectives, from which he concludes that children should be given better information and more say in the process of social work intervention, particularly in child protection cases.

One service in the voluntary sector, ChildLine, because its entire work consists of listening to the voices of children, has offered especially rich information about how and why children use its dedicated helpline and how this meshes into the broader context of their lives, their families and their other help-seeking activities (see, for example, ChildLine, 1996; undated). The rationale for conducting the research was that: 'The world of children can be impenetrable to adults ... Children's own perceptions and their experiences are usually mediated through adult preoccupations, especially when it comes to child abuse and child protection' (ChildLine, 1996, p. 6). The only solution is to talk to children directly.

Consistent themes from all this research have been that it is perfectly possible to discuss a whole range of topics with children, with very fruitful results, and that children want more say in all aspects of their lives. Though Hill's (1997b) research synthesis, mentioned above, revealed that teenagers had been more often asked for their views than younger children, it is nevertheless clear, for example from a survey of 5- to 7-year-olds on physical punishment (Willow and Hyder, 1998), that much younger children can also express their understanding and opinions – in this case on how they define smacking, what it feels like to be smacked, and where and why adults smack children. Nor are there good reasons to exclude children whose understanding or communication skills are limited for reasons other than age. It is perfectly possible to consult children with a wide range of disabilities, provided that the interviewer possesses sufficient skill and uses appropriate communication methods (Beresford, 1997). Visual and play techniques of various kinds (Marchant, Jones, Julyan and Giles, 1999; O'Kane, 2000), 'yes/no' answers or multiple choice questions help children who have difficulty writing (Ward, 1997), and group interviews with an interviewer who has built up a measure of rapport, can work well, for example, for those with moderate learning difficulties (Costley, 2000). Also, talking to children and young people can encompass extremely sensitive material, such as the experience of being medically examined following a sexual abuse allegation (Westcott and Davies, 1996), again provided that the interviewer conducts the interview appropriately. Exclusion can happen, too, where some groups of children are overlooked and it is important that sampling pays due attention to ethnicity, for example (see Chapter 6).

Children do not have to be asked pre-set questions determined by adults. Marchant, Jones, Julyan and Giles 'tried to give control of the agenda (and as far as possible the process), to the young people' (1999: 5) so that they were genuinely consulting rather than studying them. As with all participatory research (Dullea and Mullender, 1999), this means moving away from treating those we interview as 'research subjects' towards involving them in some level of partnership. The ultimate in this trend is empowering young people themselves to act as researchers (Kirby, 1999; Worrall, 2000; The Young Researchers, 1998) and giving a sense of ownership by disseminating in appropriate ways, such as directing a final report specifically towards the young people who participated in the research (Marchant, Jones and Martyn, 1999). Keeping language age- and ability-appropriate is vital, including in the way the researchers themselves talk about the project so that they do not exclude in unforeseen ways (Marchant, Jones, Julyan and Giles, 1999). Representing the full diversity of children means involving boys and girls in approximately equal numbers, ensuring that those with disabilities (see above) and those from a range of ethnic and social backgrounds can participate appropriately, and sampling across the selected age range. It also implies making the decision as to how young the children can be on research-specific grounds, not according to preconceived notions about what children can and cannot do, especially since such assumptions vary across cultures and societies (James et al., 1998).

Direct parallels with our own study in the above discussion include asking general populations of young people about social issues, asking those who have used them about the services available and their own help-seeking activities, interviewing children about sensitive topics, and extending the lower age range of children consulted to those in the middle years, not just teenagers. We also involved children and young people in the design of our research instruments and in planning our research process. Our confidence in the viability of our proposed study drew, then, upon a deepening consensus in the research world that there is enormous potential for consulting children's views on an ever-widening range of subjects and upon a background of developing skills which seek to ensure that this happens appropriately.

DOMESTIC VIOLENCE RESEARCH AND CHILDREN

Despite all of the work discussed in preceding sections, within our specialist field of domestic violence research, when we started our study, there had been no others published that placed children's own perspectives at the heart of the subject. Adult-generated research-based papers about children living in situations where their mothers were being abused had appeared in the USA and Canada in the 1980s, leading to the first book on the subject, *Children of Battered Women* (Jaffe et al., 1990). This highlighted that living with violence could adversely affect children's behavioural and emotional adjustment and cognitive development and argued, consequently, that responses and intervention with children in all settings should routinely include an assessment of exposure to violence. Jaffe et al. (1990) did not cite the words of children directly except in passing in one chapter, moderated through a small number of case studies that were gathered, interpreted and presented by adults. The research they reported was largely in the positivist tradition of developmental psychology and psychiatry, and most of the work in the USA and Canada has continued the quest for 'psychopathology' in children who have witnessed violence against their mothers. As Alderson (1995) notes of research *about* rather than *with* children more generally, this has a history where 'researchers have collected the views of parents, teachers and other adults, assuming that their views represent children's own views, although this is frequently not so' (p. 91).

The first British text on children and domestic violence came in 1994 (Mullender and Morley, 1994), offering a conceptual framework in a UK legal and comparative practice context, and the first original UK research appeared in the same year (Abrahams, 1994). Since then, a body of important home-grown work has followed. It covers, for example, how professionals respond to domestic violence in contexts of child protection (Hester and Pearson, 1998; Humphreys, 2000a), divorce (Hester and Radford, 1996), and refuge and aftercare (Hague et al., 1996; Humphreys, 2000b; Kelly, 1994a; Mullender et al., 1998), as well as more generally (Humphreys et al., 2000). The studies that have consulted children directly will be summarised below.

The early NCH Action for Children study (Abrahams, 1994) did talk to children and young people directly about domestic violence. Though mainly concerned with women's reporting of their children's experiences, the in-depth stage of the research included interviews with seven girls, aged between 8 and 17, who had lived with domestic violence: two whose mothers were attending family centres and who were also interviewed and five located through the charity's projects for young homeless people. Although there were only seven of these interviews, they furnished rich information about children's direct experiences which is presented in detail in the findings chapters of the research report, with a good many direct quotes. These illustrate all the key issues that have become familiar in the literature on children and domestic violence and may be summarised as follows:

Nature of the the indirect abuse
- details of the abuse witnessed

Overlap with direct abuse
- direct experience of physical and sexual abuse from the mother's violent partner

Impact of living with abuse
- the emotional and psychological impact of both direct and indirect abuse, including fear, distress, guilt, embarrassment, confusion, hate, depression, conflicting loyalties, jumpiness, loss of self-esteem, self-confidence and self-respect, happiness when the violence ended
- other effects, including disturbed sleep (wakefulness, nightmares), bed-wetting and eating disorders, behavioural changes (whether clinginess or aggression), impact on school attendance or performance and disrupted schooling, leaving home very young or being thrown out
- the lasting memories (or emotionally blocking them out) and continuing impact

Adverse impact on family relationships
- stigma and family secrets
- the atmosphere at home, particularly of fear and intimidation
- adverse effects on children's relationships with their mothers and siblings, including loss of respect for mother, lack of scope for mother to discipline the children (or over-chastising) or sometimes to give them adequate care or attention, aggression between siblings
- awareness of the adverse impact on mother, including psychologically (depression, self-absorption, loss of self-esteem, alcohol misuse)

Coping strategies
- attempts to make sense of what had taken place (the violence, the leaving home and returning, post-separation violence), particularly whose fault it was (mother? self?) – both then and now, for example believing now that mother should have left a lot sooner
- children creating a psychological or physical safe place
- keeping the other siblings safe and sometimes caring for them
- attempts to intervene and to summon help (or thinking about doing so, or guilt at not doing)
- concealing the abuse from teachers and social workers for fear of recriminations at home, pity and lack of understanding, or being taken away

Responses of helping agencies
- not being believed when they did disclose (one child had told a social worker but to no avail)

Long-term impact
- resentment at the loss of how childhood ought to have been
- being ambivalent about intimate relationships
- wider impact on interpersonal relationships as a young adult

All of these themes recurred in our own work, reported in later chapters of this volume. Even in the seven interviews of the NCH Action for Children study (Abrahams, 1994), there is also evidence (which, again, we also found) that children react uniquely to their circumstances so that while one will for example, intervene, another will not feel able to do so.

At the same time as the NCH Action for Children report was being written, a far larger number of children (1554 in the period June 1993 to May 1994) had talked to ChildLine about domestic violence, and a random sample of 126 of them over a six-month period had their calls analysed for the purposes of research (Epstein and Keep, 1995). Most were aged 11 to 15 (probably reflecting greater telephone use amongst teenagers than amongst younger children) and 91 per cent were girls, as opposed to around 80 per cent of ChildLine's callers in general. Boys perhaps find it more difficult to talk about sensitive subjects, or it may occur to them less readily to do so (see Chapter 3, this volume, though this was not our finding in our in-depth interviews). The ChildLine study provides a precious insight into children's experiences of living with domestic violence. This had usually occurred in their own homes and, though often not referred to by the young people as 'domestic violence', had typically been inflicted by their fathers (or less often their stepfathers) upon their mothers – sometimes after they had already separated.

Since they were ringing a helpline, the young people talked about issues of their own choice, in their own words, and not according to a pre-set research agenda. Not all had called ChildLine because of the violence. For some, it formed a constant backdrop and had already become long-term. Where it had recently or only just started, however, it was more likely to be the main reason for the call. Children told ChildLine counsellors that the violence left them anxious and confused, particularly when it was unpredictable. Their reactions ranged from feeling helpless to taking responsibility for trying to hold the family together or for attempting to end the violence; some felt personally responsible. Distress, anger, insecurity and fear loomed large and children had no difficulty in describing the intensity of these feelings to the telephone counsellors, though they did not always say how they coped with them. A range of adverse physical and adjustment symptoms were also mentioned. In addition, more than a third (38 per cent) had themselves (and/or their siblings had been) physically abused by the perpetrator and this was sometimes the main reason for calling.

This is a skewed sample in that the children had all called ChildLine and we might surmise that this means they had not received help from elsewhere. Within the family, it was impossible to turn for help to a terrifying father or a mother they wanted to protect from further anguish. Reasons for not talking to people outside ranged from covering up the abuse so as to protect parents to not being believed by a teacher. Police intervention, where it was mentioned, had not been effective in stopping the violence. Few of the young people were in touch with social services or Women's Aid (six had actually called to request being taken into care). ChildLine counsellors discussed both these potential sources of help with children on the line but in the knowledge that some would probably be talking about their problems for the first time and that it might take several calls before any further action felt possible to them.

There have been a number of other, smaller studies. The present research team conducted a national refuge-based study (Hague et al., 1996) which included individual and group interviews with children who had recently left violent situations. Individual refuge-based interviews with children in the middle years had already been tested out by Kelly (1994a), who talked to two girls, aged 10 and 11, as part of an evaluation of a particularly pioneering childwork project. 'Rosie' and 'Clare' (not their real names) had talked about the positive help they had received, so that they no longer had to keep their feelings bottled up or blame themselves for what had happened at home. Moving on from this foundation, the team again found that refuge interviews with children worked well, revealing individualized distress and fear reactions, and also resilience and coping strategies in relation to living with domestic violence. Children spoke about having to cope with moving home and school, often several times as their mothers had fled violence, and about disruptions to their schooling and to their family and friendship networks. They talked readily about why women and children come into refuges and what refuges are, what they themselves thought about living in one, both when they had first arrived and at the time of the interview, the best and worst things about refuges for children and what they would change about them if they could. They mentioned as problems the overcrowding and the presence of the naughtier children, the loss of all that was familiar, and the restrictions on going out and having friends back (because of keeping the location secret); but they liked being safe, being with other children, having play facilities and going out on trips. There tended to be less provision for teenagers (who represent only a small proportion of residents). Feedback on different refuges varied but, in general, they were not experienced as bad places by children, some of whom did not want to leave. In a related study (Humphreys, 2000b), five children interviewed by a children's worker about their needs on leaving a particular refuge all said they would have liked some continued contact with a children's programme.

Another small-scale study of the issues and needs of children living with domestic violence was conducted on a more localized basis, in Coventry (Hendessi, 1997). As well as mothers and professionals, researchers saw 22 children and young people (only 17 of them aged under 17), either individually or in a group. Fourteen were from two local refuges and eight Asian children were living in the community. Older boys were less willing than girls to be interviewed (cf. Epstein and Keep, 1995), as well as being harder to access because many refuges have an upper age limit for boys, set at about 12. All the young people had either witnessed or heard the violence and all had been affected by it emotionally, in terms of physical health, at school or in starting to truant. They had not felt able to turn for help to either adults or friends. This may reflect the young age of nine of the children (under 9) and the fact that more than half the sample was of Asian or mixed-race origin which can present additional difficulties both within the community and outside it. Some of the Asian women had been abused by other family members, notably brothers and in-laws, sometimes as well as by their partners, reflecting the complexities of domestic violence in a tight-knit, patriarchal community. As in the ChildLine study (Epstein and Keep, 1995), children did not tend to use the term 'domestic violence' but talked about 'quarrels' and 'rows' (see Chapter 3, this volume). Younger ones had a tendency to blame themselves, older ones were more likely to hold the perpetrator responsible. Ethnic minority children faced additional problems, including racial harassment, fear of abduction and the inadequacy of specialist services. All children had their own coping strategies (see Chapter 5, this volume). The youngest tended to disengage in various ways (playing, hiding, fantasizing) while the older ones showed a wider range of internalized symptoms and externalized behaviours, with truancy particularly noticeable amongst the teenagers.

McGee's (2000) was a much more comprehensive study, and the closest in scope to the qualitative phase of our own work. Based on in-depth interviews with 54 children and 48 mothers, it covered children's experiences of living with direct and indirect abuse, often in their own words: witnessing and overhearing physical, emotional and sexual abuse, and the impacts this had on their feelings, identity, health, education, relationships and friendships. Almost a third of the book is devoted to agency responses, again focusing on children's own views as well as those of their mothers. Children had had mixed experiences of social workers and teachers; some of the former failed to explain what was happening while the latter were sometimes supportive but did not always do anything practical to help. Experiences of the police were largely negative, whereas refuges were positively regarded by children as having improved their lives and given them the chance to talk freely, often for the first time. Finally, McGee considers what children see as the barriers to help-seeking. Children had tried talking to their mothers (this tended to become easier after leaving the violence), grandparents, siblings and trusted friends. They were often scared of telling professionals what was happening at home for fear of escalating the situation or causing violent recriminations, sometimes even after leaving. There were many emotional and practical barriers to disclosure, including a feeling of stigma and fear of not being believed. Children often did not know where to go for help or, if they had heard of ChildLine or other agencies, sometimes lacked access to a telephone or the freedom of movement to use one in privacy, particularly where the violent man was exerting total control over their lives. Some children, of differing ages, felt they would not know what to say or would not be believed, especially if the perpetrator denied their story.

Although McGee's book is called *Childhood Experiences of Domestic Violence*, and is rich in children's own accounts, it gives equal space to mothers' views of their own and their children's problems. By definition, though, the book is firmly in the tradition of participative research with children in that it draws on children's own experiences and understandings and also discusses their agency (in the form of coping strategies) at some length. The content is not overtly placed within this ontological/theoretical framework, however, and tends to feel somewhat descriptive overall. Owing to practical problems, interviews could not be pursued with mothers whose first language was not English and it is unclear whether any of the children's researchers were from minority ethnic communities which may have restricted what the children felt able to say to them (see Chapter 6, this volume). Also, although 13 per cent of the sample (it is not clear whether this refers to the children or to them and their mothers jointly) described themselves as black, their experiences are not separately analysed. The outcomes of the study confirm and reinforce much of what was already known, telling the stories of living with violence from children's own perspectives. The book is chiefly valuable for its richness of detail, rather than for offering new insights, but it is an essential read for anyone who works with children they know or suspect to have had violence in their background.

TALKING TO CHILDREN ABOUT DOMESTIC VIOLENCE

Does this accumulating body of research mean that we can now talk straightforwardly to children about domestic violence? Jaffe et al. (1990), writing about practice settings, considered that children would be reluctant to discuss domestic violence because they would wish to protect their parents. Disclosures might be triggered, they thought, in the course of a crisis when professionals became involved, or in reaction to relevant materials in the classroom, for example. Yet they said of their own clinical work that 'The children we have interviewed are almost universal in their need to be listened to, believed, and supported. They usually are not looking for solutions but an opportunity to share their fears about their mother and perhaps all members of the family. Children at different stages of development may express these feelings directly to adults with whom they feel safe, or indirectly through play and drawings' (p. 83). Although the link had not, at that time, yet been made with listening to children as a research method, the lessons from practice were about trust, pace, listening, believing, and using appropriate communication techniques.

Care over obtaining consent, the potential for distress, and the need for sensitivity to the risk of harm, all feature in the research literature on domestic violence and children. Abrahams (1994), in writing up the NCH Action for Children research study, talked about the dilemmas the researchers experienced as to whether they might be exploiting already vulnerable children and young people by gathering research data from them, and about the issue of knowing when consent was real or was mediated by the child's mother. In practice, in the two cases in that study where children were identified through their mothers (who were also interviewed), both mother and child were asked to give permission for the interviews to proceed. In an overlapping field, Mahon et al. (1996), in their study of the Child Support Act 1991 which involved talking to children about their parents separating or living apart, wondered whether the interviews might be distressing for children. They consequently paid particular attention to interview closure (as did we), asking the children how they felt at the end of the interview. The same authors' work on young carers (op. cit.) involved children who were in touch with professional support, and topics the children had previously talked to those professionals about, so, although there was sensitivity and sadness about the family illness or disability which had given rise to the children's caring roles, the researchers perhaps felt less necessity to build particular precautions into the interviews. Domestic violence studies, including our own, tend to have targeted children who are, similarly, in touch with services (and still living with the non-abusing parent) so that they do have supports available.

Given the uncertainty of professionals and researchers about discussing domestic violence with children who have lived with it, it is perhaps not surprising that mothers, too, may be hesitant. Both mothers and children in the NCH Action for Children study (Abrahams, 1994), described the emotional and other obstacles to this. Many mothers, it emerges from that study, considered that their children were too young to talk about the violence or believed they were unaware of it or that it was an issue best not broached with them. Children pick up on these boundaries and decide not to raise the subject themselves. This is a theme that recurs in our own research and will be discussed in some detail in Chapter 5. Yet strongly present, here and in both stages of our own study, is the theme of children wanting someone to talk to. Those young people interviewed in the NCH Action for Children study (Abrahams, 1994) felt that sharing their experiences earlier would have helped them to make sense of what was happening and to feel less isolated, sad and overwhelmed. It would have had to be someone with whom there was a bond of trust. Two had had such a person, one a friend and the other her grandparents, while a third had later been able to confide in a social worker who had treated her 'as a person' (p. 93).

Researchers were not, of course, first on this scene of talking to children about direct and indirect abuse and need not be our only sources of advice on how to do it appropriately. Practitioners in social work and child health are enormously experienced in interviewing children about their experiences of the most distressing forms of sexual and physical abuse. They learn how to hear children's voices without visibly registering shock, disgust or alarm, so that children will feel safe confiding in them (Bray, 1997). It is often crucially important, for purposes of courtroom evidence, that children talk in their own words, at their own pace, and do not have ideas suggested to them by the adult interviewer. Closer links between research and practice skills, techniques and values in work with children would be a most valuable sharing (Thomas and O'Kane, 2000).

Most notably in respect of domestic violence, children's workers in refuges have been sensitive listeners to children for over a quarter of a century now. In recent years, they have begun collecting together for publication children's accounts of the violence and what it has meant in their lives (see, for example, Higgins, 1994). A notable example is a whole volume of poetry, drawings and other writings collated by Scottish Women's Aid (undated). These could be regarded as just as much a resource for those wanting to learn about children's experiences of living with violence as more formal research outputs. Indeed, child workers' recognition that children can express very powerful views on these issues was influential in reinforcing the present authors' wish to pursue research ideas in this field, as will be explained in the next chapter.

TALKING TO GENERAL POPULATIONS OF CHILDREN AND YOUNG PEOPLE ABOUT DOMESTIC VIOLENCE

A related question is whether we can talk to general populations of children about domestic violence. NCH Action for Children (undated), in its Family Forum consultation with 250 children and young people and 1000 parents, conducted in 1997, found that children volunteered the information that they were greatly concerned about family violence, which parents in the same survey agreed was often a secret. Half the young respondents did not know where to turn for help if there was violence at home; their parents were even less sure. Teenagers who were consulted about council services in Newham similarly raised their own questions as to whether the council was encountering increasing degrees of all forms of abuse, including emotional abuse (Students from Sarah Bonnell and Brampton Manor Schools, 1997).

The only study before ours to initiate talking in any depth to a general population of young people about gendered violence in this country consisted of ten focus group discussions and a survey of 2039 young people in Scotland and Northern England, mainly aged between 14 and 21 (Burton and Kitzinger, 1998). Ranging wider than domestic violence, the study sought to ascertain the extent to which violence against women was viewed as acceptable. Amongst young men, one in five considered that abuse/violence was sometimes 'OK', rising to almost one in four if the woman had 'slept with someone else' (p. 1). (Young women were only about half as likely to think this.) Our findings (see Chapter 3, this volume) make an interesting comparison. One in five young men in the Burton and Kitzinger study also condoned marital rape, again with figures for young women very much lower. Participants in the focus groups welcomed the opportunity to talk about sex, relationships and violence and wanted to discuss such issues in depth, not just to be told what was right or wrong. They also welcomed the idea of campaigns involving young people. (Again, compare our finding in Chapter 3 that young people want to be given more information in school and to be actively involved in discussion.)

It is, if anything (and contrary to what might be assumed), in some ways more worrying to be talking to general populations of children about domestic violence than to be talking to well-supported children who have actually lived with violence but who are now in safety and in touch with appropriate support services. This is because some of the former may have hidden experiences that they have never yet disclosed (see below and Chapter 2 and 3, this volume). Nevertheless, provided that adequate preparations are made (including with relevant adults, such as teachers) and supports put in place for those who may need them, work to date has confirmed that research can open up the topic of gendered violence with children and young people, who make an enormously important contribution to potential developments in policy and practice by their ability and willingness to discuss it.

CONCLUSION

Over the course of the past decade, thinking has shifted considerably as to whether it is possible or desirable to talk to children and young people about their experiences of living with domestic violence. We now know, both from practice and research experience, that this is perfectly possible, provided communication is sensitive and age appropriate. The next chapter will chart our approach to conducting a major research study that built on this recognition.

NOTES

1. The children whose experiences form the central focus of Chapters 4 to 8 of this book have all lived with the commonest form of domestic violence: male-on-female violence or what in Canada would be called 'woman abuse'. By 'domestic violence' we mean the physical, mental, emotional and/or sexual abuse of a woman by her partner or ex-partner. Statistically, the perpetrator is usually male, although there is also violence in a proportion of same-sex relationships and, of course, this is also harmful for children where it occurs. Though women can be abusive towards their partners, women's behaviour is seldom as dangerous or frightening as that of violent men (Mirrlees-Black, 1999) and it is important to separate out violence used in self-protection from unprovoked attacks. Furthermore, women's violence has never been socially condoned, as has the violent control of women by men over the centuries. Consequently, this book is grounded in a gendered understanding of violence in intimate relationships and, where it focuses on children's experiences, takes men's violence against women as its theme.

2 Researching with Children on a Sensitive Topic

The research on which this book draws (see also Mullender et al., 2000) was based chiefly on asking children about their own understandings and experiences of domestic violence. The shift this represents in social attitudes towards children – in taking their views more seriously (see Chapter 1) – was summed up by some of the children who helped to pilot our research. They felt their statements would not count because they were 'just something that children think' and they had to be reassured that this was very far from the case. Their fears bear testimony to an 'anti-child bias' in our society (Alderson, 1995, p. 79), of which children themselves are all too aware. It can only be countered in social science research by an overt recognition that children's own perceptions and actions in all areas of their lives deserve separate study if existing gaps in our understanding are to be filled.

THE BACKGROUND

As was mentioned in Chapter 1, the project reported here built on two earlier studies. The first of these was an evaluation of children's work in a single refuge where considerable developmental work had taken place (Kelly, 1994a) and the second a telephone survey of all women's refuges in England, encompassing also individual and group interviews with children, their mothers and children's workers in a sample of refuges, funded by the Women's Aid Federation of England Trust (Hague et al., 1996; Mullender et al., 1998). Although it formed only one aspect of these studies, direct contact with children confirmed that they were well able to talk about their experiences, given a sensitively designed approach. They described, for example, the disruption of moving home and school, often several times as their mothers fled violence, the security and support they had found in the refuge, and also some of the more difficult things such as having to learn to live with many other people and worrying about the future.

Following on from that work, the research team, now slightly enlarged to include two Asian researchers, was inspired to attempt a larger-scale project based centrally upon the views of children and young people. It was clear that hearing from children about living with domestic violence could constitute an important way of informing a more coherent and appropriate response to their needs since they would be able to offer insights unavailable to most adults. It also seemed important to learn from a general population of children about their attitudes to violence in the home. Funding for the work was sought through an appropriate Research Programme of the Economic and Social Research Council

(ESRC), the major funder of social science research in the UK, entitled 'Children 5–16: Growing into the 21st Century'.

In this programme 22 different projects shared the common theme of looking at children as social actors, focusing on children's experiences of and responses to contemporary society, with the aim of drawing out implications for policy and practice. The rationale behind the programme was that, whilst recognizing diversity amongst children, it is possible to conceptualize them as a population group with important things to say about the circumstances of their own lives in their family, community and environment. They have an influence on society as well as being influenced by it (in sociological terms, they have 'agency') and are not simply the passive constructs or observers of an adult-dominated world. If children are treated as the primary unit of analysis, a whole new perspective on every area of social change opens up, with a different cross-section through family relationships and social networks, the physical environment, the economy, policies and services, and even our sense of time. This perspective could usefully inform policies aimed at improving the quality of life for all children, and for specific groups, if we listen carefully enough to their own experiences of and responses to relevant social circumstances. Indeed, the extent to which a society listens to its children is a core social indicator.

Since children do not necessarily compartmentalize their lives along the lines we expect, a multidisciplinary, multi-project programme was needed to shed new light on how they regard the changing conditions of childhood and of their everyday lives. A key aim of the programme was to hear the opinions and experiences of a wide range of children, in their own words, against a background where both the Children Act 1989 and the UN Convention on the Rights of the Child require statutory authorities to accord children the right to express their views (see Chapter 1). The decision to select middle childhood, the years of compulsory education, for detailed study was taken because far less published work had previously focused on this period than on infancy or youth (though see Borland et al., 1998, for one example).

The project reported here was the only one on domestic violence in the Children 5–16 Programme, although two others within a stream on 'Children and Household Change' considered children's experiences of divorce and its aftermath. Ours was the first competitively funded study in the UK to be focused on children's own views of domestic violence. It ran from 1996 to 1999, with research sites centred on the Universities of Bristol, Durham and North London, and with co-ordination from the University of Warwick.

THE STUDY

THEORETICAL UNDERPINNINGS

An anti-oppressive research praxis was attempted. Abused women and their children were treated with respect and, as outlined above, were viewed as having agency in their own lives, not as passive victims, despite the distressing and sometimes terrifying experiences through which they had lived. The research team was multicultural and strove to be both ethnically sensitive and anti-racist in its approach.

The overall approach to conceptualizing children was probably closest to James et al.'s (1998) model of the 'social structural child' (see also Morrow and Richards, 1996). We did not perceive children as 'socially developing' and hence as less than competent or trustworthy (as briefly discussed in the last chapter); or as 'socially constructed' if this means that everything that happens to them, including abuse, may be excused as culturally relative; or as inhabiting their own, unknowable world; or as 'adult', as if they were only part of an adult-centred world with no distinguishable perceptions, experiences or social status of their own. And, though we do consider that children are discriminated against in many ways in contemporary Western society, we do not categorize them as a homogeneous 'minority group' in a way that glosses over the differences between children and between the contexts in which they live. Rather, we see them as a diverse body of social actors with their own varying levels of competence and their own ways of communicating. Though we planned to use questionnaire and interview techniques, we aimed do so as participatively as possible, making our communication child-centred and age-appropriate as a part, not just of our research process, but of our research ethics (Thomas and O'Kane, 1998).

The team's understanding of domestic violence was theorized from feminist standpoints (as demonstrated in the authors' earlier work: Kelly, 1988; Mullender, 1996; Hague and Malos, 1998) and drew upon feminist epistemological approaches and research methods (see, for example, Alcott and Potter, 1993; Harding, 1987; Kelly, 1988; Maynard and Purvis, 1994; Nielsen, 1990; Stanley and Wise, 1993), as well as upon its own past practice in domestic violence research (Hague et al., 1996). Close links were maintained throughout the study period with the Women's Aid Federation of England and other women's services. As mentioned in Chapter 1, the gender implications of girls' and boys' responses about men's and women's behaviour were carefully considered in the way data were collected and later analysed (and proved to lead to some of the most important findings). The research team also pursued a feminist commitment to collective working in its own process. This proved enormously helpful in navigating the complexities of collaborative work across four universities and as many background disciplines. Meetings, telephone conferences and electronic communication were all used to ensure thorough discussion of the substantive and methodological issues raised by the research and to resolve ethical and practical dilemmas.

AIMS

The primary themes of the particular research study reported in this volume were children's general understandings and perceptions of domestic violence – including whether they saw it as affecting children, who they saw as responsible for it, and what they thought should be done – and, more specifically, the need to learn from children who had lived with domestic violence about how they had coped with it and what they considered to be the most helpful forms of response. This latter point included building on children's agency in the situation and not treating them as passive victims.

The specific objectives were twofold, linked to the two phases of the project. First, the study aimed to discover what a general population of children knew about domestic violence and what sense they made of it. Second, in respect of children known to have lived in situations where their mothers had been abused, we aimed to answer the following research questions:

- How do children make sense of the experience of living with domestic violence?
- What coping strategies do they use?
- What help do they consider would meet their needs and build on their coping strategies?
- What help do they currently get?
- How do children and young people consider it could be improved?

METHODS

In order to meet these aims, the research combined quantitative and qualitative methods and was conducted in two phases. In Phase I of the study, 1395 children and young people aged 8 to 16 in school settings (five junior and seven senior) in three areas of England encompassing urban and rural settings completed a questionnaire about what they knew and thought about domestic violence. Phase II was a more detailed study of a smaller sample of 54 children, interviewed individually and in groups, who were known to have lived with violence against their mothers. The researchers explored with the children and young people their views and feelings about their experiences, the coping strategies they had adopted while living through the violent situations, and ideas on the support they thought would have been most helpful to them. The groups were held after the individual interviews and the discussion within them was framed around themes that had emerged from the interviews. In addition, 24 mothers and 14 professionals were interviewed about children in the qualitative sample.

SAMPLING

Samples for both phases of the work were drawn from contrasting parts of the country, both in socio-economic terms and in relation to urban/rural contrasts. The research sites were in London, the north-east and the south-west of England. There were disabled children in both samples (see Table 3.3 in Chapter 3, and also Chapter 4) and the researchers in the qualitative phase of the work went to great lengths to ensure that children with speech problems or learning difficulties could trust them and feel that they had made themselves understood. In one case, this was achieved by spending several hours together with a 13-year-old girl with Down's Syndrome before the interview started. The researcher noted:

> After I'd been around the house for several hours, we found it much easier to communicate because of her getting used to my voice and me getting used to hers. (Research notes)

In another, an interview schedule designed for a younger age group was used where three boys in the same South Asian family had become virtually selectively mute. It also helped on some occasions to use mother tongues where children with speech and language problems that seemed to have developed as a result of living with the violence were unwilling to converse in English. A boy with severe hearing loss chose to have his mother present during the first interview to ensure he could understand what he was asked though, in fact, he experienced no difficulties. These are all examples of the lengths the researchers, and the process of research design, went to to ensure that disabled children were not excluded from the study and they were remarkably successful in helping children feel able to talk, even where their mothers had doubted that this would happen because their children had become monosyllabic at school or with other professionals. A gentle and slow interview, lasting over two hours in total, including many breaks, also allowed a very shy 13-year-old South Asian girl to participate, even though she started off by pulling her sweater over her head and covering her face with her hands.

The decision to set 8 years of age as the minimum age to participate in both phases of this particular study was taken for research-related reasons (James et al., 1998) after discussion with the children who piloted the questionnaire. Not only was reading ability a factor, but young people of various ages in the pilot suggested that 8 years old would be a good starting point since children of this age would have the maturity and comprehension to deal with the issues coherently. To exclude such children as too young, they suggested, would patronize them and mean that important information would be lost. It was also decided that the younger children (those of primary school age) needed their own, age-appropriate version of the questionnaire and the opportunity to have the questions read to them and their answers written down if they found this too difficult in the space of one lesson. It was a particular aim of the team not to exclude younger or less bright children (Costley, 2000, and see Chapter 1, this volume) and not to have teachers making this kind of selection in advance either. There were usually two researchers present in the class and available to offer practical support.

A sample of 1200 to 1500 children was planned for Phase I and, in common with many research studies involving general populations in the middle years of childhood, it was decided to recruit the children through their schools. The complexities inherent in the then recent move towards local autonomy for schools meant that, in place of the one-off decision to participate that might at one time have been taken at local education authority level, the research team had to negotiate access with each school individually. A letter was sent to selected school heads in the three parts of the country concerned, outlining the project, its standing within a prestigious national research programme, and the research team's prior experience. This was followed by telephone contact and, where sufficient interest was shown, a preliminary meeting with relevant staff. Although it was very complicated and time-consuming to recruit, the desired sample was achieved, with 1395 children participating in Phase I.

There was no overlap between the Phase I and Phase II samples. For reasons of confidentiality and safety, the researchers had made no attempt to identify which children in the schools' sample had lived with domestic violence so they could not funnel such children through into Phase II. Rather, children to be interviewed were accessed through inter-agency domestic violence forums, Women's Aid groups, women's support groups, family centres and statutory organisations providing services for abused women and their children. Making contact via agencies was considered to be important, because the researchers did not want to approach families who did not have supports in place in the event that the research contact proved to be in any way distressing for the children. However, it emerged as enormously time-consuming to work through the complex layers of consent and practical co-operation needed from agency management structures, individual workers, mothers and then individual children. Another obstacle to obtaining a sample was that the majority of children resident in refuges in the research areas during the period of the study were too young to be interviewed. (This was partly to be expected, given the age profile in refuges – see Hague et al., 1996 – but was exaggerated at this time.) It had been anticipated that boys might be harder to recruit to the sample because they might not want to talk about their feelings but this turned out not to be so. Boys were just as willing to be interviewed as girls and, in many cases, talked very openly about their experiences. Indeed, mothers were far more often an obstacle to research access than children themselves, fearing that interviews would be upsetting for children (see Chapters 5 and 7 on mothers' general underestimation of children's desire to talk).

The sample eventually achieved for Phase II after attempts lasting well over a year, 45 children and a further 9 in groups, was about half what had been hoped for but it did meet the parameters of a purposive sample in that the children were of both sexes and from diverse ethnic and social backgrounds, ages, abilities and areas. Seven had disabilities, two of which (Down's Syndrome and hearing loss) might have affected the interview process. The resultant interviews produced some very interesting and useful material about what had been witnessed and the impact it had had. As planned, no more than half of the sample came through refuges, thus avoiding a bias which has been built into much domestic violence research in the past simply because of ease of access to an otherwise hidden population. The research team is aware that the most distressed and fearful children are likely to have been excluded from the sample, through their own or their mothers' choice that they should not participate, so that some of the worst experiences may not have been described. This was ethically inevitable and must be allowed for when reading the results, although these are shocking enough.

Families with more than one child were sought where possible, the earlier study by the research team (Hague et al., 1996) having shown that siblings often have markedly different experiences of and reactions to the same set of events and their aftermath. Recruiting sibling groups also helped to ensure an age range.

Care was taken in both phases of the research to include ethnically and culturally diverse voices because there is so little in the domestic violence literature on the needs of minority ethnic children (see Imam, 1994). In Phase I, this was achieved by approaching some schools that were known to have very mixed student groups. In Phase II, it was decided to have three sub-samples of children, two of diverse ethnicity in contrasting parts of the country, and one black (see Chapter 6 for a fuller discussion of the latter). The work of obtaining a separate sample of black children proved to be much more complex even than had been anticipated. Intensive contact with 35 agencies over a period of many months by two members of the research team was needed to secure a sample of 14 children (instead of the target of 30). Difficulties chiefly arose because the agencies concerned were even more overstretched than those contacted for the general sample (see below), with insecure funding leading to temporary or permanent closures of projects, staff leaving part way through negotiations, and so on. In the event, most of the 14 children contacted were of South Asian origin (two were from south-east Asia) which, though it did not achieve the intended diversity in the sub-sample (though this *was* possible in the study overall), does mean that interesting things can be said about the lives and perceptions of a group of children of sufficient size and commonality to allow shared themes to emerge. They were tracked as for the general sample (see below), but with a view to the possibility of identifying any additional relevant factors in their lives such as issues relating to culture, community and family, as well as experiences of racial abuse and harassment. The specific focus of South Asian researchers with appropriate language skills and community involvement made it possible to gain access to experiences that are not typically given sufficient attention and which have not been fully reported elsewhere in the literature.

ETHICAL CONCERNS

One of the issues that most concerned the research team in its earliest days was the ethics of talking to children about such a sensitive topic as domestic violence. We decided to think about relevant ethical issues in both phases of the research under three headings: consent, confidentiality and child protection. The latter issue extended beyond the normal statutory concerns into thinking about possible harm that might be inflicted by the research process itself, if not properly thought through. It was consequently broken down into three sub-issues: arrangements for disclosure, distress and danger. Whereas disclosures and distress are referred to constantly in the literature covering the ethics of research with children, danger is an issue more specific to work on domestic violence. In this context, any ill-advised practice or research intervention can inadvertently threaten the safety of women and children escaping violence if, for example, their abuser finds out about and feels threatened by their participation or if their confidentiality is inadvertently breached.

These 'three Cs and three Ds' provided a handy mnemonic which could be applied in all research team discussions, and in access negotiations, thus ensuring that ethical dilemmas were fully explored at all stages. Thomas and O'Kane (1998) suggest that all of what we refer to here as 'the three C's' are made more complicated where children are concerned by the power dynamics between them and adults. Adults are likely to become involved in questions of consent, carers may expect children not to have wholly confidential private lives, and there are particular legal and policy requirements concerning child protection that differ from the protection of vulnerable adults. Thus all three issues need particularly careful consideration.

CONSENT

The decisions the present research team reached were that adult consent should be sought before children were approached to give their own consent, not only because of the sensitivity of domestic violence as a topic but for the essentially practical reason that children would need to be accessed through their schools and families. The research project was clearly explained to both the adults and children concerned.

In light of the complexity of negotiating with every school individually, it was decided to leave it to the head to determine the number of levels of consent that would be seen as required. Some heads felt it necessary to consult with governors, some involved the whole staff group or the teachers of relevant classes, some asked parents' permission, ar any combination of these. The schools that decided not to participate gave a whole range of reasons, including OFSTED inspections, exams and, in some cases, explicit unease about the topic. The research team was aware that the process of seeking access gave a number of powerful adults the opportunity to silence children by ruling them out of the research but, as this phase of the research constituted a large-scale quantitative survey intended to represent all children in the relevant age group, we concluded that, provided there was no bias in the type of schools or children that were excluded, the children we did recruit would speak for all their peers.

Once the researchers had gained access to the classroom, the children's own individual involvement was sought by giving a clear explanation of the research and its purpose and by taking particular care to ensure that children knew they did not have to participate or to answer all the questions (see section on piloting, below). The children in the schools-based survey were thus accorded at least 'informed dissent' (Morrow and Richards, 1996, p. 101), made real by being given alternative things to do, as well as tasks for those who finished more quickly (drawing on the back of the questionnaire, reading a book).

Children at home, in the qualitative phase of the research, had a more active 'informed consent' in that their mothers asked them individually whether they would like to participate before inviting the researchers to their homes. The children also had a further 'informed dissent' in that they could still change their minds at any point and not be interviewed. This was checked at various stages before and during the interviews. A small number did decline to be interviewed. One mixed-race[1] boy was receiving considerable police attention at the time and it was also unclear whether his mother had fully checked that he was in agreement. Two sisters had just returned from witnessing quite serious violence between family members in Africa and, now that they were back, preferred to put it behind them and not talk about it. A couple of boys had forgotten the researcher was coming and gone out, but agreed to the interview when they got home. Other young people chose to exercise a different kind of control over the interview process, for example by deciding where it would be quiet or whether they would agree to be tape-recorded (see Chapter 6).

In the home context, it was decided to make the first approach to children through their mothers because we considered it vital not to usurp the right of the women concerned to decide what would be safe or harmful for their children. The women in question had themselves only recently become free of the power and control of their abusers and were newly established as the heads of their households (Bilinkoff, 1995). Both they and their children were often still having to observe very real precautions in order to remain safe. We assumed that they would want to assure themselves and their children that we had no connection with their abusers. We therefore decided to ask mothers for access to talk to their children, but not for a proxy consent to conduct the research interview, which would involve asking the child separately. The reverse would also apply, in that neither the child's mother nor any key professionals in their lives would be interviewed unless the child agreed to this and only then would that adult's consent be obtained to be interviewed themselves. Also, the child would be interviewed before the adult so that they could see that their views were not an afterthought but were particularly valued by the researchers. (Practicalities occasionally intervened, for example in one case where the children had not yet returned home when the researcher arrived and their mother was interviewed in the meantime.) Children were also told that their mothers were not being seen to check up on what they themselves had said. They were interviewed without their mothers present, so that they could talk freely, except where the child chose otherwise. The researcher always checked that the child was prepared to talk to her and that he or she freely agreed to be tape-recorded. The children in the South Asian sub-sample did not give permission to be tape-recorded and generally demanded a particularly high level of confidentiality. Detailed notes were kept instead. The children chose names for themselves so that their real names did not have to appear, even in the researchers' field notes. With these safeguards in place, they did talk freely to their South Asian interviewers, who they felt would understand what they were saying, for example about family and community relationships (see Chapter 6). All children were told that the purpose of the interviews was to try and 'make things better for other children'.

For the group interviews, consent was once again complex, involving the refuge staff, the children's mothers and the children themselves all being in agreement. The refuge children's workers helped to explain the research in advance, and this was also done by the interviewer at the start of the group to ensure that the children's consent was fully informed. The usual 'what, why, who, how' information about the study was covered, in an age-appropriate way. Children were told that the research was to find out what children think about domestic violence and how they cope with it, that it was hoped the findings would be useful for other children in the future and to their mums and also to refuges, that the researchers were from four universities working in three different parts of the country and that they were women who worked very closely with Women's Aid refuges and with other community-based women's services. The planned conduct of the group was also explained to those involved. The children's agreement to participate and to be tape-recorded was again confirmed at the start of the group. They were told that their names would not be used and that the tape would not be played back to their mothers or the refuge workers. Their permission was obtained to quote from what they said in writing up the research but in a disguised way, without using their names. They did not have to share anything they did not want to in the group; for example, they need not talk about what had happened to them and their mum personally, unless they wanted to, because the discussion would mainly be more general than that.

CONFIDENTIALITY AND CHILD PROTECTION

We offered confidentiality within the familiar parameters of any disclosures of current risk or harm to the child or others needing to be shared with the appropriate authorities. Some researchers have moved beyond this into offering children complete confidentiality, only to be broken with their agreement (Butler and Williamson, 1994; Thomas and O'Kane, 1998; see fuller discussion in Chapter 1, this volume). However, our research focused so directly on violence and abuse, and the overlap between woman abuse and child abuse is so high (Edleson, 1999; Farmer and Owen, 1995; Goddard and Hiller, 1993; Hester and Pearson, 1998), with dangers continuing in the post-separation phase (Hester and Radford, 1996; Radford et al., 1999), that it was considered essential to put measures in place for potential disclosures. Any child protection issue would be handled through the school's normal procedures if it occurred in Phase I of the research.[2] In Phase II, the matter would be brought to the full research team to decide, in conjunction with the child and the child's mother if at all possible (though not to the point of ignoring real concerns), whether it needed to be referred onwards. In the event, there were no fresh disclosures of abuse, although safety levels were checked with children and their mothers in two or three instances where the perpetrator appeared to be on the scene (see above). In one case, the researcher reached the point of considering making a child protection referral but did not need to do so as a legal adviser passed on all the information to the relevant authorities.

DISTRESS AND DAMAGE

The researchers determined that every possible measure would be taken to ensure that the research itself was not unreasonably distressing or in any way damaging.

In Phase I, the issue of support for pupils who might become distressed or want to disclose something was carefully considered and it was decided to handle it in three ways. First, the role of the children's teachers, both during and after the research visits, was recognized and they were offered resources based on training materials developed by a group within the research team,[3] to learn more about domestic violence, together with training on request. Second, the research team members would remain available in the school for a time after the completion of the questionnaires, and would explain that they would be doing so, in case any child wanted to talk to them individually. Third, all participating children would be given a ChildLine contact leaflet to keep, which contained the free-phone number. ChildLine was regarded as the most appropriate support agency to recommend because it operates a dedicated, confidential helpline for children, can be contacted by children direct without gatekeeping by adults in whom they may not want to confide, has had previous experience of dealing appropriately with calls about domestic abuse (MacLeod, 1996), and can also deal with any other issues that may be triggered for children as a result of completing research questionnaires. It would not have been appropriate within research boundaries for the research team itself to act in this open-ended support role, despite including three qualified social workers and individuals with child care, children's work and youthwork experience. As well as avoiding a blurring of roles, this was because there was no way of remaining actively available to the children or of operating in a professionally supported environment while so doing. The team was conscious, in planning to distribute the ChildLine leaflets, that only a proportion of calls get through to that agency because demand outstrips the available supply of lines, but there is reason to believe that children do persist with their calls (Epstein and Keep, 1995) and this remained the most suitable alternative, particularly when backed up by teacher and more limited researcher availability. Children were encouraged to take the leaflet away with them and, using a strategy devised in a previous project (Kelly et al., 1991), were told that, whilst they might never need it, a friend of theirs might. Not all did, however, with more leaflets left behind by older groups than by younger.

In Phase II, the possibility of children becoming distressed was a matter for individual researchers to handle. Children were always put at their ease through the creation of a trusting atmosphere and sharing of full information about the research. All research team members who undertook these interviews were mature women with relevant professional and research experience and a sensitive manner. They were in a position to offer referral to helping agencies if needed. Also, as with any research interview, they would pause if the child or young person being interviewed became upset or overcome with shyness, and perhaps suspend the interview for a time, only resuming when the interviewee was calmer and able to make a clear decision to do so. Interview closures were carefully handled. Researchers did not just rush off but might stay for a while and chat, or look at or play with toys. If appropriate, they might telephone next day to check that all was well.

One 14-year-old boy actually chose to complete an interview despite being in tears for much of the time because he really wanted to talk about his experiences. This was his free choice and he was given several opportunities to stop, which he declined because he felt he had important messages to share. The harm involved in silencing him could have been threefold: denying him a voice, denying him the opportunity to try and help others, and denying him the catharsis involved in ventilating his feelings. He was above all concerned that other people should know what he had lived through. Also, he had a most sensitive interviewer with a social work qualification, considerable experience of direct work with young people, and many years' research experience. She did not cross the boundary into offering counselling or therapy (Mahon et al., 1996), but she was well equipped to empower the young person concerned to make a decision he felt comfortable with about continuing the interview and she was able to empathize with his distress without being 'fazed' by it into a precipitate decision to terminate the interview. At the same time, she was making a judgement that the young man concerned was 'Gillick competent' to make this decision about his own wellbeing (Alderson, 1995 and see Chapter 1). At the end of the interview, and by phone next day, she again checked that the young man felt OK and that he was happy for his interview transcript to be included with the others for analysis. This young man was re-interviewed in subsequent stages of the research when he stated that he was pleased he had taken part. Other young people, too, gave evidence of having found the interviews a productive experience which had been appropriately handled and had caused them no ill effects.

At the same time that some children found the interview process sometimes upsetting because it re-awoke painful memories, others were keen to talk to the researchers. One 15-year-old girl made a special request to be included when she heard about the study through her youth club. A 6-year-old South Asian girl, too, young to be included in the sample, did not want to be left out and was asked to draw and write something for the interviewer who was talking to her 9-year-old sister. Both sisters asked the interviewer lots of questions about herself and thanked her warmly for coming.

DANGER

This issue was handled by attempting to select only children for the sample who were not living in continuing danger, by choosing families who had current supports in place, and by being in a position to offer contact details of relevant agencies if needed. In order not to compromise their safety, as far as could possibly be known the children in the sample were in families no longer living with or in current danger from the abuser. There were a small number of reconciliations or resumptions of contact over the period of the research, which meant that the perpetrator was back on the scene, and contact had continued throughout in other cases. In one of these, the child's mother had just come through a long drawn-out criminal prosecution of the abuser for a repeat attack against her, in the context of his contact with their daughter. Safety was not at issue by the time of the research, but the situation was still emotionally fraught for the girl concerned, which came through in the interview content (see Chapter 5, for example). Also, one teenager who was still living with both parents particularly asked to be interviewed by one of the researchers at a youth centre which she attended and where she had heard that other interviews would be taking place. In all these cases, it was considered safe to proceed with the interviews. One family was dropped from the sample because an incident involving the perpetrator occurred outside their house. Although the woman concerned reported satisfactory assistance from the police, had current social services involvement and felt reasonably confident that she and the children were safe, she agreed with the interviewer that it was best not to proceed since there were still unresolved issues and possibly an ongoing risk. In all the more complex cases, the research team held full discussions about how to proceed and made the safety of the women and children concerned their first concern.

PREPARATORY WORK WITH WOMEN

Members of the research team undertook preliminary consultation on two occasions with women who had considerable experience of working with children who had lived with domestic violence. This was never seen as an alternative to talking to children directly, but was viewed as an additional precaution taken because of the sensitivities and dangers inherent in situations of domestic violence and as part of clarifying our initial thinking about the three Ds (see above) and whether we might inadvertently do more harm than good through our research (Alderson, 1995).

In the very earliest stages of planning the project, we attended a national meeting of Women's Aid children's workers (convened by WAFE's then National Children's Officer who was also consultant to our project), at which we outlined the research proposal and sought suggestions about both content and process. The children's workers were very encouraging about the viability and importance of the proposed study, particularly the qualititative phase. From their own extensive experience of listening to children, they assured us that children would be quite prepared to talk about the violence. They considered it crucially important to hear the voices of children and to let this be as wide-ranging as possible. The research would inevitably collect valuable information and they hoped this could be channelled into indications for practice. Issues of trust, consent and confidentiality were emphasized. Mothers, and children's workers for those in refuges, could help support children both before and after the interview.

Later, prior to the second (qualitative) phase of the research, two of the researchers ran a workshop at the Women's Aid Federation of England annual conference, part of which was devoted to asking participants for their ideas on conducting the research. Again, they confirmed our view that it would be important to build rapport and trust, allowing ample time and never forcing any issue in the interviews. Mothers would need to be somewhere on hand, with parameters of confidentiality made very clear both to the children and their mothers. Older children and young people were likely to find a one-to-one interview most enabling. They might also respond to keeping a notebook. Younger ones might need some non-verbal communication methods. Safety issues were emphasized for all participants, including checking whether it felt safe to talk about what had happened.

The research team was encouraged by these sessions with highly experienced workers to proceed with interviewing children on the topic of domestic violence, feeling reassured that the research was unlikely to do more harm than good, provided an appropriately sensitive approach was adopted.

DEVELOPMENT AND PILOTING OF RESEARCH INSTRUMENTS WITH CHILDREN

We endeavoured to work with children at all stages of research design. Our questionnaires were developed in conjunction with groups of children, who also helped to draw out the themes for the in-depth interviews. Thus we were open to children's own agendas and understandings (Thomas and O'Kane, 1998). The questionnaires and interview schedules were piloted both with individuals and with groups of children and young people, the latter including both mixed ethnicity and Asian-only groups.

It proved enormously valuable to involve children and young people very fully at this early stage of the work. They were able to point out any draft questions they did not understand and one or two *non sequiturs* or awkwardnesses in the ordering of questions which confused them. For example, some questions which asked respondents to 'tick one box only' caused difficulty because those completing the pilot thought that some children might need more than one choice fully to represent their views or experiences. Similarly, a few questions needed to ask more specifically what the respondent would do *first*, not just what they would do, because, over time, they might take a number of actions. Older children liked the tick-box lay-out of the closed questions because it resembled quizzes in popular magazines (for example, we asked 'How many women do you think are victims of domestic violence?', with six possible responses to choose from, from '1 in 2' to '1 in 500').

The research team had first thought of seeking children's own definitions of domestic violence and then using this as the baseline for subsequent answers so as to avoid directing their perceptions. However, the children in the pilot exercise perceived this as leaving them without a definition of what we really meant. Consequently, it was decided to ask for children's own ideas on one page and then, on turning over to the next page, to include a commonly accepted definition as the basis for later answers. This greatly improved the questionnaire since it gave a point of comparison for all children's level of understanding without stifling their own contribution. For the younger children, the definition we offered built on children's published accounts in earlier publications (e.g. Higgins, 1994) and was worded:

Some children have told us that domestic violence means:
  'When your dad hits your mum and makes her cry'
  'When your dad shouts, makes everyone frightened, and hurts your mum'.

For the older children, it simply read:

The next set of questions is about domestic violence which means violence between adults in the home.

In practical terms, it transpired that the typical time taken to complete the first draft of the questionnaire was 20 to 30 minutes but that some children could take up to 40 minutes, thus leaving the quickest ones with a lot of time to fill. The idea emerged of leaving the back page blank for the younger age group and asking children who had finished to do a drawing. These illustrations were later used to throw further light on, and to give presentations about, the research findings. (Older children were asked to read a book if they finished before the others.) Children wanted bigger print in the questionnaire than had been used initially but for it to be printed on both sides of the page so that it did not look too long and put people off before they had started. Even so, it was decided to make cuts after the pilot because children felt the questionnaire was 'a bit too long'. The research team had not made sufficient allowance for mixed ability classes where, children advised us, some pupils might take the whole lesson to write one sentence, meaning that lots of questionnaires might not have been completed in time. The version of the questionnaire intended for younger children ended up shorter than that for teenagers, allowing for slower reading and writing times, and help was available in completing it if required. (In practice, the younger children took about 15 to 25 minutes to complete their questionnaires.) Children themselves advised on which questions could be left out because they were too confusing, upsetting or 'no good'.

Children in the pilot were also very helpful to us in thinking through how others might feel when they completed the questionnaire. They were sensitive to the fact that some children might have experienced domestic violence at home and thought this might make the child 'go red, feel awful, think everyone is looking at them'. Or, they might be relieved to find out that it happens to others. Others, too, might be upset by the content, for example being asked what made them unhappy, and the children wanted to know whether anyone would be on hand at the end, and whether the teacher might give an opportunity later on to ask how everyone had found completing the questionnaire, in case anyone had been upset but not shown it: 'Just gone out to break or something'. Also, the research team learned that they might need to say several times that 'You don't have to fill in the questions if you don't want to'. One of the pilot groups suggested the wording: 'Remember you don't have to answer these questions if you don't want to or if they upset you'. The group also thought it was important to repeat this on the questionnaire, even if it had already been explained at the beginning of the session, because not everyone would pay attention or remember, and others might be frightened of the teacher or the researcher and think they had to answer everything. These were very helpful and sensible responses to the difficulties of obtaining voluntary consent in a school context (Costley, 2000; Solberg, 1996).

Although the research was only conducted in mainstream schools, the research team was anxious not to exclude any children with a degree of learning difficulty who might have been integrated into the classes visited (Costley, 2000) and, indeed, was aware of the wide range of reading ages present in all schools. The pilot helped us decide that two different, age-appropriate versions of the questionnaire would need to be designed, for 8 to 11 and for 12 to 16-year-olds. It would also be particularly important to allow plenty of time to complete the task, to explain it adequately and to provide support. During the pilot, it became clear that the younger children, particularly, had a tendency to ask for help when a question was not understood or where the whole task was experienced as rather difficult for an individual, who could therefore become excluded if assistance was not given. The research team discussed this issue at length and decided that, with two people present in the room (either two researchers, or one researcher and the class teacher), it would be possible to offer help, even to the level of reading out every question to a child who was struggling and then writing down his or her answers. Explanations would be given, if requested, that stayed within what was written on the questionnaire and did not offer any new material that might influence an answer.

It was also evident from the pilot that younger children assumed there would be right and wrong answers (Solberg, 1996), as if the questionnaire was a piece of school work, and wanted to know whether they were 'doing it right'. This has been previously discussed in terms of consent (see Chapter 1) but struck us, also, as an issue of how much explanation and reassurance needed to be given, both in introducing the task and in answering any questions during it, that what we wanted was children's own ideas and understanding – there were no 'right' answers. Children in one of the pilot groups also pointed out where the team needed to insert 'If you don't know, go on to the next question'.

The children and young people were extremely helpful to the research team in thinking through the gender implications of Phase I of the research. Both older and younger participants reacted against what they saw as a male-on-female bias in the first draft of the questionnaire. Many of the children involved in the pilot knew that it was mainly men who abused women, but they wanted the questionnaire to include violence in both directions, not because they held simplistic views about mutual fighting (see discussion in Mullender, 1996) but for a whole range of more sophisticated reasons such as *knowing* that there are social stereotypes and differential impacts and wanting to explore these in their own terms. This helped the research team to develop questions that more subtly recorded the young people's own views about who does perpetrate the violence/abuse and whether a man hitting a woman is different from a woman hitting a man, rather than appearing to prejudge this. Another point was that the older girls wanted a girls-only section in the questionnaire if there was to be a boys-only one as had originally been intended (to ascertain boys' attitudes). In the event, neither was included and it was boys' and girls' different answers to the same questions that were analysed, thus providing data for comparison. The teenagers in the piloting also helped us decide to include a question about sexuality in the demographic section of the questionnaire, where we asked the secondary-aged children how they would define their sexuality, offering the options: 'heterosexual (straight)', 'lesbian/gay', 'bisexual', 'not sure' and 'don't want to say'. (This question was omitted from the primary-age form.) Young people were 'cool' about including such a question and we were more fearful of losing access if parents or schools did not approve but, in the event, this did not happen.

Piloting the questionnaires with Asian children revealed a number of inadvertently ethnocentric assumptions underlying the initial draft of the questions and vignettes. First, households might be more complex than had been thought about, so more options were added to cover different family forms and other adults living in the home. Secondly, the team had written a vignette about a young woman with a jealous boyfriend. A group of Asian young women told us that this worked for fictional scenarios that were about other people because everyone knew that other people had boy- and girlfriends. However, direct questions such as 'Have you ever been hit by a boy/girlfriend' would be outside some young people's own experience, either because they were not yet dating or because they came from a non-dating culture. Consequently, only the fictional question was retained. Also, asking children to tick a box best describing their ethnic origin was quite complicated. In the Asian pilot group, some children described themselves by their religion: 'I'm Muslim', while a mixed group thought the long list of categories might be confusing, for example the difference between African-Caribbean and Black British – which one should someone tick if they felt both applied? In the event, for reasons of practicality, we retained the list with five options (Asian, African-Caribbean, Black British, Mixed Race, White) and added a further question: 'How do you describe yourself in terms of race, culture or religion?' Many children did not complete this latter question but it helped reveal diversity since 34 different categories were filled in. One point the team did get right first time was in naming the child in a vignette about violence between parents. We chose a deliberately ambiguous name, 'Jaz', in the hope that children of different sexes and ethnic origins would potentially be able to identify with an imagined child of this name, as opposed to seeing it as indicating someone who was definitely male, female, or from a different cultural group. This worked well in piloting where, although not everyone said they knew a child of this name, all could accept it as a real name and no one thought it would sound odd in their own context. It might suggest, for example, someone called Jasmine, Jaswinder or Jazza.

The young people who piloted the questionnaire were quite safety conscious. They felt there was a danger of inadvertently suggesting, through the options provided for response or the way a vignette was presented, that children should intervene in situations of domestic violence where this might in fact be dangerous. Children were therefore asked open-ended questions ('What should Jaz do?', 'Who do you think could help Jaz?'), rather than being asked to tick one or more options.

In addition to designing and piloting the questionnaires with groups of children, the drafts of the in-depth interview topic guides for Phase II of the research were checked over by the staff of a refuge and were piloted with a small number of children and their mothers. Slight adaptations were made as a result. There was also some bridging between the two phases of the research in that findings from

Phase I influenced some of the questions in Phase II as, of course, did the team's earlier research.

The research team was struck by the care with which all the pilot groups and individual children who assisted in developing the research tools approached their task. They were thorough, animated, and totally committed to helping. They contributed energy, fun and careful reflection, teasing out sensitive issues in what can be a distressing and demanding topic.

PHASE I: THE SCHOOL SURVEY

The schools-based survey was undertaken in order to access a broad, general population of children. Age-appropriate questionnaires were administered to 1395 children in classroom settings in twelve schools in contrasting parts of England.

Since there is no way of knowing with certainty which children within a classroom population have lived with domestic violence in their own home and which have not, the team had to act on the assumption that within the sample there would be children who had had these experiences and who might or might not previously have talked to someone about them. Appropriate training was offered to teachers, every teacher at participating schools (not just participating teachers) received an information sheet (on the impact of domestic violence on children, its widespread incidence and prevalence, and ways of handling disclosures), and a training pack for every participating school was developed in conjunction with the then WAFE National Children's Officer who was acting as a consultant to the project. However, teachers were asked not to cover the subject matter in advance, which could have planted ideas in the children's minds and contaminated the findings. Research team members were equally careful when introducing the questionnaire in class. Questions of consent, confidentiality and child protection were all discussed with the schools (see above).

Questionnaires were completed in one period of class time. With the youngest children, the researchers began by asking if anyone knew what a researcher was and what 'confidentiality' was. Once a good description of each had been provided by children themselves, they explained that there was a free choice whether to fill in the questionnaire and this was also printed on the front. Children tended to ask a good many questions at the beginning of the session but then settled down and worked hard, clearly being attentive to the explanations given and thinking about what to write. As planned, questions were read out to any child who asked for this and were explained where necessary, but only by rephrasing the question, never by giving any hint as to what to write. Completed questionnaires were handed to the researchers in sealed envelopes.

All coding and analysis was undertaken at one research site. Coding frames for open-ended questions were built up using content analysis and subsequently recoded into more inclusive categories for analysis. Coding was checked in a random one in ten of all questionnaires. Analysis was made using SPSS for Windows, and any anomalies checked. Basic frequency counts on a number of variables and cross-tabulations were produced. Data is stored at London Metropolitan University and has been deposited in the ESRC Data Archive. Responses to open-ended questions were all transcribed, together with the questionnaire number, age and sex of respondent.

PHASE II: THE IN-DEPTH INTERVIEWS

Phase II of the research comprised an in-depth study of 54 children known to have lived with domestic violence; 45 were interviewed individually and 9 in groups. The children who were seen individually were members of 25 households. The largest number of siblings individually interviewed was four, with four sets of three and the remainder in singletons or pairs. Where possible, children were tracked from the time of being recruited to the sample through to the end of the study period (up to 18 months), to obtain information on their changing situations and views and to increase validity by making the researcher more familiar to the child and hence more likely to be trusted with accurate information (Rubin, 2000). Wherever contact could be retained (renewed danger might lead women to move suddenly), respondents were interviewed twice, with a telephone contact in between. This always required some effort on the part of the researchers since it was clearly not a priority in the lives of the domestic violence survivors to remain in touch with the team. Some women were still moving on, attempting to remain safe and to rebuild their lives. The London sample, in particular, was hard to keep track of, perhaps because people are more mobile there. Anyone who had returned to the violent relationship was not recontacted, for fear of placing them in danger if the perpetrator discovered that they had been talking to an outsider about his behaviour.

For some of the younger children, there was communication through drawing, and all participants were given a notebook in which to record their impressions in any way they wished so that they could discuss these when the interviewer returned. Sadly, the child who made fullest use of the diary mislaid it on having to make an emergency move in order to stay safe; others did not complete or chose not to pass their notebooks back to the researchers. All the children were interviewed in their own homes, following contact with their mothers by letter and then by telephone. Wherever possible, they were seen on their own, in a separate room, unless they chose otherwise. It is important in ensuring validity in qualitative research that respondents should feel able to talk openly and independently (Mahon et al., 1996), so the context and process of the interviews were very important. The researchers worked hard to put the children at their ease. They emphasized that a child could refuse the interview, could withdraw his or her consent at any time, stop talking at any point, and/or decide not to answer any of the questions. The interviews were never rushed but were lengthy enough to build the child's trust, again to enhance validity (Rubin, 2000). As has been noted by many researchers with children (e.g. Mahon et al., 1996), it is always impossible to know how far children are impeded by the way they perceive the researchers (adults, authority figures, and so on). Like Williamson and Butler (1997), the interview team used their own personal styles to engage the young people, in this case taking a warm, respectful, supportive approach. The team's backgrounds in social work, youth work, child care, sociology and social policy, and in activism with women and children, helped them to reduce the social distance between themselves and the young people they were interviewing. The interviews followed a semi-structured format, using a pre-piloted interview guide. There was a wide range in how forthcoming children and young people were able and chose to be. Some found it difficult to speak, while others talked without stopping. Amongst sibling groups, one child was often more vociferous than the others, with perhaps another who said very little. This may have been a pattern they had developed amongst themselves.

As a form of triangulation, and because they can sometimes be a more natural environment for children than individual encounters, two group interviews were held with nine additional children in refuge and aftercare settings. The children were aged 8 to 13 and were from a range of ethnic backgrounds. A quiet space was found to conduct each group. The sessions started with refreshments and then some name games and setting of ground rules, including reconfirming the children's consent to participate and to be tape-recorded. Agreement was obtained to conduct the group seated and in relative quiet, with an attempt not to interrupt other people while they were speaking, so that voices would be heard on the tape. The group discussion itself was focused around the four key research questions outlined earlier in this chapter, but always in age-appropriate language and bearing in mind children's shorter concentration spans. The main focuses were what children think about domestic violence (what it is, why it happens), how children cope with it (themselves and other children), what sort of help children need so that they can do the things that help them cope, what other sort of help they need, and how the help they get now could be made better. The interview framework for the groups included a range of sub-questions and possible probes to ensure that roughly comparable ground was covered in each group. At the end, the children were asked whether they wanted to hear the tape played back (which they all did), whether they felt OK, whether they wanted to stay and talk individually, and whether they wanted to see the children's worker. They were also thanked and given a token parting gift after further refreshments.

In addition to talking to children, 24 interviews were conducted with mothers, several of whom were mother to more than one child in the sample. All but one mother of children in the sample were interviewed. (One woman was not up to being interviewed, although she had been willing in principle.) Altogether, the women were mothers to 76 children, 45 of whom were interviewed – at least one in each family. Most of the children who were not interviewed fell outside the parameters of the research because they were either adult or very young. A further 20 interviews were conducted with professionals whom the children considered to have been significant in their lives. This last number was smaller than had been anticipated but one finding of the research was that families who have gone through a period of upheaval, and who have frequently moved around, rarely have clear memories of which agencies workers have come from and often do not remember their names. Hence it was hard to trace a sample of practitioners from what family members (mothers and children) could recall. Also, because professionals in relevant settings work under such pressure themselves, a surprising number were on long-term sick leave with stress-related illnesses or their projects had lost their funding; clearly, people could not be contacted under these circumstances. We also chose to interview only professionals who had been involved directly with the children, which further decreased the sample pool.

All interviews were transcribed, coded and analysed using the NUD*IST package. The coding categories began with base data on demographics and whether there had been any contact with statutory agencies and/or women's organisations. This was followed by a coding for the children that encompassed whether they had left home at any time and the impacts on them of this; whether they had heard/seen/been aware of the violence and the impacts on them of that; whether they attributed blame and, if so, to whom and why; whether their parent(s) had talked to them about the violence; whether they themselves had ever talked to anyone about it and, if so, to whom and with what response (especially whether this had been experienced as helpful); whether anyone had ever helped their mother; what would have helped; what they wanted now; how safe they felt; whether they still saw the perpetrator, how often, under what circumstances, and whether or not this was OK; and what changes there had been in their lives. A separate coding for interviews with the children's mothers included whether they had tried to prevent the child(ren) from knowing about the abuse and if so how and with what result; whether the man had used the children in any way within his pattern of abuse and if so how and with what result; how the violence had affected the children and whether this had varied between siblings; whether she had talked to the child(ren) about the abuse; whether she had sought help from anywhere, where from and with what results; the impact of the abuse on her ability to care for the children; whether the children still saw the perpetrator and with what impact; and any particular concerns she now had for them.

Analysis took place under general themes and then under specific questions for children and mothers, both separately and in combination. Where it had been possible to maintain contact, copies of their own transcripts were offered to individual participants (both to share ownership with them and as a useful way of enhancing validity) but relatively few took up the offer. While it is acknowledged that the samples of children and women are small and cannot be used to arrive at any 'cause and effect' conclusions, the resultant interviews were rich in detail and, in Chapters 4 to 7, will offer considerable insight into the impact of domestic violence in children's lives and their responses to it.

CONCLUSION

The research study outlined in this book followed the high standards listed by Alderson (1995) for research with children: the children and young people were fully informed about the project in which they were being asked to participate; their consent was not only requested but was renegotiated throughout, thus putting the children as far as possible in charge of participation; their non-abusing parents' consent was also sought (or, in school, that of those *in loco parentis*); respondents knew that they could refuse to participate in the research or to withdraw from it at any point if they wished to do so, and some did; their confidentiality was respected within the limitations of child protection concerns (although it never became necessary to talk to an outside agency about any child's safety); and their own views, often in their own words, are being disseminated in this book and through other channels. In a field in which parents, teachers, psychologists and a host of other professionals and academics have been interviewed over the years about the impact on children of living with violence, it is still innovative to request children's permission before this is done and to raise the children's own accounts, if anything, above those of the adults who purport to talk for them (Alderson, 1995). Our research *with* children rather than *about* them will now be reported in the ensuing chapters. The concepts we employ in our discussion will, as far as possible, be grounded in the way the children and young people talked about their own lives (Williamson and Butler, 1997), as opposed to the adult perspectives which have preoccupied the literature up to now.

NOTES

1. The term 'mixed race' is used throughout this book because it is the term children most often used to describe themselves. The research team is aware that it is problematic in that, for example, it retains the outmoded concept of 'race' and may also be considered discriminatory because it tends to be used to emphasize black and white parentage, as against any other combination. The term 'dual heritage' is perhaps more celebratory of the richness of a shared parentage and family background, but is not in such wide-scale use and, certainly, did not form part of the children's language in either the completion of the questionnaires or the conduct of the in-depth interviews.

2. Children were not asked to indentify themselves in the questionnaire, so such issues would have been the outcome of children choosing to disclose directly to the researchers during the time they spent in the school.

3. These had been developed by the Child and Woman Abuse Studies Unit, when conducting a prevalence study of child sexual abuse in further education colleges (Kelly et al., 1991), and updated for a study done in schools on attitudes to violence against women (Burton et al., 1999).

3   What Children Know and Understand about Domestic Violence

Whilst a number of studies had previously begun to explore children's experiences of and responses to living with domestic violence (see Chapter 1), as far as we know the study reported in this book was the first to ask a general population of children what they knew and thought about the topic. In this chapter, we present the findings of Phase I of the research, the schools survey, which was designed to seek the views of a wide range of children and young people in primary and secondary schools (see Chapter 2 for methodology). By sampling in this way, we knew we would be including some children who had personally lived with domestic violence, along with many who had not. We did not consider it appropriate, under the circumstances of this survey, to try and identify who had or had not had this experience because we were not offering any opportunity for direct follow-up. Instead, we assumed that the experience would be present somewhere in every school and proceeded accordingly: by preparing the staff, working with sensitivity, and leaving ChildLine leaflets with all the children we met. We hoped, too, that having their own lives validated as part of a named, recognised and widespread phenomenon might be reassuring to some children who were living a 'family secret' (Peled and Edleson, 1995).

A total of 1395 questionnaires were completed in six primary and seven secondary schools in three contrasting parts of the country. The gender balance achieved was good, with 51 per cent of respondents (n = 715) female and 48 per cent (n = 671) male (less than 1 per cent, n = 9, unknown). Of those children and young people who answered the question about ethnicity, 76 per cent were white and 24 per cent came from a range of minority communities (see Table 3.1). There was a deliberate strategy to over-represent minority ethnic children in the sample, in order to ensure that we could make sensible comments about their experiences and not have to discount them because the numbers were too small. The age range across the board was 8 to 16 (40 per cent, 8–11; 60 per cent, 12–16 – see Table 3.2). A total of 89 children reported having a disability (see Table 3.3). This constituted 6 per cent of the total, falling comfortably between the 3 per cent and 16 per cent in 30 years of childhood disability surveys overviewed by Gordon et al. (2000). We can therefore say that disabled children were not excluded from the survey (see Chapters 1 and 2).

Analysis of the data included basic frequency counts, with additional analysis to explore variations across age, gender and ethnicity, and the difference it made to children's responses if they knew someone who had experienced domestic violence. Numbers of 15- and 16-year-olds were lower than other secondary school

TABLE 3.1 *Ethnicity of sample*

	Female		Male		Total	
	n	%	n	%	n	%
White	506	37	525	39	**1031**	76
Asian	58	4	58	4	**116**	9*
Mixed Race	33	2	28	2	**61**	5*
Afro-Caribbean	26	2	27	2	**53**	4
Black British	15	1	29	2	**44**	3
African	19	1	8	< 1	**27**	2
Turkish/Cypriot	5	< 1	16	1	**21**	2
Total	**662**	**49**	**691**	51	**1353**	100

42 children did not provide information on their ethnicity.
*Rounding error.

year groups (see Table 3.2) – perhaps because schools protect pupils from outside interruptions during their vital exam years – so it is necessary to interpret the statistics with more caution where the highest age group is concerned. Results on ethnicity are not reported in this chapter since they revealed no significant differences in this phase of the research.

THE MEANING OF DOMESTIC VIOLENCE

Children at both primary and secondary level were asked what they understood by the words 'domestic violence'. As would be expected, secondary school children reported a higher level of familiarity with the term (71 per cent) than primary school children (37 per cent), with few gender differences. However, analysis of what children understood the words 'domestic violence' to mean revealed considerable confusion. Only 9 per cent of primary and 28 per cent of secondary school children restricted those involved to parents and/or adults at home. A much higher number defined domestic violence as involving 'violence/hitting' (59 per cent of the sample), with 'fighting' being cited by 28 per cent of primary and 19 per cent of secondary and 'arguing' by 8 per cent and 6 per cent respectively. Combining responses of 'violence/hitting', 'fighting' and 'arguing' with those involved as 'parents and/or adults at home' reveals that only 5 per cent of the whole sample referred to the definition of domestic violence now commonly used by service providers and in legislation. A small proportion of children included child abuse within their definition. This suggests that, unless the commonly held definition has been explained, the combination of the word 'domestic' – which the majority of children understood as meaning 'within the family' – and the word 'violence' leads to all conflicts within the family, including arguments, being included. While a viable view, this nevertheless constitutes a strong argument for providing children with information on the topic, a proposal on which they have their own views and to which we shall consequently return below.

We also asked where children had heard the term 'domestic violence' (see Table 3.4). Younger children reported that they had learnt about it primarily from school and to a lesser extent from the television. The reverse was true for

TABLE 3.2 *Age of sample*

		8	9	10	11	Sub-total 8–11	12	13	14	15	16	Sub-total 12–16	Total
Female	n	41	51	93	88	273	92	106	132	47	4	381	654
(48%)	%	6	8	14	13	41	14	16	20	7	<1	58*	99*
Male	n	50	68	76	78	272	119	113	146	49	5	432	704
(52%)	%	7	9	11	11	38	17	16	21	7	<1	61*	100
Total	**n**	**91**	**119**	**169**	**166**	**545**	**211**	**219**	**278**	**96**	**9**	**813**	**1358**
	%	**7**	**9**	**12**	**12**	**40**	**16**	**16**	**20**	**7**	**<1**	**60**	**100**

37 children did not provide information on their age.
*Rounding error.

TABLE 3.3 *Disability in sample*

Type of Disability		Asthma	Sight	Dyslexia	Mobility	Hearing	Other (specified)	Other (unspecified)	Total
Female	n	8	6	5	4	3	6	6	38
	%	21	16	13	11	8	16	16	101*
Male	n	14	11	4	1	4	9	8	51
	%	27	22	8	2	8	18	16	101*
Total	n	22	17	9	5	7	15	14	89
	%	25	19	10	6	8	17	16	101*

*Rounding error.

older children who cited television at a higher rate the older they were. Younger children also mentioned their parents as their source of knowledge at a much higher rate than teenagers. Clearly, children's current sources of information are *ad hoc* and, for older children in particular, may not be offering them a sensitive or balanced view.

WHAT IS VIOLENCE?

Further questions probed what children understood by violence, and variations between the genders and across age ranges were minor here. Children were provided with a list of possible actions and asked to say whether they thought these did or did not constitute violence. Psychological abuse, excluding threats to hurt, was defined as violence by over a third (39 per cent) of secondary school children and by a slightly higher proportion of younger children. Controlling behaviour (in this instance illustrated by 'stopping them seeing friends') was also seen as violence by a third of the sample overall. Threats to hurt were defined as equally violent as physical acts of aggression by the majority of secondary school children (73 per cent) and by just over half of primary school children (57 per cent). These responses (in no way suggested by the researchers but representing the children's own views) were in line with contemporary thinking on domestic violence which sees it as a pattern of behaviours encompassing physical, emotional and sexual abuse, as well as threats and intimidation.

We also asked children to say if they thought the same acts constituted violence if the perpetrator was male and the victim female and if the sex of the actors was reversed. Primary school girls were slightly more likely to define various acts (such as pulling hair) as violence when committed by men towards women than by women towards men, but such distinctions were not evident in the responses of the other children. Clearly, children and young people's own view is that violence is equally wrong, whoever commits it. Complexities of context, motivation and outcome were introduced in later questions, through the use of vignettes.

PERSONAL KNOWLEDGE AND AWARENESS

Rather than ask whether children had themselves witnessed domestic violence, we explored whether they knew anyone this had happened to. Since we were

TABLE 3.4 *Where children learnt what the words 'domestic violence' mean*

Age	8–10 n = 177 (19%)				11–13 n = 427 (47%)				14–16 n = 309 (34%)				Total n = 913 (100%)	
	Female		Male		Female		Male		Female		Male			
	n	%¹	n	%	n	%	n	%	n	%	n	%	n	%
Television	36	40	38	43	89	43	114	51	88	56	87	58	452	50
School	55	62	49	56	99	48	98	44	69	44	54	36	424	46
Magazine	1	1	0	0	29	14	20	9	65	41	13	9	128	14
Mother	19	21	14	16	34	17	30	14	21	13	8	5	126	14
Friends	5	6	5	6	23	11	25	11	33	21	30	20	121	13
Father	18	20	22	25	20	10	28	13	12	8	9	6	109	12
Other media	5	6	3	3	<1	1	1	1	0	0	0	0	10	1
Other people	5	6	10	11	9	4	9	4	7	4	9	6	49	5
Total	89		88		205		222		158		151		913	

1. Percentages are based on those of that age and sex answering the question; multiple responses possible so do not total to 100.

interested in children's knowledge and what their sources of knowledge had been, this was both a more appropriate question and avoided inviting direct disclosure where support and follow-up possibilities were limited. In order to ensure consistency, a common definition of domestic violence was provided at this point, after children's own perceptions had been canvassed.

Just under a third (30 per cent) of children reported that they knew someone who had experienced domestic violence. We conducted a series of analyses to see whether personal contact had any impact on knowledge and understanding. It appears to have had little, if any, effect on younger children's responses but for secondary school children some small differences were evident, with those who had direct knowledge displaying more, and more complex, understandings. It was also the case that the older children were more likely to realize that they knew someone with this experience. In two unrelated studies by two of the present authors, with groups of young people aged 14 to 23, samples covering Ireland, Scotland and England revealed a picture consistent with this finding. In the most recent of these (Regan and Kelly, 2001) – a survey of 302 Irish young people – half knew someone who had been hit by a partner. An earlier study (Burton et al., 1998) which had investigated young people's attitudes to violence against women, found that, on average, just over half knew at least one woman or girl who had been hit by a partner. Young women were more aware of the violence around them than young men. Again, this parallels gendered awareness amongst teenagers in the present study (see below).

Taken together, these findings indicate that a substantial proportion of children and young people have contact with domestic violence within their family, friendship and community networks. Members of the research team have noted elsewhere (Regan and Kelly, 2001; Kelly et al., 1991) that this has extensive implications for education and prevention programmes, especially since our previous and current research indicates that friends are the most likely people who children and young people will tell about abuse and violence in their lives. Thus, many children have direct contact with domestic violence, not just in their own homes but also in their wider networks, and the older they get the more likely it is that this knowledge will involve at least one of their peers. Again, this is an argument for providing them with more information and equipping them to deal with worrying events in both their own and their friends' lives. We will return to this issue at the end of the chapter.

KNOWLEDGE OF PREVALENCE

One interesting area of knowledge is how common various groups think domestic violence is. Asking such questions amongst professionals (Kelly, 1999) produces widely varying estimates, as do prevalence studies (Hagemann-White, 2001; Schwartz, 2000; Walby and Myhill, 2001). In research projects with adults, we have provided numeric options (such as 10 per cent, or 1 in 10) for this type of question but since some of the children in the present study were as young as eight and might have had difficulty with percentages and proportions the question used across age groups offered options ranging from 'very common' to 'very rare'.

TABLE 3.5   *Answers to the question 'How common is domestic violence?'*

	Male		Female		**Total**	
	n	%	n	%	n	%
Very common	134	16	108	13	**242**	29
Common	216	26	209	25	**425**	50*
Rare	42	5	82	10	**124**	15
Very rare	20	2	36	4	**56**	7*
Total	412	49	435	51	**847**	100

*Rounding error.

Over three-quarters (79 per cent) of the older children thought that domestic violence was 'very common' or 'common' (85 per cent of females and 73 per cent of males), and those who knew someone who had experienced it were more likely to opt for 'very common'. Girls were more likely than boys to think that it is 'very common' (see Table 3.5).

HOW CHILDREN AND YOUNG PEOPLE UNDERSTAND PARENTAL CONFLICT

Again, rather than ask directly about domestic violence, we posed open-ended questions about what happened and how children reacted when there was an argument at home. Analysis (see Table 3.6) shows that the largest single group (25 per cent) reported that their parents did not argue in front of them, but that this was closely followed by 19 per cent who wrote about shouting or screaming and things being broken. Only 4 per cent reported events that would clearly fit within the definition of domestic violence used in the questionnaire, with this being more common amongst the 11 to 13 age group (though numbers are small throughout). Other responses to the same question referred to the way either parents or children reacted to conflict at home. Twelve per cent reported that, when parents argued, they subsequently 'made up' or talked about it, 8 per cent that one parent 'took time out' or left, and 7 per cent that their parents did not speak for some time. Children's own reactions to arguments fell into three main categories: ignoring the conflict (10 per cent); intervening (8 per cent); and being emotionally affected (7 per cent). A predominantly emotional impact was most commonly reported by the youngest girls. Interestingly, all three kinds of response echo the coping strategies reported by children who have lived with domestic violence (see Chapter 5).

We then probed further, becoming more explicit about violence and using a series of attitude questions about whether arguing, fighting and hitting are ever OK between parents. To keep the layout simple, the measure used here was somewhat crude – simply asking children whether they thought each statement was 'true' or 'false' (they could also opt for 'not sure'), rather than using a scaled response. Tables 3.7 to 3.10 present the responses analysed by gender and age. Some interesting patterns emerge, with older children far more willing to accept

TABLE 3.6 *What happens if parents argue*

Age	8–10 n = 248 (27%)				11–13 n = 398 (44%)				14–16 n = 256 (28%)				Total n = 902 (99%)*	
	Female		Male		Female		Male		Female		Male			
	n	%[1]	n	%	n	%	n	%	n	%	n	%	n	%
Parents don't argue/ not in front of child	36	30	31	25	64	34	47	22	22	18	26	20	226	25
Shouting/screaming/ swearing/damage to object	24	20	23	18	27	14	37	18	28	23	33	25	172	19
Parents make up/talk about it	8	7	15	12	18	10	29	14	19	15	23	17	112	12
Child/sibling avoids/ignores	9	7	14	11	19	10	18	9	13	11	19	14	92	10
Parents take 'time out'/leave	6	5	10	8	15	8	20	10	10	8	9	7	70	8
Child/sibling intervenes	7	6	11	9	15	8	16	8	11	9	8	6	68	8
Parents don't speak for a time	9	7	5	4	18	10	15	7	10	8	9	7	66	7
Emotional impact on child/siblings	16	13	8	6	16	8	14	7	2	2	4	3	60	7
Domestic violence in past/present	1	1	3	2	9	5	12	6	6	5	1	1	32	4
Other[2]	6	5	7	6	8	4	18	9	16	13	7	5	62	7
Total	122		126		189		209		123		133		902	

1. Percentages are based on those of that age and sex answering the question; multiple responses possible so do not total to 100.
2. 'Other' here includes: 'parents takes it out on everyone', 'child tells someone else about it', 'parent hits child', 'one parent backs down', 'nothing happens', 'not sure'.
*Rounding error.

TABLE 3.7   *Attitudes to conflict and violence between parents – primary school*

		Female				Male				Total
		True	False	Not sure	Sub-total	True	False	Not sure	Sub-total	
Some arguing	n	60	88	75	**223**	55	86	77	**218**	**441**
between parents	%	27	40	34	101*	25	39	35	99*	
is OK										
Some fighting	n	13	161	51	**225**	15	162	43	**220**	**445**
between parents	%	6	72	23	101*	7	74	20	101*	
is OK										
Some hitting	n	10	181	35	**226**	7	178	35	**220**	**446**
between parents	%	4	80	15	99*	3	81	16	100	
is OK										

*Rounding error.

arguing between parents than younger children (70 per cent as against 25 per cent). Whereas two-fifths of primary age children did not consider parental arguing to be OK, and over a third of them were not sure (with no gender differences), just over 7 out of 10 secondary age children appeared to accept it as a fact of life. The more detailed age breakdowns in Tables 3.9 and 3.10 reveal a dramatic jump in tolerance of parental arguing between the 8 to 10 and the 11 to 13 age groups, with a continuing incremental rise thereafter. Taken together with the response, above, that showed younger girls admitting to finding parental arguing emotionally upsetting, we might conclude from this that parents could usefully explain to their younger offspring that arguments do happen, what their own arguments are about (in an age-appropriate way) and that it is possible to argue safely, without hurting anyone (where this is the case). None of the age groups considered hitting between parents to be 'OK' in the abstract. We will see later in this chapter, though, that when specific incidents are described, both age and gender differences start to appear in tolerance levels.

Three additional questions were used in the secondary school questionnaire to explore whether children thought men or women were more or similarly violent in families (see Tables 3.9 and 3.10). Only a tiny proportion of respondents of all ages and both genders thought that women were more violent than men. There was not a marked difference between seeing men and women as equally violent or men as more violent, with girls just a little more aware than boys of men's violence, particularly at 14 and above. Interestingly, older children who knew someone who had experienced domestic violence were more likely to think that men were more violent in families, perhaps demonstrating that, in the absence of information being provided, life is the best teacher.

Of course, asking whether men are 'more violent' risks confusing prevalence with impact. We are able to throw more light on children's recognition of this. Overall, young people declared themselves around a third more likely to be sure that violence was equally a problem amongst men and women in families than to be sure that it was not. Yet, when subsequently asked whether there was a difference between a man hitting a woman and a woman hitting a man, only a quarter overall felt sure there was no difference (see Table 3.11). In response to an open-ended question (see Table 3.12), the overwhelming reason given for

TABLE 3.8   *Attitudes to conflict and violence between parents – secondary school*

		Female				Male				Total
		True	False	Not sure	Sub-total	True	False	Not sure	Sub-total	
Some arguing between	n	306	73	45	424	315	90	42	447	871
parents is OK	%	72	17	11	100	70	20	9	99*	
Some fighting between	n	29	343	50	422	39	382	31	452	874
parents is OK	%	7	81	12	100	9	85	7	101*	
Some hitting between	n	7	384	34	425	13	424	11	448	873
parents is OK	%	2	90	8	100	3	95	3	100	
Men are more violent	n	172	109	141	422	171	140	139	450	872
in families	%	41	26	33	100	38	31	31	100	
Women are more	n	20	233	165	418	24	273	156	453	871
violent in families	%	5	56	39	100	5	60	34	99*	
Women and men are	n	161	114	138	413	165	140	146	451	864
equally violent	%	39	28	33	100	37	31	32	100	

*Rounding error.

TABLE 3.9 *Attitudes to conflict and violence between parents – girls*

Age		8–10 True	False	Not sure	Sub-total	11–13 True	False	Not sure	Sub-total	14–16 True	False	Not sure	Sub-total	Total True	False	Not sure	Sub-total
Some arguing between	n	38	70	66	**174**	174	66	38	**278**	153	22	15	**190**	365	158	119	**642**
parents is OK	%[1]	22	40	38	100	63	24	14	101*	81	12	8	101*	57	25	19	101*
Some fighting between	n	10	121	44	**175**	14	226	40	**280**	18	152	17	**187**	42	499	101	**642**
parents is OK	%	6	69	25	100	5	81	14	100	10	81	9	100	7	78	16	101*
Some hitting between	n	8	135	32	**175**	7	251	25	**283**	2	174	12	**188**	17	560	69	**646**
parents is OK	%	5	77	18	100	2	89	9	100	1	93	6	100	3	87	11	101*
Men are more violent	n					97	61	77	**235**	75	48	64	**187**	172	109	141	**422**
in families	%					41	26	33	100	40	26	34	100	41	26	33	100
Women are more	n					13	125	95	**233**	7	108	70	**185**	20	233	165	**422**
violent in families	%					6	54	41	101*	4	58	38	100	5	55	39	99*
Women and men are	n					94	63	71	**228**	67	51	67	**185**	161	114	138	**413**
equally violent	%					41	28	31	100	36	28	36	100	39	28	33	100

1. Percentages are based on those of that age and sex answering the question, including those who responded 'not sure'.
*Rounding error.

TABLE 3.10 *Attitudes to conflict and violence between parents – boys*

Age		8–10				11–13				14–16				Total			
		True	False	Not sure	Sub-total	True	False	Not sure	Sub-total	True	False	Not sure	Sub-total	True	False	Not sure	Sub-total
Some arguing between parents is OK	n	39	70	64	**173**	177	79	38	**294**	154	26	15	**195**	370	175	117	**662**
	%[1]	23	40	37	100	60	27	13	100	79	13	8	100	56	26	18	100
Some fighting between parents is OK	n	13	127	35	**175**	14	264	18	**296**	27	151	20	**198**	54	542	73	**669**
	%	7	73	20	100	5	89	6	100	14	76	10	100	8	81	11	100
Some hitting between parents is OK	n	7	139	29	**175**	7	278	11	**296**	6	83	5	**194**	20	600	45	**665**
	%	4	79	17	100	2	94	4	100	3	94	3	100	3	90	7	100
Men are more violent in families	n					92	85	78	**255**	79	55	61	**195**	171	140	139	**450**
	%					36	33	31	100	41	28	31	100	38	31	31	100
Women are more violent in families	n					16	157	82	**255**	8	116	74	**198**	24	273	156	**453**
	%					6	62	32	100	4	59	37	100	5	60	34	99*
Women and men are equally violent	n					101	82	72	**255**	64	58	74	**196**	165	140	146	**451**
	%					40	32	28	100	33	29	38	100	37	31	32	100

1. Percentages are based on those of that age and sex answering the question, including those who responded 'not sure'.
*Rounding error.

TABLE 3.11 *Is there a difference between a man being violent to a woman and a woman being violent to a man?*

| | Primary n = 431 | | | | Secondary n = 875 | | | | Total n = 1306 | | | | Total | |
| | Female | | Male | | Female | | Male | | Female | | Male | | | |
	n	%	n	%	n	%	n	%	n	%	n	%	n	%
Yes	104	47	113	54	167	39	187	41	271	42	300	45	**571**	44
No	28	13	40	19	131	31	140	31	159	25	180	27	**339**	26
Not sure	89	40	57	27	125	30	125	28	214	33	182	27	**396**	30
Total	221	100	210	100	423	100	452	100	644	100	662	99*	**1306**	100

*Rounding error.

TABLE 3.12 *Why answered previous question the way they did*

| | Primary n = 212 | | | | Secondary n = 532 | | | | Total n = 744 | | | | Total | |
| | Female | | Male | | Female | | Male | | Female | | Male | | | |
	n	%[1]	n	%	n	%	n	%	n	%	n	%	n	%
Why there is a difference														
Men are bigger/stronger	72	71	79	71	108	39	97	38	180	47	176	48	**356**	48
Men hit the most	6	6	1	1	17	6	12	5	23	6	13	4	**36**	5
Not right for a man to hit a woman	3	3	6	5	5	2	6	2	8	2	12	3	**20**	3
Women less violent	0	0	0	0	2	1	5	2	2	<1	5	1	**7**	1
Why there is no difference														
Both can hit	12	12	18	16	84	30	72	28	96	25	90	25	**186**	25
Violence is wrong	1	1	1	1	16	6	11	4	17	4	12	3	**29**	4
Other[2]	8	8	10	9	33	12	39	15	41	11	49	13	**90**	12
Total respondents	101		111		278		254		379		365		**744**	

1. Percentages are based on those of that age and sex answering the question; multiple responses possible so do not total 100.
2. 'Other' here includes: 'illegal for men to hit women', 'men use weapons', 'men can do sexual violence', 'women don't like fighting'.

differentiating – by 71 per cent of primary and 39 per cent of secondary-aged children – was that men are stronger. This combination of answers picks up the complexity in real-life research on domestic violence. Whilst women and men may use violence in some form or another at similar rates (though not necessarily in similar patterns), the meaning and consequences of violence to men and women are not the same (see Hagemann-White, 2001; Mirrlees-Black, 1999; Schwartz, 2000). Men inflict more harm and are often differently motivated, with men's power and control tactics and women's self-defence completely obscured within simple frequency counts of violent incidents. Our survey shows that men's and women's use of violence is understood as not the same by a substantial proportion of children, once again suggesting that they would be perfectly able to benefit from more widespread and quite sophisticated education about the less attractive side of personal and social relationships.

LIVING WITH DOMESTIC VIOLENCE

One of our major interests was to discover what children in general think might be the impacts on children of living with domestic violence. We therefore asked an explicit question about this and also explored the issue further, using a short vignette (see next section and Chapter 2). The explicit question asked how children would feel if they were living in a family where domestic violence was happening (see Table 3.13). The most common responses to this open-ended question can be grouped into one category, related to the emotions: 'upset'/'unhappy'/'sad'. Over half of the entire sample responded in this way, and as many as two-thirds of the under 11s. Another 40 per cent of the sample, with more girls than boys at all ages, said they thought children would feel 'afraid'/'scared'/'worried'. These two themes predominated, with other reactions such as 'unwell'/'hurt', 'unloved'/'alone' and 'angry' suggested by smaller numbers. The theme of sadness in children in relation to domestic violence is perhaps less predictable by adults than that of fear, yet it occurred in both phases of this study (see Chapter 4); that is, it was raised both by children who had actually lived with violence and by others who were imagining their experiences. It has also arisen in other studies where children report their own experiences of living with domestic violence and talk about being unhappy or crying all the time (McGee, 2000; Saunders et al., 1995), whereas adults tend to be far more aware of children being frightened (e.g. mothers' reports in Abrahams, 1994). Clearly, then, as well as recognizing that children's understandings of living with domestic violence are felt at an emotional level and that it has meaning in their lives, we need to be aware that children have their own complexities of emotion and that we need to ask them directly if we want to appreciate fully what they are going through. At different times, or at one and the same time, they may be feeling upset, angry, scared and confused, for example.

Secondary school age children were more likely to include reactions beyond sadness and fear in their suggestions of how domestic violence might make

TABLE 3.13 *How children feel living with domestic violence*

Age	8–10 n = 270				11–13 n = 508				14–16 n = 334				Total n = 1112	
	Female		Male		Female		Male		Female		Male			
	n	%¹	n	%	n	%	n	%	n	%	n	%	n	%
Upset/unhappy/sad	91	66	90	68	137	53	121	48	72	41	87	55	598	54
Afraid/scared/worried	75	54	54	41	122	47	78	31	69	39	44	29	442	40
Unwell/horrible/hurt	6	4	5	4	38	15	14	6	31	18	14	9	108	10
Unloved/alone	6	4	2	2	28	11	17	7	18	10	12	8	83	7
Angry	7	5	6	5	8	3	3	1	16	9	4	3	44	4
Other	16	12	7	5	63	24	85	34	84	48	62	39	317	29
Total respondents	138		132		258		250		176		158		1112	

1. Percentages are based on those of that age and sex answering the question; multiple responses possible so do not total to 100.

children feel, perhaps reflecting their maturing understanding of the range of emotional responses that can occur. Additional questions, for secondary children only, explored potential variations in response in more depth, asking whether respondents thought there might be different impacts according to the age and sex of the children who lived with domestic violence. Approaching a quarter of respondents thought that young children would have less understanding than teenagers and one in five saw the situation as likely to be more difficult emotionally for the younger ones, as they might be more 'vulnerable'/'fearful'/'upset' (see Table 3.14). Interestingly, almost one in five of these secondary-aged respondents volunteered the suggestion that younger children who lived with abuse might grow up to be abusers themselves, with boys more likely than girls and older respondents more likely than younger to support this idea. They saw it as far less relevant to their own age group, however, with only 2 per cent making this point about a potential effect on teenagers. This is not very logical and perhaps suggests that it is easier to assume such an effect on people at a distance (in this case, the younger age group) than on one's immediate peers. In fact, the concept of transgenerational transmission, or a 'cycle of abuse', though widespread, is highly contentious regardless of age group (see overview of research in Morley and Mullender, 1994). With respect to their own age group, in the main they thought that teenagers would be less affected (13 per cent) and more able to take some form of action (11 per cent), although a minority cited intervention as increasing the possibility of direct harm (2 per cent). In terms of whether reactions would be gendered (see Table 3.15), a greater adverse impact on girls was predicted by both genders, with girls being seen by both sexes (but particularly by 14- to 16-year-old boys) as 'more sensitive' and (particularly by 11- to 13-year-old girls) as more likely to be frightened. Boys were regarded as more likely to be able to intervene, although more girls thought this than boys themselves. The minority who thought that girls would be more likely to intervene saw this more in terms of telling someone or showing understanding of what was happening than through a physical intervention. (Later chapters will say more about how children actually do intervene when they live with domestic violence.)

A HYPOTHETICAL CASE

The vignette of Jaz was carefully constructed in order not to presume the child's sex or ethnicity in the hope that as many children as possible would identify with the fictitious child and think themselves into the story. It also included simple elements of victim-blaming on the part of the perpetrator in order to explore how children allocate responsibility for abuse. It was in response to the ensuing questions that some of the most marked age and sex differences began to emerge. The account went as follows:

> Jaz is about your age. Jaz's father becomes angry and violent sometimes. One Saturday afternoon, Jaz is at home with Mum and Dad. Dad hits Jaz's mother because the house is untidy and knocks her down. He shouts that he has told her loads of times to sort it out. Jaz tries to intervene, but Dad threatens Jaz.

TABLE 3.14 *How would domestic violence affect young children differently from teenagers?*

Age	11–13 n = 280				14–16 n = 241				Total n = 521	
	Female		Male		Female		Male			
	n	%¹	n	%	n	%	n	%	n	%
How children would be affected										
Children don't understand/know it is wrong	39	27	24	18	36	27	20	19	119	23
Children would be more vulnerable/fearful/upset	22	15	34	26	28	21	18	17	102	20
Children could grow up to become abusers/abused	18	12	23	17	28	21	31	29	100	19
Children could/would get hurt more	5	3	5	4	1	1	3	3	14	3
How teenagers would be affected										
Teenagers would be less affected	24	16	14	11	12	9	16	15	66	13
Teenagers can intervene/do something	20	14	13	10	16	12	6	6	55	11
Teenagers would be more affected	8	5	2	2	6	5	6	6	22	4
Teenagers could go on to become abusers/abused	3	2	7	5	1	1	1	1	12	2
Teenagers can evade/avoid violence	3	2	4	3	4	3	0	0	11	2
Teenagers can get hurt because they intervene	4	3	2	2	1	1	1	1	8	2
Other²	16	11	20	15	13	10	7	7	56	11
Don't know/not sure	4	3	2	2	0	0	3	3	9	2
Total respondents	147		133		133		108		521	

1. Percentages are based on those of that age and sex answering the question, multiple responses possible so do not total 100.
2. 'Other' includes: 'children's education could be affected', 'teenagers are more aggressive'.

TABLE 3.15 *How would girls react differently to domestic violence from boys?*

| | 11–13 n = 146 | | | | 14–16 n = 152 | | | | Total n = 298 | |
| | Female | | Male | | Female | | Male | | | |
	n	%[1]	n	%	n	%	n	%	n	%
Girls' reaction										
Girls are more sensitive/emotional	31	35	19	33	43	45	30	53	123	41
Girls would be more frightened/scared	24	27	10	18	13	14	8	14	55	18
Girls are just less violent than boys	5	6	2	4	8	8	2	4	17	6
Girls more likely to intervene/tell someone/understand	9	10	1	2	6	6	6	11	22	7
Boys' reaction										
Boys are more aggressive, likely/able to intervene	17	19	7	12	17	18	5	9	46	15
Other[2]	12	13	21	37	10	11	5	9	48	16
Don't know/not sure	1	1	0	0	3	3	2	4	6	2
Total respondents	89		57		95		57		298	

1. Percentages are based on those of that age and sex answering the question, multiple responses possible so do not total 100.
2. 'Other' includes: 'roles of victim and perpetrator', 'boys seeing as joke', 'boys less likely to show their feeling'.

The first question asked how Jaz would be feeling. Sadness and fear recurred as the predominant emotional responses suggested, again with the younger children more likely to mention sadness, but with anger also more in evidence than before, including specifying anger at the father (see Table 3.16). This may have been because children had an actual scenario to react to this time, rather than just the abstract idea of domestic violence. Secondary children were somewhat more likely to mention anger than primary age children.

Further open-ended questions asked children to speculate on what they thought Jaz, Jaz's mother and Jaz's father should do. Almost all of the older children (90 per cent) and over half of the younger children (62 per cent) thought Jaz should do something. The most common courses of action recommended were to call the police (38 per cent) and/or to tell someone (30 per cent) – more older children opting for the latter, and more younger children placing their faith in Jaz's telling both parents to stop (see Table 3.17). Secondary children had some awareness of the possibility of phoning for advice: ChildLine or the NSPCC, for example. With respect to Jaz's mother (see Table 3.18), two main possibilities were recommended: leaving (39 per cent) and calling the police (30 per cent), with older children preferring the former and younger children the latter. Only 1 per cent, all but one of whom were older children, suggested she should contact Women's Aid, revealing a low level of knowledge amongst these children about support services, and 2 per cent, all of secondary age, suggested taking Jaz's dad to court. Five per cent (with slightly more younger children) suggested physical retaliation. Falling into the victim-blaming motivation attributed to Jaz's dad, small numbers of children thought Jaz's mum should apologize or be a better wife.

The commonest view (held by 30 per cent) as to what Jaz's father should do was to stop being violent/arguing (see Table 3.19). Other possibilities included calming down (suggested more by older children), apologizing (proposed more by younger ones), and being more considerate to Jaz's mother. There is a clear theme here of the perpetrator needing to take responsibility. As before, older children had more awareness of services available, with a third of secondary age girls and 18 per cent of their male peers suggesting that Jaz's father should get some form of counselling or other help. A tiny minority of the sample, at all ages but slightly more commonly amongst boys, made strongly victim-blaming responses to the effect that Jaz's father should 'sort out' Jaz's mother.

We also asked what would help Jaz (see Table 3.20). The commonest response, including from over a third of secondary age children, focused on the importance of Jaz being able to obtain support or advice. A third of primary children thought the most important thing would be for the violence to stop, with 15 per cent making clear statements that Jaz should be removed from the situation altogether. Older children were more likely to recommend talking with both parents. Age differences were par-ticularly marked here, and were much more significant than any variations by sex.

When asked who was responsible for the violence – 'Whose fault was it that Jaz's mum got hit?' – secondary school children were far more likely than their younger counterparts to blame Jaz's father (see Table 3.21) and girls of all ages were more willing to do so. Boys displayed more ambivalence, increasing with age and with the divergence between the attitudes of girls and boys peaking at 13 to 14 years of age (p = .003) and remaining significant amongst the 15- to

TABLE 3.17 *What form of action individuals should take*

| What Jaz should do | Primary n = 190 | | | | Secondary n = 712 | | | | Total n = 902 | |
| | Female | | Male | | Female | | Male | | | |
	n	%¹	n	%	n	%	n	%	n	%
Call the police	31	29	34	41	136	36	139	41	340	38
Talk to/tell someone	13	12	8	10	158	42	88	26	267	30
Call ChildLine/helpline/NSPCC	7	7	2	2	58	15	56	17	123	14
Tell both parents to stop	28	26	22	27	24	6	42	13	116	13
Jaz might get hurt	13	12	8	10	14	4	7	2	42	5
Get help	0	0	3	4	19	5	11	3	33	4
Support Mum	0	0	0	0	16	4	15	4	31	3
Evade/avoid the situation	4	4	3	4	13	3	10	3	30	3
Tell Dad to stop	1	1	2	2	6	2	16	5	25	3
Talk to Mum	2	2	0	0	8	2	9	3	19	2
Should not get involved/interfere	4	4	1	1	7	2	5	2	17	2
Other²	14	13	7	8	15	4	13	4	49	5
Total respondents	107		83		377		335		902	

1. Percentages based on those of that age and sex answering the question, multiple responses possible so do not total 100.
2. 'Other' includes: 'Could cause more trouble', 'should do something', 'could get into trouble', 'tell Dad to stop', 'might make it worse', 'can't do anything', 'scream out/yell'.

TABLE 3.18 *What Jaz's mother should do*

| | Primary n = 341 | | | | Secondary n = 746 | | | | Total n = 1087 | |
| | Female | | Male | | Female | | Male | | | |
	n	%[1]	n	%	n	%	n	%	n	%
Leave (and take Jaz with her)	34	19	20	12	200	53	165	45	419	39
Call the police	70	40	69	42	92	24	97	26	328	30
Talk to/tell someone	14	8	10	6	58	15	25	7	107	10
Get help	2	1	6	4	31	8	28	8	67	6
Be a good wife (cook etc)	9	5	6	4	19	5	25	7	59	5
Walk away/evade the situation	22	12	25	15	3	1	3	1	53	5
Physically retaliate	12	7	10	6	10	3	20	5	52	5
Talk to Jaz's dad	0	0	0	0	12	3	2	1	31	3
Ask/get Jaz's dad to leave	8	5	4	2	4	1	7	2	23	2
Apologize to Jaz's dad	6	3	6	4	2	1	4	1	18	2
Take Jaz's dad to court	0	0	0	0	7	2	10	3	17	2
Defend herself	1	1	0	0	9	2	4	1	14	1
Ring Women's Aid	1	1	0	0	4	1	9	2	14	1
Tell Jaz's dad to stop	3	2	2	1	4	1	2	1	11	1
Other[2]	15	8	15	9	22	6	20	5	72	7
Total respondents	177		164		379		367		1087	

1. Percentages based on those of that age and sex answering the question; multiple responses possible so do not total 100.
2. 'Other' includes: 'get counselling/help for Jaz's dad', 'calm the situation down', 'yell/scream', 'not listen to Jaz's dad', 'take care of Jaz', 'marriage counselling', 'contact social services'.

TABLE 3.19 *What Jaz's father should do*

| | Primary n = 323 | | | | Secondary n = 734 | | | | Total n = 1057 | |
| | Female | | Male | | Female | | Male | | | |
	n	%[1]	n	%	n	%	n	%	n	%
Stop the violence/arguing	49	29	42	28	112	30	109	31	**312**	30
Get counselling/help	6	4	4	3	126	33	65	18	**201**	19
Calm down	20	12	8	5	77	20	66	19	**171**	16
Say sorry/apologize	38	22	32	21	44	12	55	15	**169**	16
Tell Jaz's mother if going to be late/be more considerate	24	14	14	9	35	9	34	10	**107**	10
Leave the house/go away	18	11	28	18	20	5	27	8	**93**	9
Talk to Jaz's mother/make up	9	5	9	6	11	3	10	3	**39**	4
'Sort her out'	3	2	5	3	3	1	7	2	**18**	2
Call the police/ambulance	9	5	2	1	3	1	2	1	**16**	2
Other[2]	18	11	20	13	27	7	38	11	**103**	10
Total respondents	171		152		379		355		1057	

1. Percentages based on those of that age and sex answering the question; multiple responses possible so do not total 100.
2. 'Other' includes: 'think about his actions', 'take care of Jaz's mum', 'stop blaming Jaz's mum', 'nothing', 'forget about it'.

TABLE 3.20 *What would help Jaz?*

| | Primary n = 310 | | | | Secondary n = 346 | | | | Total n = 656 | |
| | Female | | Male | | Female | | Male | | | |
	n	%[1]	n	%	n	%	n	%	n	%
Opportunity to talk/reassurance/support	49	28	23	17	67	34	45	31	**184**	28
Give 'Jaz' advice	0	0	0	0	79	40	50	34	**129**	20
Stop the violence	56	32	45	33	10	5	16	11	**127**	19
Talk to the parents	13	7	5	4	30	15	23	16	**71**	11
Take child somewhere else	26	15	20	15	0	0	0	0	**46**	7
Involve the police/arrest perpetrator	12	7	15	11	8	4	3	2	**38**	6
Other[2]	32	18	30	22	25	13	21	14	**108**	16
Total respondents	175		135		200		146		**656**	

1. Percentages based on those of that age and sex answering the question; multiple responses possible so do not total 100.
2. 'Other' here includes: 'checking whether mother is hurt', 'talking to father', 'removing mother' and 'pratical help'.

TABLE 3.21 *Responsibility for violence (by sex and educational level)*

			Father	Mother	Both Parents	Unsure	Total
Primary	Female	n	102	14	55	37	208
n = 394		%	49	7	26	18	100
	Male	n	74	16	51	45	186
		%	40	9	27	24	100
Secondary	Female	n	295	15	39	57	406
n = 822		%	73	4	10	14	101*
	Male	n	252	34	58	72	416
		%	61	8	14	17	100
Total n = 1216		n	**723**	**79**	**203**	**211**	**1216**
		%	59	6	17	17	99*

*Rounding error.

TABLE 3.22 *Responsibility for violence (by sex and age)*

Age			Father	Mother	Both parents/ unsure	Total n = 1201[1]
8–10	Female	n	79	8	72	159
n = 303		%	50	5	45	100
	Male	n	59	15	70	144
		%	41	10	49	100
11–12	Female	n	104	10	57	171
n = 335		%	61	6	33	100
	Male	n	92	6	66	164
		%	56	4	40	100
13–14	Female	n	172	10	47	229
n = 467		%	75	4	21	100
	Male	n	145	23	70	238
		%	61	10	29	100
15–16	Female	n	36	0	10	46
n = 96		%	78	0	22	100
	Male	n	28	5	17	50
		%	56	10	34	100
Total	Female	n	**391**	**28**	**186**	**605**
		%	65	5	31	101*
	Male	n	**324**	**49**	**223**	**596**
		%	54	8	37	99*

1. The precise age of 15 children not known.
*Rounding error.

16-year-olds (p = .022) (see Table 3.22). Given that the vignette made it perfectly clear that Jaz's father had hit his partner and knocked her down, and that the violence was entirely in one direction, it is worrying that so many male respondents blamed both parents or were unsure as to who was responsible. Overall, 50 boys (and 29 girls, though none in the 15 to 16 age group) even considered Jaz's mother to be solely at fault. There is surely strong support here for the argument that lessons are needed in school to help children and young people – and especially teenage boys! – better understand that domestic violence is a crime and that the perpetrator is responsible for his own actions. We will return to this point below.

EMERGING DIFFERENCES BETWEEN GIRLS AND BOYS

A second series of attitude questions, for secondary school pupils only, followed the Jaz scenario. The responses elicited confirmed the emerging gender differences, especially in the 15- to 16-year-old age group, and presented a particularly worrying picture of teenage boys' attitudes towards domestic violence that was widely picked up from this research by the news media (though girls' views allow no room for complacence). The research team has reached the conclusion, as a result of these findings, that preventative work in schools needs to start at the beginning of secondary school, or even back in primary school, if it is to stand any chance of influencing boys' thinking about women and about relationships between the sexes. Girls do seem to acquire some greater understanding as a facet of maturing, but the same does not happen for boys.

The questions we posed involved a series of five statements with which young people were asked to agree or disagree. The first two involved levels of victim-blame, the third a misconception (that pregnancy protects women from violence whereas, in fact, it can be a time of particular risk; see, for example, Stanko et al., 1998), the fourth the idea that perpetrators are sick or mentally ill (which would give them some level of excuse, whereas domestic violence is actually endemic throughout society), and the fifth the commonsense notion that it is easy for victims to leave, when it is really very difficult. Table 3.23 presents the findings.

Boys were more likely than girls to agree with the statement that 'women get hit if they have done something to make men angry', though it is a matter of some concern that a majority of both sexes agreed with this. Whereas that first statement has clear overtones of victim-blaming but also implicates men's anger, the second quite explicitly places the responsibility for violence on women: 'Some women deserve to be hit'. Despite two decades of widespread action against domestic violence, a third of all the boys questioned (34 per cent), in this large-scale survey agreed with a view that wider society no longer considers tolerable. Even amongst girls, one in five agreed, which is a horrific comment on the way our nation is preparing young women to view themselves and their expected quality of life in the twenty-first century. A more detailed breakdown of the findings reveals an intensely worrying trend by age, in that boys' attitudes harden as they reach the teenage years; 31 per cent of 11- to 12-year-olds, rising to 33 per cent of 13- to 14-year-olds, and again to 41 per cent of 15- to 16-year-old boys agreed with this woman-blaming statement. Girls, on the other hand, grew somewhat in awareness that women are not to blame, with the percentage agreeing dropping from around one in five to under one in six for the

TABLE 3.23 Attitudes to violence

Statement		Female 11–12		Male 11–12	
		Agree	Disagree	Agree	Disagree
Women get hit if they have done something to make men angry	n	57	44	81	25
	%	56	44	76	24
Some women deserve to be hit	n	18	67	26	59
	%	21	79	31	69
Men don't hit women when they are pregnant	n	43	50	54	40
	%	46	54	57	43
Men who hit women are 'crazy'/mentally ill	n	79	30	66	41
	%	73	27	62	38
Women could easily leave if their partner is violent to them	n	69	25	82	22
	%	73	27	79	21

Statement		Female 13–14		Male 13–14	
		Agree	Disagree	Agree	Disagree
Women get hit if they have done something to make men angry	n	126	68	152	74
	%	59	41	67	33
Some women deserve to be hit	n	39	161	70	143
	%	20	80	33	67
Men don't hit women when they are pregnant	n	64	145	89	130
	%	31	69	41	59
Men who hit women are 'crazy'/mentally ill	n	156	62	127	102
	%	72	28	56	44
Women could easily leave if their partner is violent to them	n	141	70	159	65
	%	67	33	71	29

Statement		Female 15–16		Male 15–16	
		Agree	Disagree	Agree	Disagree
Women get hit if they have done something to make men angry	n	27	14	28	17
	%	66	34	62	38
Some women deserve to be hit	n	6	33	16	23
	%	15	85	41	59
Men don't hit women when they are pregnant	n	10	27	22	19
	%	27	73	54	46
Men who hit women are 'crazy'/mentally ill	n	29	15	31	14
	%	66	34	69	31
Women could easily leave if their partner is violent to them	n	20	20	37	6
	%	50	50	86	14

oldest group (15 per cent), though this is still a worryingly high number in an age group of girls who are heading towards choosing the partners with whom to spend their young adult lives. A similar pattern can be discerned in the responses to the 'men don't hit women when they are pregnant' statement; with the disparity between girls and boys growing across the age range, this time chiefly because girls appear to become more aware of the dangers. Thus, while girls decrease their agreement from almost half at 11 to 12 to only just over a quarter by age 15 to 16, more than half of boys agree in both the younger and older age brackets.

The tendency to assume that there are individual and psychological explanations of the use of violence was explored through the statement 'men who hit women are "crazy"/mentally ill'. A clear majority of both sexes agreed with this although at age 11 to 14 more girls agreed than boys (almost three-quarters as against between a half and two-thirds). Perhaps boys are less ready to condemn men with these labels whereas, for us as the question-setters, there was an implication of offering men an excuse for their violence if it were to be explained in these terms. This finding echoes a study undertaken for the Zero Tolerance Trust (Burton et al., 1998) that also asked young people aged over 14 a similar question, using the term 'sick' rather than '"crazy"/mentally ill'. Nearly two-thirds of that sample agreed with the statement, a figure remarkably close to that in the present study. This widespread perception amongst young people that men's use of violence against their female partners is linked to some form of mental disorder is not supported by the literature on male perpetrators (see Mullender, 1996, for an overview).

Similarly, the majority of the total schools sample reported in this chapter agreed with the common misconception that 'women could easily leave if their partner is violent to them'. Three-quarters of the youngest group agreed, with a slight fall at 13 to 14. By age 15 to 16, however, a marked sex difference becomes evident, again because girls begin to show greater awareness. Thus we see only half the girls now agreeing, but boys' level of agreement jumping up to 86 per cent. Though numbers are smaller in this age band and thus must be read with some caution, these figures appear to suggest that boys do not grow out of the widespread belief that leaving a violent relationship is both relatively simple and, by implication, that it stops abuse. As they get older, girls, on the other hand, appear to develop a more realistic perception that leaving a bad relationship is not necessarily easy, though whether they glean this from experience, observation, the media or other influences, we do not know. The marked differences associated with age and sex reported here raise a number of questions about perception, knowledge and experience that would merit more detailed investigation. Yet again, they also point towards the value of offering lessons in school that could include learning about perpetrators' responsibility for their own violence, the criminal nature of domestic violence, its prevalence, particular risk factors, and the dangers of post-separation violence – actually one of the most likely times for an abused woman to be killed (Wilson and Daly, 1992; 1998).

PUTTING THEMSELVES IN THE PICTURE

The questionnaire to secondary school students was longer than that for the younger children because of the time taken to complete it at different levels of ability and because some material was not considered age appropriate for the younger ones. As well as the question just cited, it contained two additional sections in which we explored the potential for violence in relationships. The first looked at various issues that might be considered triggers for violence and at what respondents thought they would do if they were the victim or the perpetrator of violence. The second contained a story of 'dating violence' and a series of questions linked to it.

Tables 3.24a and 3.24b record responses, broken down by age and sex, about the likelihood of violence being used in relation to five specific things a woman might do, including refusing to cook or do housework, or to have sex, focusing her attention on the children, or making fun of her partner at a party. Here it should be noted that boys were being asked to answer in terms of their own probable actions against a wife or girlfriend, if they had one, whereas girls were being asked what a man might do to a woman in identical circumstances. Both sets of answers are hypothetical, but only one involves the respondents thinking about their own likely behaviour. Perhaps because of this (the boys may have been reluctant to own their probable reactions), or perhaps because girls are more aware of the danger of violence, for all of the scenarios girls rated the likelihood of violence being used much higher (both in terms of overall ratings, and in the proportions saying that it was 'very likely') than did boys. The two sexes agreed, however, that the most likely context for violence was unfaithfulness, with three out of four boys and nine out of ten girls (rising to 97 per cent of 14- to 16-year- old girls) stating that violence was possible or likely where a woman had sex with another man. Most of the girls considered it probable rather than possible and half the boys' sample agreed. If we reflect on these figures for a moment, they tell us that teenage girls consider it almost inevitable that sexual jealousy can lead to violence and that a clear majority of boys agree, even when their own future behaviour is implicated. Both the extremely high levels of expectation of violence amongst young women and the significant levels of potential willingness to use violence expressed by young men are cause for concern, and echo findings from a number of other studies with young people (see Price et al., 2000). The theme of sexual jealousy and possessiveness recurs in the domestic violence literature, and is one of the key areas where control over women's behaviour is exerted (Wilson and Daly, 1998) so the young people in our sample were unfortunately not being unrealistic in their replies. Again, we did not ask whether this lesson had been learnt from personal experience, or from the media or popular culture. Intervening to change these attitudes should surely start in school, preferably before they are so entrenched. Girls have a right to expect better and it is profoundly depressing that boys have such low expectations of their own behaviour.

When asked specifically what they themselves would do if they were either hitting their partner (boys: see Table 3.25) or being hit (girls: see Table 3.26), over half the girls said they would end the relationship and, whilst none of the boys gave this response, the majority (58 per cent) opted for calming down/stopping. Most of the responses from girls involve taking some form of action: telling someone; fighting back; informing the police; telling him to stop. Fewer of the boys mentioned actions involving others, although about one in five (22 per cent) wrote 'getting some form of help'. Rather, their proposed actions focused more on the relationship itself: apologizing; leaving the situation; talking to the girl. Since this was an open-ended question, a wide range of responses was possible and, alarmingly, only a few more boys made a clear statement that they would not hit a girlfriend (n = 16: 6 per cent) than wrote that they would continue the abuse

TABLE 3.24a   *Whether it is likely that he would hit a wife/girlfriend in certain circumstances – boys*

		Male 11–13			
Statement		Likely	Maybe	Unlikely	Total
She refused to cook or do housework	n	20 (12)[1]	28	121	169
	%	12 (7)	17	72	101*
She had sex with another man	n	90 (28)	44	41	175
	%	51 (16)	25	24	99*
She refused to have sex with you	n	38 (23)	28	106	172
	%	22 (13)	16	62	100
She made fun of you at a party	n	41 (15)	48	84	173
	%	24 (9)	28	48	101*
She gave all her attention to the children	n	29 (16)	23	121	173
	%	17 (9)	13	70	100

		Male 14–16			
Statement		Likely	Maybe	Unlikely	Total
She refused to cook or do housework	n	23 (8)	14	128	165
	%	14 (5)	8	77	99*
She had sex with another man	n	80 (48)	43	44	167
	%	48 (29)	26	26	100
She refused to have sex with you	n	26 (15)	25	115	166
	%	16 (9)	15	69	100
She made fun of you at a party	n	30 (13)	54	80	164
	%	18 (8)	33	49	100
She gave all her attention to the children	n	17 (9)	17	128	162
	%	10 (6)	10	79	99*

1. Figures in brackets refer to those boys who said it was 'very likely' they would hit in these circumstances.
*Rounding error.

TABLE 3.24b *Whether it is likely that he would hit a wife/girlfriend in certain circumstances – girls*

Statement		Female 11–13			
		Likely	Maybe	Unlikely	Total
She refused to cook or do housework	n	85 (26)[1]	55	31	171
	%	50	32	18	100*
She had sex with another man	n	139 (110)	18	16	173
	%	80	11	9	99*
She refused to have sex with you	n	100 (52)	48	23	171
	%	59	28	13	99*
She made fun of you at a party	n	101 (54)	48	25	174
	%	58	28	14	100*
She gave all her attention to the children	n	68 (30)	49	53	170
	%	40	29	31	100

Statement		Female 14–16			
		Likely	Maybe	Unlikely	Total
She refused to cook or do housework	n	75 (21)	58	24	157
	%	48	37	15	100*
She had sex with another man	n	137 (108)	15	5	157
	%	87	10	3	100
She refused to have sex with you	n	89 (28)	60	7	156
	%	(57)	39	4	100
She made fun of you at a party	n	87 (36)	47	22	156
	%	56	30	14	100
She gave all her attention to the children	n	39 (14)	75	42	156
	%	25	48	27	100

1. Figures in brackets refer to those girls who said it was 'very likely' that a man would hit in these circumstances.
*Rounding error.

TABLE 3.25 *What he would do if he was hitting his girlfriend – boys only*

Age	11–13 n = 129		14–16 n = 135		**Total** n = 264	
	n	%[1]	n	%	n	%
Calm down/stop	77	60	76	56	**153**	58
Get help	30	23	27	20	**57**	22
Apologize	11	9	18	13	**29**	11
Leave/go away	10	8	11	8	**21**	8
I would not hit a girlfriend	7	5	9	7	**16**	6
Talk to the girl	6	5	8	6	**14**	5
Continue the abuse	2	2	8	6	**10**	4
Other[2]	7	5	5	4	**12**	5

1. Percentages are based on those of that age and sex answering the question; multiple responses possible so do not total 100.
2. 'Other' here includes: 'inform/get the police', 'talk to someone', 'sort myself out'.

TABLE 3.26 *What she would do if she was being hit by a partner – girls only*

Age	11–13 n = 160		14–16 n = 153		**Total** n = 313	
	n	%[1]	n	%	n	%
End the relationship	80	50	88	58	**168**	54
Tell someone	65	41	52	34	**117**	37
Fight back	24	15	37	24	**61**	19
Inform the police	24	15	22	14	**46**	15
Tell him to stop	10	6	17	11	**27**	9
Other[2]	6	4	6	4	**12**	4
Don't know/not sure	2	1	0	0	**2**	1

1. Percentages are based on those of that age and sex answering the question; multiple responses possible so do not total 100.
2. 'Other' here includes: 'cry', 'not talk to anyone about it', 'warn others' and 'try to help them'.

(n = 10: 4 per cent). Yet again, this reinforces the normative presence of domestic violence in the thinking of young men.

The vignette we included in the secondary school questionnaire was designed to elicit young people's views on violence in their own relationships, whilst containing a number of themes that are common in the domestic violence literature: sexual possessiveness; controlling behaviour; ambivalence. It ran as follows:

> A boy and a girl have been going out for six months. They often argue, the girl thinks the boy doesn't respect or trust her, because he's always checking up on her and gets very jealous if she talks to other boys. The girl likes the boy a lot, but she also likes going out with her female friends for a laugh. This is what they argue about the most – her nights out with her friends. Sometimes when the boy gets really upset he hits the girl and calls her all sorts of names, but he always apologizes afterwards.

The first of the ensuing questions asked whose fault it was that the girl got hit (see Table 3.27). Both sexes were relatively clear that the responsibility for the violence lay with the perpetrator (68 per cent overall) although a gendered difference did again emerge, with at least 10 per cent more girls in each age group opting for this response. Boys of all ages were more likely to think both parties were to blame, and a minority of both sexes and all ages (5 per cent overall) blamed the girl. Boys of all ages were slightly more likely to do this than girls and, overall, to be uncertain whose fault it was. Thus even in response to a scenario deliberately designed to name who was violent to whom, and with no reciprocal violence involved, almost a third of respondents (32 per cent) were unable or unwilling to hold the perpetrator responsible for his own behaviour, with two out of three of these thinking the blame was shared. Routine discussion of these matters in the classroom, at even the most basic level, would certainly not be time wasted.

Sexual jealousy emerged for both sexes and across the age groups as the commonest understanding of why the boy was acting in this way, never dropping below half of the responses from the age/sex cohorts to an entirely open-ended question and rising to virtually two-thirds of 11- to 13-year-old girls (see Table 3.28). Much lower numbers provided explanations based on fear of losing the girl (16 per cent overall) – a politer version of jealousy, perhaps – and that he loved her (10 per cent overall). Violence as an expression of love is a powerful, if perverse, theme in many romantic stories but, interestingly, somewhat higher proportions of young men at all ages drew on this as an explanatory framework. Having problematic attitudes to women and wanting to control his girlfriend were offered by only a very small minority as explanations, yet these are the issues that emerge from domestic violence research and practice (Gondolf, 1988; Pence and Paymar, 1990 and 1996). A few young people (more girls than boy at all ages), as we saw in response to an earlier question, surmised a transgenerational effect on the boy of having lived with child abuse or domestic violence, even though there was nothing in the vignette to indicate such a history in the boy's life. All these themes could be usefully explored in the classroom, combining accurate information with the opportunity to discuss why people continue to offer excuses for men who are violent. Story lines from TV serial dramas ('the soaps') could, for example, open up useful debate.

Consistent with the responses to the Jaz story, when asked what the girl in the dating vignette should do, two-thirds thought that she should end the relationship (see Table 3.29). Girls were slightly clearer about this than boys, the more so as they got older. A smaller proportion of the sample (21 per cent) thought that the girl should discuss the situation with the boy, although this was far more often seen as an option by girls than by boys and, again, more so as they got older (n = 27: 16 per cent overall). A small number of assertive young women (4 per cent) and a tiny number of boys (1 per cent) said the girl should demand that the boy must change, but a larger number of young women (6 per cent), and considerably more young men (10 per cent) advised that she should comply with her boyfriend's wishes, and even apologize for her own behaviour! As we noted above, this casts a depressing light on the self-esteem of today's young women

TABLE 3.27 Whose fault is it that the girl gets hit?

| Age | 11–13 n = 443 | | | | 14–16 n = 361 | | | | Total n = 804 | | | | Total | |
| | Female | | Male | | Female | | Male | | Female | | Male | | | |
	n	%	n	%	n	%	n	%	n	%	n	%	n	%
The boy	157	70	134	61	133	76	121	65	290	73	255	63	545	68
Both at fault	36	16	56	25	28	16	38	20	64	16	94	23	158	20
The girl	10	4	13	6	6	3	12	6	16	4	25	6	41	5
Not sure	20	9	17	8	7	4	16	9	27	7	33	8	60	7
Total	223	99*	220	100	174	99*	187	100	397	100	407	100	804	100

*Rounding error.

TABLE 3.28 *Why is the boy acting this way?*

Age	11–13 n = 403				14–16 n = 333				Total n = 736						
	Female		Male		Female		Male		Female		Male		Total	
	n	%[1]	n	%	n	%	n	%	n	%	n	%	n	%
Jealousy	133	65	123	62	102	60	86	52	215	57	209	58	**424**	58
Fear of losing her	33	16	22	11	40	24	26	16	73	19	48	13	**121**	16
He loves her	13	6	18	9	17	10	23	14	30	8	41	11	**71**	10
Possessiveness	15	7	3	2	15	9	10	6	30	8	13	4	**43**	6
Attitude problem (to women)	5	2	6	3	4	2	4	2	9	2	10	3	**19**	3
Lack of trust	8	4	4	2	6	4	1	1	14	4	5	1	**19**	3
Wants to control her	6	3	2	1	4	2	5	3	10	3	7	2	**17**	2
His experience of child abuse/domestic violence	4	2	2	1	7	4	3	2	11	3	5	1	**15**	2
He has problems	3	1	2	1	3	2	6	4	6	2	8	2	**14**	2
Other[2]	11	5	19	10	5	3	11	7	16	4	30	8	**46**	6
Don't know/not sure	0	0	10	5	1	1	1	1	1	<1	11	3	**12**	2
Total	206		197		169		164		375		361		**736**	

1. Percentages are based on those of that age and sex answering the question; multiple responses possible so do not total 100.
2. 'Other' includes: 'he is stupid', 'lack of respect', 'because he wants to'.

TABLE 3.29 *What should the girl do?*

| Age | 11–13 | | | | 14–16 | | | | Total n = 736 | | | | Total | |
| | Female | | Male | | Female | | Male | | Female | | Male | | | |
	n	%¹	n	%	n	%	n	%	n	%	n	%	n	%
Leave him	134	64	126	63	120	70	109	65	254	67	235	64	**489**	66
Discuss the situation with the boy	46	22	26	13	55	32	31	19	101	27	57	16	**158**	21
Do as he wants/ apologize/comply	15	7	21	11	7	4	16	10	22	6	37	10	**59**	8
Talk to friends	22	11	11	6	7	4	7	4	29	8	18	5	**47**	6
Physically retaliate	3	1	10	5	4	2	5	3	7	2	15	4	**22**	3
Inform the police	4	2	9	5	4	2	4	2	8	2	13	4	**21**	3
Demand the boy changes	9	4	0	0	8	5	4	2	17	4	4	1	**21**	3
Get help (general)	6	3	3	2	6	3	3	2	12	3	6	2	**18**	2
Other²	4	2	8	4	1	1	5	3	5	1	13	4	**18**	2
Don't know/not sure	2	1	6	3	0	0	1	1	2	1	7	2	**9**	1
Total	208		199		172		167		380		366		**746**	

1. Percentages are based on those of that age and sex answering the question; multiple responses possible so do not total 100.
2. 'Other' includes: 'get help for the boy'.

and on what they think they will have to do to keep a boyfriend. The equally distressing views held by their male peers, together with boys' slowness to see talking about the problem as a potential solution, suggest that the girls may well be right to hold such low expectations, unless society intervenes to raise these issues in a non-threatening way, much earlier in their educational careers.

We went on to ask the young people to think of two things the boy might do to stop hurting his girlfriend and, since this was an open-ended question, a wide range of responses was proffered (see Table 3.30). There was considerably less consensus here than we saw in the actions recommended for the young woman. The commonest response (from almost four in ten) was that the boy should learn to control his jealousy, followed by just under a quarter suggesting he should learn to trust his girlfriend (with more girls, of all ages, in both cases). Around a fifth of the sample (more boys) said he should stop abusing, and another fifth framed this in terms of giving the girl her freedom. Again, more girls than boys (n = 59: 42 per cent) said that the boy should discuss the situation with his girlfriend. Interestingly, one in five boys but only around one in eight girls suggested that the boy should end the relationship (whereas we saw above that more young people overall, including a somewhat higher proportion of girls than boys, thought the girl should end it). It is not clear whether this implies that he would be better suited with a more compliant girl, as opposed to needing to look at his own behaviour, but the majority of responses overall did imply that the boy was at fault and needed to change not just his conduct but his orientation to the relationship. Several referred, for example, to respecting his partner, not trying control her, and to other strategies such as undertaking activities together and spending time with his friends (while she spent time with hers, presumably). This is more encouraging than some of the other sets of answers because it has emerged from research into the effectiveness of domestic violence perpetrator programmes that changing violent men's attitudes to women may be linked with better outcomes (Gondolf, 1988). Unlike the suggestions made with respect to Jaz's father (see above), apologizing was recommended by only a tiny minority. Somehow, young people were less able to see this as an option for their own age group.

The response to questions as to whom both the girl and the boy could talk to reflects responses to earlier questions. Friends are the most likely confidants for both sexes, being cited by half the sample overall and by considerably more girls than boys, particularly in the teenage years (see Tables 3.31 and 3.32). The importance of friends has been under-recognized and underplayed in work with children and young people, although peer counsellors have been trained in some non-violence initiatives in Canada and elsewhere (Mullender, 1994b; Hague et al., 2001). Aside from talking with the partner concerned, parents (mentioned by just over a third overall) and the family generally were the next major source of support suggested, with mothers singled out most often for the girl and fathers for the boy. (We shall see in Chapter 6 that the family takes on even greater significance for South Asian children and also in Chapter 4 that siblings emerge as important for many children, regardless of ethnicity.) ChildLine, and helplines generally, featured to some extent but professional help, and especially from teachers, came low on the list, perhaps not being seen as relevant or accessible to young people facing this kind of difficulty. These findings echo those from a

TABLE 3.31 *Who could the girl talk to?*

| Age | 11–13 n = 395 | | | | 14–16 n = 328 | | | | Total n = 723 | | | | Total | |
| | Female | | Male | | Female | | Male | | Female | | Male | | | |
	n	%[1]	n	%	n	%	n	%	n	%	n	%	n	%
Friends	97	49	85	44	110	66	68	42	207	57	153	43	**360**	50
Her parents	71	36	65	33	53	32	65	40	124	34	130	36	**254**	35
Family	34	17	27	14	42	25	19	12	76	21	46	13	**122**	17
The boy	29	15	28	14	39	23	25	15	68	19	53	15	**121**	17
Mother	38	19	23	12	31	19	13	8	69	19	36	10	**105**	15
ChildLine	32	16	14	7	16	10	9	6	48	13	23	6	**71**	10
Counsellor	8	4	8	4	9	5	4	2	17	5	12	3	**29**	4
Helpline	4	2	3	2	12	7	8	5	16	4	11	3	**27**	4
GP/psychiatrist/ professional	4	2	5	3	7	4	5	3	11	3	10	3	**21**	3
School/teacher	3	2	3	2	5	3	4	2	8	2	7	2	**15**	2
Police	3	2	6	3	4	2	2	1	7	2	8	2	**15**	2
Other[2]	9	5	11	6	4	2	13	8	13	4	22	6	**35**	5
Total	200		195		166		162		366		357		**723**	

1. Percentages are based on those of that age and sex answering the question; multiple responses possible so do not total 100.
2. 'Other' includes: 'an adult', 'father', unspecified 'someone'.

TABLE 3.32 *Who could the boy talk to?*

Age	11–13 n = 378				14–16 n = 313				Total n = 692				Total	
	Female		Male		Female		Male		Female		Male			
	n	%[1]	n	%	n	%	n	%	n	%	n	%	n	%
His friends	79	41	54	29	67	42	38	25	146	42	92	27	238	34
The girl	43	23	48	26	56	35	44	28	99	28	92	27	191	28
His parents	48	25	43	23	32	20	36	23	80	23	79	25	159	23
Counsellor	22	12	16	9	26	16	16	10	48	14	32	9	80	12
Family	21	11	20	11	8	5	14	9	29	8	34	10	63	9
ChildLine	24	13	6	3	13	8	8	5	37	11	14	4	51	7
Father	18	9	13	7	13	8	6	4	31	9	19	5	50	7
Social worker/psychiatrist/ professional	5	3	3	2	12	8	12	8	17	5	15	4	32	5
Helpline	4	2	2	1	10	6	4	3	14	4	6	2	20	3
Her friends	3	2	4	2	2	1	5	3	5	1	9	3	14	2
School/teacher	3	2	3	2	4	3	3	2	7	2	6	2	13	2
Police	2	1	6	3	1	1	2	1	3	1	8	2	11	2
Other[2]	10	5	12	6	10	6	14	9	20	6	26	8	46	7
Total	191		187		158		155		349		343		692	

1. Percentages are based on those of that age and sex answering the question; multiple responses possible so do not total 100.
2. 'Other' here includes: 'no excuse', 'male friends', 'her parents', 'mother', 'an adult', unspecified 'someone', 'no one'.

study in Dublin (Regan and Kelly, 2001) that also found young people tending to look to one another for support, with only a minority considering professionals likely to be helpful despite having a good knowledge of the services available. Active suggestions included enhancing opportunities and locations where peer support could be available. Responses to an additional question in the present study, 'How could boys/men show more respect to girls/women?', demonstrate the concern of these young people about male violence. Almost a quarter of responses could be grouped into a category concerning 'being non-violent/ abusive/aggressive' (23 per cent), with an additional 18 per cent suggesting 'treat them equally' and 'by loving/caring for them'. 'Trust', 'listening/talking' and 'sharing housework/child care' also all came up.

WHAT CHILDREN NEED AND WANT

Several questions towards the end of the questionnaire probed the support needs of children living with domestic violence, and explored the extent to which children want to know more about the issue.

The whole sample was asked to whom they would talk if they were living with domestic violence and secondary children were asked what would help (see Tables 3.33 and 3.34). Peers again featured strongly, with friends and siblings being the most common reference points – the former preferred by older children, especially girls. Grandparents, albeit in choices made from a tick-list of options we had suggested, were preferred over parents as a specific source of support, though a third of older children and a quarter overall recommended talking with mothers. (See Chapter 7 for an exploration of the complexities involved in mother-child relationships in the context of domestic violence.) The police were preferred over teachers (n = 21: 16 per cent), especially by the youngest age group, though they had featured very little in response to the vignette (which had, though, not been included for primary age children). These age-related differences are important since they suggest that children and young people may know about or look towards different potential support networks from the ones adults would predict or suggest and that, for older children, it is their peer group rather than adults who are most likely to be approached. These varying patterns of preferred confidants need to be taken into account when thinking about educational interventions and other forms of support work with children and young people.

Secondary school children were asked what would help children living with domestic violence. The opportunity to talk, together with reassurance and support, was seen as the single most appropriate form of help that could be provided (see Table 3.34), again with a predominance of girls over boys (n = 48: 29 per cent) seeing talking as the basis of a solution. A combined majority of responses, however, involved a range of direct strategies that would have the effect of ending the presence of violence in children's daily lives, including someone intervening to stop the violence, removing the child to a relative's or into care, or separating the parents. There is a clear message from both phases of this study that children do not think they should have to live with domestic violence, with a sizeable minority of a general population of children recommending even quite drastic

TABLE 3.33 *Who children living with domestic violence would talk to*

| | Primary n = 415 | | | | Secondary n = 775 | | | | Total n = 1190 | | | | | |
| | Female | | Male | | Female | | Male | | Female | | Male | | Total | |
	n	%[1]	n	%	n	%	n	%	n	%	n	%	n	%
Friend	38	18	36	18	233	60	148	38	271	45	184	31	455	38
Siblings	87	40	80	40	118	30	114	29	205	34	194	33	399	34
Grandparents	68	31	72	36	98	25	110	28	166	28	182	31	348	29
Mother	16	7	19	10	141	36	125	32	157	26	144	25	301	25
Police	72	33	59	30	53	14	67	17	125	21	126	21	251	21
Another relative	2	1	1	<1	123	32	103	27	125	21	104	18	229	19
Teacher	58	27	36	18	55	14	44	11	113	19	80	14	193	16
Father	6	3	16	8	17	4	15	4	23	4	31	5	54	5
Helplines	1	<1	0	0	5	1	5	1	6	1	5	1	11	1
Other	2	1	2	1	4	1	0	0	6	1	2	<1	8	1
Total	216		199		387		388		603		587		1190	

1. Percentages are based on those of that age and sex answering the question; multiple responses possible so do not total 100.

TABLE 3.34   *What would help children living with domestic violence*

| | Secondary n = 357 | | | | | |
| | Female | | Male | | **Total** | |
Type of help	n	%[1]	n	%	n	%
Opportunity to talk/reassurance/support	106	48	39	29	**145**	41
Take child into 'care'	50	22	21	16	**71**	20
Stop the violence	24	11	42	31	**66**	18
Child to live with other relative	33	15	19	14	**52**	15
Protect child	34	15	17	13	**51**	14
Split parents	20	9	11	8	**31**	9
Help parents	16	7	11	8	**27**	8
Other[2]	68	30	34	25	**102**	29
Total	223		134		**357**	

1. Percentages are based on those of that age and sex answering the question; multiple responses possible so do not total 100.
2. 'Other' here includes: 'unspecified general help', 'telling someone' and 'punishing the perpetrator'.

measures to avoid it, such as removing the child into care (one in five suggested this). If we are serious about listening to children, this call for an end to violence in children's lives is one of the most powerful messages of this study and it is reinforced by the direct experiences and recommendations made by children who have lived with violence in their own household, as we shall see in later chapters. The need for someone to talk to will also strongly recur.

The vast majority of secondary school children (84 per cent) – girls even more strongly than boys (87 as against 81 per cent) – and a majority at primary school age (52 per cent) would like lessons on domestic violence in school (Table 3.35). Respondents cite a varied list of reasons for having these lessons, including wanting to understand what domestic violence is and why it happens and wanting to know what to do if it should occur (see Table 3.36). The older group, in particular, also want to know how to stop it. These responses alone ought to be reason enough to ensure that children have access to information, strategies and the opportunity to talk, especially if there is a commitment to listening to children and taking their views seriously. The confusions, variations and contradictions in children and young people's knowledge, understandings and attitudes revealed by our data reinforce the necessity of engaging directly and honestly with children and young people about domestic violence. Though there have been some initiatives to introduce such work in the UK, the work remains patchy and is not a required part of the National Curriculum (see Chapter 9). Far more has been done in parts of Canada, for example (Mullender, 1994b; Hague et al., 2001), including with official backing, to show that anti-violence work can fit well into the school curriculum and can help children and young people learn how all their interpersonal relationships can be healthy and conflict-free, both now and in the future.

CONCLUSION

This chapter, reporting the first ever survey of a general population of children about their understandings and perceptions of domestic violence, can be seen as

TABLE 3.35 Lessons on domestic violence in school

| | Primary n = 422 | | | | Secondary n = 597 | | | | Total n = 1019 | | | | Total | |
| | Female | | Male | | Female | | Male | | Female | | Male | | | |
	n	%	n	%	n	%	n	%	n	%	n	%	n	%
Yes	120	55	100	49	299	87	205	81	419	75	305	67	724	71
No	33	15	50	25	43	13	46	18	76	14	96	21	172	17
Unsure	65	30	54	26	1	<1	3	1	66	12	57	12	123	12
Total	218	100	204	100	343	100	254	100	561	101*	458	100	1019	100

*Rounding error.

TABLE 3.36 *What lessons about domestic violence in school should address*

| | Primary n = 252 | | | | Secondary n = 363 | | | | Total n = 615 | | | | | |
| | Female | | Male | | Female | | Male | | Female | | Male | | Total | |
	n	%[1]	n	%	n	%	n	%	n	%	n	%	n	%
To understand what it is and why it happens	58	43	41	35	105	45	42	32	163	44	83	33	246	40
To know what to do it if happens	34	25	23	20	97	42	34	26	131	36	57	23	188	31
To stop it happening	10	7	5	4	32	14	24	18	42	11	29	12	71	12
Effects of domestic violence	0	0	0	0	20	9	8	6	20	5	8	3	28	5
So don't do it in the future	7	5	10	9	0	0	0	0	7	2	10	4	17	3
Other[2]	29	21	41	35	29	13	25	19	58	16	66	27	124	20
Total	136		116		231		132		367		248		615	

1. Percentages are based on those of that age and sex answering the question; multiple responses possible so do not total 100.
2. 'Other' here includes: 'domestic violence is wrong'; 'stop violence in school'; 'sad/hard to talk about'; 'someone can get hurt'; 'fighting back'; 'sex education/ relationships' and 'child abuse'.

a combination of good and bad news. The downside lies in the depressingly traditional attitudes revealed by teenage boys towards male–female relationships and the use of violence within them. Even girls, though they grow in awareness as they get older – in a way that does not seem to happen for boys, though we cannot say why – still often have low expectations of heterosexual relationships and of how they will have to behave within them. There is further bad news in the confusion as to what domestic violence actually is and what causes it and, of course (though not surprisingly) in the high number of respondents who knew someone with direct experience of it. The good news from the schools survey, however, is that children and young people themselves recognize that they do not know enough and are positively asking for lessons in school where they could learn more about domestic violence, what causes it and how it could be stopped. We know from another study (Burton et al., 1998) that children prefer an approach to such learning that is based in debate and discussion – not adults telling them what to think but an opportunity to explore their own views and opinions with one another.

Other crucially important findings from this chapter are that children do not think other children should have to live with violence – with an implication that adults should intervene more effectively to stop it – and that young people may turn more readily to their friends than to adults (especially professionals) for help and support, particularly to talk over what is happening to them. There are major implications in all of this for the services that should be provided for younger people, to which we will return at length in Chapter 9 where we will draw together key messages for policy and practice.

Meanwhile, in the next five chapters we turn to a detailed presentation and analysis of the qualitative phase of the study: the in-depth interviews with children and young people who have lived with domestic violence and also with their mothers and, in some cases, key professionals who had been involved in helping them. We will hear first about the children's own experiences, the coping strategies they have used, and the particular issues and experiences from a sub-sample of South Asian children. We will then look more closely at issues between children and their mothers and between them and their fathers. We will see throughout the rest of the book that children who have known violence in their own lives would be a rich source of information and advice to other children, both those who are facing specific risks and those who have a general need to learn more. If the need for work in schools is taken seriously, then it becomes clear that the preparation of appropriate learning materials could be based, at least in part, on what children and young people themselves have to tell us and not only on what adults think they need to hear. Both children and adults have concrete information to convey, and lessons they have learnt the hard way, which could help the generality of young people to rethink some of the myths and misconceptions that are peddled by the popular media and carried over from earlier habits of thinking, before men's violence towards women was recognized as criminal behaviour and as not tolerable in a civilized society.

4 Children's Experiences of Living
   with Domestic Violence

This chapter provides an overview of the qualitative sample of children and their mothers who had lived with domestic violence. It locates the families and briefly explores children's knowledge and understanding of violence and their contact with helping organizations, setting the scene for subsequent chapters on children's coping strategies, the particular experiences of South Asian children, children's relationships with their mothers and their fathers and their advice on what helped. We have chosen to emphasize findings and analysis that extend, and even at times question, current knowledge and understanding. For children, living with domestic violence requires negotiating, making sense of, and managing a number of complex and overlapping issues: the behaviour of the abuser; the responses of, and impacts on, their mother and siblings; danger and risk to themselves; their emotions; and kin and friendship relations. In the chapters that follow we endeavour to make children's thinking and decision-making central to our explorations of this difficult terrain. Our interest is in reflecting children's perceptions, their actions, and their comments and opinions. At the same time, we seek to go beyond reportage, however powerful and moving the content, and to offer our engagement with children's realities in relation to previous knowledge in the field and the implications for policy and practice.

WHO ARE THE CHILDREN?

As outlined in Chapter 2, the main qualitative sample comprised 45 children, from 25 families. For two-thirds of the sample it was their father who had been violent, and for the remaining third it was their mother's partner. Fifteen of the families were contacted through a refuge and ten through community support groups, although the number of children accessed through each of these channels was virtually equal. Again as mentioned in Chapter 2, we deliberately sought to interview sibling groups as a way of exploring differences between children who had similar experiences in terms of age and gender. Of those interviewed, 24 were girls and 21 boys, half were aged 11 or under and half aged 12 to 16. More than half of the children were from minority ethnic groups or were 'mixed race'. Fourteen (31 per cent) defined themselves as Asian, three (7 per cent) as African, five (11 per cent) as black British, seven (15 per cent) as 'mixed race' and sixteen (35 per cent) as white. The over-representation of minority ethnic families is partly due to deliberately seeking to develop a sub-sample of black (but eventually South Asian) children (see Chapter 6). Seven children (approaching 16 per cent) had disabilities, ranging from Down's Syndrome and a serious hearing impairment to asthma. This puts the sample at the top end of estimates of disabled children in the population nationally (somewhere between 3 and 16 per cent, according to Gordon et al., 2000) and demonstrates that we achieved our aim of being inclusive in our approach to sampling and interviewing.

In some respects, our data extend beyond the main sample to a further 29 siblings who were either too young to be interviewed (17) or who were not currently living with their mothers (12). The latter group included a few children who had not been allowed to leave home when she did or who had chosen to live with their father, but most were over 18 and did not live with either parent. Whilst neither the adult siblings nor the youngest ones participated in the research, both their siblings and their mothers included them in their accounts.

The range of experience within the sample was extremely broad, with some children having lived with domestic violence for lengthy periods and others for a much shorter time. Some had left home many times to try and find safety, others only once. This variation offers us sources of insight, but also makes it impossible to offer anything beyond an analytic description of their experiences and reflections. The sample is too small to control for more than one variable, yet even analysis at the qualitative level makes clear that factors such as age, sex and the severity and frequency of violence interact in children's experience, understanding and responses.

PART OR MOST OF CHILDHOOD

Some children (about a fifth) had lived with domestic violence for a year or less, about a third had lived with it for between one and seven years, but the largest group comprised those who had spent the majority of their childhood dealing with violence in their household. Several sibling groups had the experience of escaping one violent man, only to have the violence recur with their mother's new partner. These children's lives were full of disruption and lost hopes. On the other hand, there were several children whose mothers had left after the first serious incident of violence. This, however, is only part of the story since the frequency and severity of the violence had also varied, as did the extent to which children were direct witnesses of it, overheard, intervened – or a combination of all of these. The richness and detail of qualitative data provides us with windows into the experiences of others; it also warns us against creating models and stereotypes that flatten out the complexity of lived experience. Even children in the same family had different experiences of violence, due to their age. Some older children had periods of family life they remembered fondly, when there had been far less conflict and much less violence. Mothers also reflected on the fact that their youngest children (often those under three) had known nothing but a household ruled by fear and insecurity. Whilst it is undoubtedly true that lengthy exposure to domestic violence takes a toll on a child (Jaffe et al., 1990; McGee, 2000), shorter periods where the abuse has escalated and their mother's resources have been depleted can also have significant impacts:

She used to freeze wherever she was, basically, then she learnt to scuttle out the room when he was coming home. (White mother)

Some children were chillingly matter of fact about their encounters with abuse:

Just Dad being horrible. So we left, then we came back. (8-year-old white boy)

In terms of differences between siblings, being older meant that children had more experience of abuse, but also had more knowledge and resources to draw on both to make sense of what was happening and to protect themselves physically and emotionally. Being younger meant the reverse. Whilst siblings share many things, our interviews made clear the importance of each being able to explore memories and feelings. What featured strongly in one child's account often was less significant for their brother or sister. Older children had seen more, were more likely to have intervened at some point, and had developed (in the main) a heightened sense of responsibility towards their mother and siblings, yet, with some notable exceptions, they also appeared to have sustained less damage. Since we were not able to collect data systematically about impacts, this is a suggestive rather than a definitive finding. Mothers' accounts of developmental delays and withdrawal were most noticeable when discussing younger children, especially those whose early childhood had involved extensive violence or periods when their mothers had felt depressed and hopeless and thus had been less able to mitigate their children's distress and anxiety. Our qualitative sample is not large enough to do anything other than raise these observations, which need to be explored in more depth. It is possible, for example, that as they grow and develop all children are able to draw upon understanding and resources that enable them to cope more effectively, or that the impacts of domestic violence become more subtle and less obviously expressed through behaviour. On the other hand, it may be that being born into a household where domestic violence has reached recurrent and potentially lethal levels has a greater effect. In particular, whether this may be a background factor in diagnoses of 'failure to thrive', as some practitioners suspect, deserves explicit attention.

WHAT THEY HEARD AND SAW

When asked directly what they knew, four children said they had not really been aware at all of what was happening but the majority talked of overhearing arguments and, at times, witnessing violent incidents or their aftermath:

I used to hear them sometimes. (8-year-old white boy)

That was the only time I saw it. It was behind closed doors. But I used to know and I would see the bruises that she had before that. (12-year-old white girl)

I saw my dad fighting with Mum. I saw them arguing, shouting at each other and hitting each other. My dad used to do the hitting. (10-year-old South Asian boy)

Over a third reported both overhearing and witnessing abuse. These children were also the ones who were most likely to talk about threats to, and abuse of, themselves or their siblings:

> He used to say, 'I am going to kill you at night-time when you are all asleep.' He used to come with an axe and say, 'I am going to kill you.' I used to get very frightened. We had a lock on the bedroom doors in case he did what he said. He once made a hole with an axe in my sister's bedroom door. Then he used to look through the hole. (8-year-old South Asian girl)

> I heard my dad swearing and I saw him grab my mum's throat and push her against the door and, later, I saw him slap her around the face and push her over the sink. (10-year old white girl)

> He tried to get her to drink the bleach, to pour it into her mouth while he held her there and, when he couldn't make her, he poured bleach all over her face and hair. He was trying to kill her. (15-year-old white boy)

Later in the interviews, in response to further questions, more children recalled at least one incident where they had observed often quite brutal and frightening incidents. And some talked of lives suffused with fear, unpredictability and multiple abusers:

> I've seen it all the time. First from my real dad and then from this one and my brothers. (14-year-old white girl)

> It was the worst part of my life – constantly being shouted at, frightened, living in fear. You will never know what it is like, thinking that every day could be your last day. (16-year-old South Asian girl)

One sibling group revealed the differences that age and children's own choices can make. The oldest child, a boy, reported having seen little of the violence. As he had got older, his choice had been to leave the house if he could. The next oldest, a girl, had the greatest awareness of the violence but had tried to avoid witnessing it and to protect her younger sisters. The youngest child interviewed, also a girl, had clearly seen more than the other two, partly because she tried to protect her mother (and another, much younger, sister) by being present:

> Interviewer: So what did you do?
> Child: … cry and say stop it and he says, 'No I won't.' And I start to cry and [he takes] the mickey out of me by making funny noises and saying, 'Stop being a baby.'
> Interviewer: Did you ever leave the room and go away from it?
> Child: No.
> Interviewer: Just stayed there?
> Child: Yes, because I like my mum. (10-year-old mixed-race girl)

MAKING SENSE OF ABUSE

We asked children how they had become aware of the abuse, what they had thought was happening, and whether and how this had changed over time. Unless their awareness had been prompted by an explicitly violent incident in which obvious external injury had been caused, children talked about having been uncertain. They had been aware of something, but were not sure what it meant:

> I don't know. I thought perhaps they were just weren't getting on. (16-year-old white boy)

> I wasn't really sure what was happening at the time. I didn't really understand what was going on, but I know my mam and dad were fighting every day. I understand more now. (13-year-old South Asian boy)

Other children were more able to detect or name conflict – often calling it 'arguing and fighting' – and sometimes saw their mothers as equally, if not more, to blame for this, at least when they were young. (See Chapter 7 for more discussion on mother-child relationships.)

> I was about six when I first realized Mum and Dad were fighting. (8-year-old black British girl)

> There was lots of arguing between my parents but I didn't understand why this was happening. (11-year-old South Asian boy)

> I just thought that my mum and dad didn't love each other any more. I knew my mum wasn't doing anything wrong. I had no idea that it was going to be this bad ... Up until then I really was – I sided with my dad most of the time. (13-year-old African girl)

Even at an early stage, some children seem to have had insight into the dynamics of power and control that lay behind the violence. Rather than using words like 'fighting' and focusing on incidents of conflict, these children located the actions they witnessed within a context and it was this that revealed the gender relations underpinning abuse:

> When my mum went out, I reckon Dad was jealous because Mum was having a good time and I don't think he liked it. (10-year-old white girl)

At the same time, several younger children were eloquent in attempting to describe the way their experiences had been not just anxiety provoking but also extremely confusing and difficult to make sense of:

> Do you want to know how I feel about it? It gets me all confused and muddled up. When it happens, I feel as if things are growing in my head, outwards and pressing on my head. Do you want me to give you an example? I'll tell you what, I'll tell you a good example, but you'll have to have lots of paper to write on when you write it down!

There was a big argument one day. My dad didn't want his tea. He bought me an ice cream. He punched her three times. Someone came running out. He kept kicking her. Mum was crying and crying. And then I got mad – I'm not a nasty person, really I'm not, but I just got mad. Then he kicked his car. Then he got in it and then he got out again, and he came for me so I ran away. Later, I played with my sister on the computer. My mum was being looked after by our neighbour. Then we saw the police and I went to my auntie's. Have you understood it? It just gets me so muddled up. I'm frightened I'll be like it when I grow up. I know what she is going through and I want to help her. I get worried for her. (8-year-old mixed-race boy)

It was both the rapid succession of events he had witnessed and the feelings they had evoked in this child that he had found so distressing. The conjunction of his fears that he might grow up to be an abuser like his father (a common belief but a highly contentious one; see Morley and Mullender, 1994, for an overview of relevant research) with his evident concern for his mother were still agonizing, both for him and for the researcher who talked with him.

We also asked children whether anyone had explained what was happening during the abuse and on the occasions when they had left. There was a clear divide here between children who felt they had received explanations and those who had not. Endeavouring to make sense of complicated and frightening realities is obviously much more difficult in the absence of information. (See Chapter 7 for a discussion of the barriers that can limit communication between mothers and children in the aftermath of domestic violence.) One of children's most heartfelt pleas about what they needed was to be given information and to be allowed to express an opinion. There are similar findings in the literature about parental separation and divorce which suggest that children are often not given full explanations or the chance to ask questions yet that having an active role in decisions helps them cope with disruption and moves (see, for example, Dunn and Deater-Deckard, 2001). Judith Wallerstein's (1980; 1989) longitudinal study of divorce confirms children's need for clarification, especially when they are being required to leave their home and familiar surroundings.

Some young people, like the 13-year-old African girl quoted earlier in this section who had initially sided with her father and the young woman speaking below, were able to reflect on the limited awareness they had had when they were younger, and on their gradual realization of what had actually been happening:

I don't know really – it just kind of crept up on me. All I know is, one day I did know, so it probably happened bit by bit from me not knowing to me knowing. Then I could remember back to when things happened when I was younger, but I didn't think anything of it – like when my mum had bandages and she said she banged herself. But now I realize my dad must have done it, but they hid it from me and I just accepted that at the time. We even made jokes about it – like how clumsy she had been to bash herself ... Mum and Dad, me, we all made those jokes. (15-year-old white girl)

The process here involves an emerging understanding, a perspective that enables children to make sense not just of the present but also of the past. Whilst some younger children did display perceptive insight into their situation, they were less likely to have had the intellectual or emotional resources that enabled reflection and reassessment. This should not, however, be understood as meaning that younger children are either unaware or unaffected. Both other research (e.g. McGee, 2000 which includes interviews with children as young as five) and mothers' comments in the present study about their youngest children confirm that they can be profoundly affected.

THE DECISION TO INTERVENE

Whilst much of the research on children to date has emphasized the extent to which they witness abuse and that on occasion they intervene (see Hester et al., 2000, for a summary), this has not previously been explored from the perspective of children's own decision-making processes. Indeed, much of the advice given to children, and also the development of safety planning,[1] advises children not to intervene since they run the risk of being hurt themselves (Loosley et al., 1997). Though it is sensible to harness children's concern and energies in ways that place them in less danger, our research reveals that more is going on in children's reactions than adults may understand. Children do not just react unthinkingly. They make their own rapid and complex decisions as to what to do for the best, and these are deeply embedded in particular contexts – both what they think is going on, and their assessments of the extent to which they can influence swiftly evolving events. To insist that children should never intervene, for example, may interfere with their own sharpened assessment of the potentially lethal danger their mothers are facing and leave them very distressed. This section will argue for a more nuanced understanding – one that recognizes both the potential harm to children of becoming physically involved in a violent incident and the reality that they do act, in a variety of ways that actually extend beyond the most obvious meanings of 'intervention'. There was in fact a range of things that children talked about doing to try and help, not always what adults might expect or worry about.

Half the children in this sample talked about having intervened to protect their mother and half did not (see also Chapter 5). Unsurprisingly, older children were more likely to have done so, and the majority of those who had not were under 12 at the time of the interview. Many children explained their choice not to get involved in terms of age. 'No, I never tried to stop them because I was too young and couldn't really do anything' (13-year-old South Asian boy). Interestingly, most of the mothers (there were only two exceptions) reported their children attempting to intervene, compared to only 50 per cent of the children reporting that they had. This is partly explained by the fact that mothers were responding on the basis of whether any of their children had acted in this way, beyond the immediate sample, whereas children were speaking only for themselves. In a number of sibling groups, some had intervened and others had not. Also, for children, the question of whether they had intervened seems to have been understood in terms of explicit attempts to stop the abuse, so that some clearly discounted what they saw as more minor actions such as telling the abuser not to shout or swear at their mother.

> My daughter would say, 'Don't smack my mummy!' when he used to send her to her bedroom. (White mother)

For mothers, however, these actions 'counted'. It mattered that their children had named the abuse and challenged its legitimacy, and these things were seen and remembered by women as acts of bravery and support.

Contrary to the impression that intervention primarily involves children trying physically to place themselves between the adults, or to seek help, the strategy used most commonly by the children in our sample had been to shout – to try to distract attention and thus interrupt a particular assault. This strategy had limited the risk of violence to children (although not always), whilst also being aimed at making the man reflect on what he was doing:

> When my dad started all of this, right, I would really get angry and start shouting at him, telling him off. (13-year-old African girl)

> Yeah, but that made things worse actually ... he would start shouting at me and everything. Most of the time I used to scream at him to leave my mum alone. (17-year-old mixed-race girl)

A number of older girls seemed to have developed a form of assertiveness where they had stood up to the man in ways their mothers either could not, or chose not to. The mother of the 13-year-old girl speaking above commented:

> One time, with my first daughter – she was 11 at the time – he was going to hit her and she said, 'If you touch me, I'm going to call the police to you. I won't take it.' (African mother)

Another young woman had over the years adapted her strategies as she came to understand what might or might not make a difference:

> No, when he gets drunk like that, it goes on for hours. You just get out. You can't try and stop him – he's too big and fat to take on. (14-year-old white girl)

A number of children had taken the actions which current safety planning advice supports (Loosley et al., 1997), such as calling the police or seeking help from friends, neighbours or family:

> Half the time we had to call the police in. I think every house we moved to we had to call the police. (17-year-old white girl)

Amongst the sample of 45 children, there were just two examples of intervention that had moved onto a different level, where violence or the risk of it was involved on both sides, and in each case this involved boys who were over 12 at the time:

One day he was going to hit Mum really hard and I pushed him out of the way, and he hit the wall with his hand really hard … And he broke his hand. It was my birthday. I remember I had this money – it was my present – and it was the only money there was, so he took my birthday money off me to pay for the taxi to the hospital. (15-year-old white boy)

Interviewer: Did you ever intervene?

Young Person: Once or twice … last time I done it I had a knife in my hand and he tried to make me stab him with it, so I didn't bother trying to stop him no more. (13-year-old mixed-race boy)

His mother also discussed this last incident and the fears it had evoked in her:

I've said to him, 'I don't want you to be like that when you've got your girlfriends.' He said, 'I'll never hit a woman.' So I'm, like, well that's what he says now, but I – it's like, too much has been seen for them to forget it. (Black British mother, again verbalising the widespread fear that children 'grow up like it')

Here again a clear age-related pattern of changing responses emerges, with younger children having felt limited in the actions they could take and older children having tended to intervene, at least on the occasions they judged the most dangerous for their mothers. It was also clear from our interviews that South Asian children had been less likely to intervene, although some of them had. Within this overall pattern, however, there were exceptions – including very small children intervening, as this mother illustrates:

She was always the one that told him off and shouted at him, even from two years old, she'd go and say, 'Don't!'. I'd always give excuses and she'd see through them. Sometimes it got me into trouble, but she didn't realize it – because she was saying things that an adult would say and he'd presume I'd put the words in her mouth. She would say things like, 'How can you be skint, and go up to the pub and come back drunk – you must be the only person that can do that. Are you magic?'… Even at three or four, she could tell him that. He'd say, 'You are putting words in their mouths again,' but children are innocent and they are honest. (White mother)

The accounts children gave of their own, complex and changing decision-making about whether and how to intervene, raise complicated issues for children's advocates. As the next chapter shows, many children had chosen to hide, or had frozen when violence began. These strategies, especially hiding, had undoubtedly protected them from being hurt directly and from witnessing distressing events. At the same time, children also talked of the anxiety of not having known whether their mother was being seriously hurt, and of feeling powerless. Shouting, and making clear their opposition to the abuse, was a way in which children had exercised agency and made their voices and opinions heard within the household. Whilst we are certainly not suggesting that children be encouraged to act in dangerous ways, some thought is needed concerning the relationship between children's understandings of violence and their decision-making. For example, further research could explore in much more detail the impacts children's interventions have on perpetrators and on mothers, and at the meanings their actions have for children themselves. With respect to the latter issue, much of the commentary to date has focused on children feeling responsible for the violence and on needing to lift the burden of guilt (Loosley et al., 1997). Within our small sample, however, it appeared that finding their voice and expressing anger served, for young women particularly but also for several of the young men, as one foundation on which they could build a determination to construct different kinds of intimate relationships for themselves in the future.

This research project was designed to explore children's perspectives and needs within a framework that views children as social actors. In this context, it is crucial to pay close attention to how children act, and to the various meanings and consequences their actions might have for themselves and for others. From this angle, while the potential for children to place themselves in immediate danger is a critical factor, it is not the only question to be asked. Rather, it suggests that both researchers and children's advocates need to explore with children and young people their nuanced and contextual decision-making processes, in order to enhance our understanding of the role intervention plays in children's own ways of making sense of and dealing with domestic violence.

SEEKING AND GETTING SUPPORT FROM OTHERS

One of the aims of this research project was to locate children as potential service users in their own right, and to explore their experiences and assessments of service provision and what they thought children like themselves most needed. (See Chapter 9 for a discussion of the policy and practice implications.) We therefore asked from whom they had received the most support.

FAMILY MEMBERS

Children invariably saw their mothers or siblings as having been most supportive, although almost half the children reported not talking to either their mothers or their siblings about the abuse whilst it was occurring. Clearly, support was experienced as something more diffuse than explicit acknowledgement and discussion of the violence.

> Just being with my sister – the fact that I could talk to her about anything, and that we could go somewhere else until it was over. (12-year-old mixed-race boy)

Even the apparently simple choice to talk to their mother, sibling or relatives about events in their household is fraught with dangers for children who are living with domestic violence. In Chapter 7, we will explore the complex dynamics between mothers and children. With respect to siblings, older children had tended to offer their brothers and sisters reassurance ('He would tell me not to worry') but to avoid detailed discussion. In the extract below, this impulse to protect takes a slightly different form. Since the eldest sister (by one year) has Down's

Syndrome, the younger girl had made her decisions based on perceptions of her sister's needs and the context:

Interviewer: Did you ever talk to her about it?
Young Person: No, because she was too scared to talk about it.
Interviewer: She was too scared?
Young Person: Yeah. And I used to – she didn't really know, and I didn't want to tell her. (12-year-old white girl)

A few children had strong support structures within their extended family or through adult friends, usually of their mother's, but this was dependent on there being both a wider knowledge of the violence within the informal network *and* a willingness on the part of both children and others to discuss it explicitly. For the children concerned, these contacts had represented forms of physical and emotional sanctuary – places they could escape to if necessary, even staying for a few days without their mothers, and people with whom they could cry, be angry and discuss their conflicts and confusions. There is an important lesson here for the way in which friends and the wider community can help children and young people survive domestic violence, even if they do not know how to intervene to stop the abuse. There is also perhaps a message for women about confiding in others, if it is at all possible to do so without placing themselves in greater danger, though we are fully aware that violent men often take care to cut women off from just this kind of supportive network.

REFUGES AND OTHER VOLUNTARY SECTOR PROVISION

A close second to immediate family members in the numbers of children saying they had been the source of most support came specialist provision such as refuges and community domestic violence projects. This contrasts to some extent with the hypothesizing of the general population sample in the last chapter, who did not see professionals as people who children would be likely to call on for help. The schools sample was right to be sceptical about children's views of statutory workers (see below), but specialist services had been appreciated because they had paid specific attention to children's own needs and perspectives. Indeed, children's workers were high amongst those to whom children had elected to talk about their problems. Having been given the opportunity to tell their own stories and to explore their fears and anxieties, when engaged either in a process of leaving and returning or of more permanent separation from the abuser, mattered intensely to those children who had been able to access it. It was also clear that safety had created a context in which it had become possible to relax and begin to enjoy outings and activities:

The people at the refuge helped the most. They did this by making our life happier, by taking us out. They made us feel better by taking everything out of our minds as if it didn't happen. (9-year-old South Asian girl)

Within our relatively small sample were a number of children who had had multiple contacts with different specialist services. In a way, they had conducted their own 'consumer test' on these vital resources and were markedly able to articulate the differences between them, especially the extent to which children's needs and realities were or were not effectively responded to. It was fascinating how closely children's positive assessments of what mattered to them were reflected in the expert interviews we conducted with specialist workers, which suggests that these hard-pressed individuals are 'getting it right' for children. They stressed the importance of consistency and continuity in specific support, moving at the pace of each child, whilst seeking to enable them to talk about their experiences, perceptions and needs. Children's feedback on what they needed from refuge provision included: children's workers who both arranged activities that 'took you out of yourself' and facilitated discussions about domestic violence; support for their mothers so that they could also tell their stories and 'get it out' (of their system); and staffing levels (both in terms of numbers and amount of time available), so that when there was a crisis or someone needed to talk this was possible:

> Someone to trust – a nice environment, homely, that will raise their confidence. Toys and games to occupy their time. Someone to talk to them about what they are feeling and to help them to understand why it is better that they have left ... You need people to understand how you are feeling and help you to cope with the changes. (14-year-old South Asian boy)

> Someone to talk to, not to keep it all bottled up – I do, but I know it is better not to. Refuges are good ... It is good for young people to get away from the situation and have their own lives. Because your life can just be tangled up with your parents and you are worrying about them all the time, so it is good to get away and just be you. (15-year-old white girl)

Children clearly made distinctions between those refuges where it had been possible to open up – to explore the complicated mess of emotions they and their mothers had kept a lid on for long periods of time – and provision that had been largely limited to housing:

> The workers could have talked to me about it, but they just never used to say anything ... There was one worker who was always wanting to bring us out places, but then she'd always ring in and say she was sick. (12-year-old white girl)

> I didn't like that refuge, there was nothing to do. I was bored all day and you couldn't go out ... The first time [in previous refuge], the workers were really helpful, very good with us [children], talked to us, spent time with us. The second lot were not as good – they asked about you, but you could tell they were not really bothered and were too busy with Mum. (11-year-old South Asian boy)

And interviews with mothers further elaborated this picture. As one South Asian mother put it:

Sort out the mother's problems, but don't forget the kids. Mothers will go back [to the abuser] if the kids are unhappy. (South Asian mother)

There was one child, however, a 12-year-old girl, whose reason for not liking the refuge, or other professional help she had been offered, was that she had been asked to talk too much. She had not been ready to open up, yet had clearly felt compelled to participate which consequently did not get to the heart of what she was feeling. This is why children's workers emphasize going at the child's pace.

First of all, I used to go to this place and, like, it's not really like you sit in a chair and talk all the time. You just play with toys and they just ask you questions like: 'How was your day at school? Did you have any problems?' And I don't think many children like it when they have to talk about their problems … Like, when I was in the refuge you have to talk, you have to at least say something. And, sometimes, you didn't really – you just made up what you were saying – you didn't really mean it. (12-year-old white girl)

Added to this, at least one South Asian family had experienced explicit racism in a refuge, despite this being contrary to national Women's Aid policy. Unfortunately, there has been minimal evaluation of refuge provision, in the UK or internationally, meaning that we have a limited basis from which to explore what factors contribute to a positive experience for women and children, nor to what extent inadequate and insecure resources contribute to the problems. A study undertaken by members of the research team reporting here (Hague et al., 1996) did find that resources for work with children in refuges in England are patchy, and that statutory funders typically fail to recognize that children constitute the majority of refuge residents or their potential status as 'children in need' under the Children Act 1989. It also included some feedback from children about refuge stays and is supplemented by increasing numbers of 'exit surveys' and other data collection exercises by refuges and outreach projects themselves. Nevertheless, the formal evaluative work that has begun in Germany (Bruckner, 2001) and South Australia (Ministerial Implementation Advisory Committee, 1997) is not paralleled here and, even there, it has concentrated on women's needs and views. Systematically exploring the contribution of refuges from the standpoint of children remains a gap in the research agenda.

FRIENDS AND PEERS

A smaller group, especially older girls, had found important support within their peer group. In several instances this relationship involved mutual exchange since one young person had recognized something familiar in the other:

Just being friends with people at school, because I only told one person – that was my friend in class. And she said that her dad's done it to her mum, so we'd been in the same situation and we just talk about it. (12-year-old mixed-race girl)

In fact, the most likely person children had actively told about the violence – as opposed to those who knew anyway by virtue of being part of the family or staff in a domestic violence project – was a friend. This pattern is confirmed by two large projects, one conducted in Australia (National Crime Prevention, 2000) and the other in Ireland (Regan and Kelly, 2001). The violence could also threaten these friendships that were so important to children, although they sustained them whenever they could:

> I have really good friends at school. But they couldn't come round when he was here, he would be so violent to everyone. He drove everyone away. I'd be too embarrassed. It was too frightening for them but they come round now. Just this last few weeks – I had a sleepover last week. But we couldn't when he was here. Also, he's a racist and he's violent and two of my friends are black, so – but now they come round. (14-year-old white girl)

Other children, however, talked of not having known what to say or that it could be dangerous to tell friends since, if you fell out with them, they might tell others and, whilst many children wanted to talk, they also wanted their confidentiality respected. Even these kinds of barriers could be surmounted by ingenuity, however:

> I talked to my friend at school and said, 'If this happened to you what would you do?' He said, 'I would go and help my mum and call the police.' (9-year-old South Asian boy)

These interviews, and material from other studies (Burton et al., 1998; National Crime Prevention, 2000; Regan and Kelly, 2001), demonstrate that over and above the children and young people who have to cope with living with domestic violence in their own families there are many others who live with knowing that it is a reality in the lives of their friends. For teenagers, this knowledge expands to include violence in intimate relationships between peers (National Crime Prevention, 2000; Regan and Kelly, 2001). Taking this aspect of children and young people's knowledge seriously, together with the uncertainties they express about what to say and do (Regan and Kelly, 2001), requires serious attention in the context of awareness-raising and educational programmes in schools and youth settings (see Chapters 3 and 9).

Almost all the children whose contact with refuges and other specialist domestic violence services had been positive mentioned the importance of being able to talk with other children who had shared their experience. Much of this interaction appeared to have taken place independently of the involvement of adults, be they mothers or children's workers:

> We helped each other … the other children helped. There were two children who helped me very much when I first went to the refuge. (12-year-old white girl)

What was clear, however, was that, whilst a number of refuges had created environments conducive to this sharing between children, others had not, resulting in much more conflictual relationships and children preferring to keep themselves to themselves.

STATUTORY SERVICES

Only three children referred specifically to professionals from statutory agencies as sources of personal support, one mentioning a police officer, another a social worker, and the third a teacher. The most common encounter had been with the police. No child had purely positive things to say about the police, and many noted either that the actions taken had been ineffective or that they had felt invisible to the officers who responded to the call (despite guidance in most areas recommending checking on the children's safety and needs, and even where it was the children themselves who had made the call):

I called the police, but they only let him back out after[wards]. (13-year-old white boy)

Interviewer: When the police came did they ever talk to any of you [the children]?
Young Person: No.
Interviewer: And had it ever been you who had called them?
Young Person: Yeah! (13-year-old mixed-race boy)

One group of siblings recalled an experience where they had run out of the house to the local police station; the three children had all been aged under ten at the time. Once there, they had been taken to a room and left on their own whilst the officers went to interview their mother. These three small children had then spent 45 minutes (a very long time to a child) fantasizing about what might be happening. Was their mother being arrested? Were they going to be taken away from her? The woman had merely been giving a statement and, presumably, the police had considered that it would better for all parties if she did not have to do this in front of the children. Taking one minute to explain this to the children would have allayed their fears and, strictly speaking, they should have had another officer with them. That these things did not occur suggests that the children were not being seen as individuals who have a right to be respected and given appropriate information. A child from another family also noted the importance of this for children:

Children need someone to look after them. If their mum or dad is taken to prison or the police station to answer questions, children need someone to be with them. They should think about this. (9-year-old South Asian girl)

A smaller group of children had been referred to other agencies, such as education welfare or an educational psychologist, but none reported that these encounters had been anything other than difficult and tense. Clearly, little if any rapport had been established and the focus appeared to have been on the problems they were experiencing either in terms of schoolwork or behaviour. No protocols appear to have been in place for routine enquiries as to abuse they might have experienced, either directly or indirectly. As they were not asked about domestic violence, far from these encounters having been used as opportunities for exploring the underlying causes of their problems, children had felt judged and anxious. Their resistance to a process that had failed to address their experience or needs had been expressed by withdrawing and refusing to communicate in anything other than a defensive manner. This young man is recalling being interviewed by a succession of court welfare officers (now 'family court advisors' in the amalgamated Children and Family Court Advisory and Support Service, known as CAFCASS) following an application by his father for contact, in a manner that reveals the widespread official bias towards maintaining contact even with dangerous men and reluctance to understand women and children's fears in the post-separation phase (see Chapters 8 and 9):

> To be honest, I did not know what to say. I used to think I was saying the wrong thing … [T]he worst thing I could think of was actually having to see him again … I remember saying – sometimes not answering the question, because I couldn't … Most of the time, as soon as they came, the first thing I was thinking of was that I've got to make sure that I don't ever have to see him … I spent about 15 minutes thinking about the question, trying to remember what it was. (15-year-old mixed-race boy)

Several children reported knowing that professionals had information about their home situation, but that they had done nothing about it:

> Mum told the teachers at school about trouble at home, that we were moving. They didn't really say or do anything to help. They could have asked if I was OK, if I wanted to talk about it. (8-year-old South Asian girl)

Interestingly, a young South Asian woman thought that social workers had been the most helpful. Although her account is not one that most domestic violence advocates would appreciate, since there is no sign of partnership with her mother or of any actions being taken to help her be safe, it does at least involve the kind of firm intervention that respondents in the schools sample thought children should have a right to expect (see Chapter 3):

> The social workers – they were always there. The teachers had contacted them after I had told them a bit what was happening … I thought the social workers would help me and my mum, and if he harmed me they would know what happened. I think they finally made my mum see how risky it was for all of us to be living with him. They threatened that we would be taken into care if she stayed on after he had hit me so badly. (16-year-old South Asian girl)

Within this overall landscape of failure on the part of statutory agencies were several beacons of hope – professionals whose openness and perceptiveness had unlocked children's trust and whose actions had served to reinforce it. One teenage boy told a story of having had a sense of dread, whilst at school, that something was terribly wrong at home. The staff were hugely supportive, allowing him to go home accompanied by his head of year. There was no answer at home, which alarmed him even more. The teacher contained the situation, brought the child back to school, and made enquiries to discover what had happened. There had in fact been an incident, his mother was at the hospital, and her abuser had been arrested:

> I was so scared. I thought he must have killed my mum and I kept asking and she [the teacher] kept saying no, he hadn't killed her. But I was sure she was just hiding it from me, and I was so frightened. I kept crying and screaming out, 'He's killed her, he's killed her!' [Respondent becomes distressed and cries. Interview temporarily suspended until he insists on resuming his account.] (15-year-old white boy)

WHAT CHILDREN NEED

When asked what children living with domestic violence need, our sample of children were astonishingly clear and consistent. Most commonly cited was safety, closely followed by someone to talk to. One or both of these themes featured in every response to this question:

> They need someone to talk to. Because, if they were like me, sometimes I'm really sad and I need someone to talk to … [They may not be able to] speak to the mum because maybe their mum don't want to talk about it. I think they should have someone to talk to. (9-year-old white girl)

> They need to get away – a long way from him, so that he can't find them. If it is that bad, mums should leave. They can go and live with their family, but these troubles won't stop – he will break down their door. They need to go away so that he can't find them. (16-year-old South Asian girl)

Within the safety theme, many children noted the need for more refuges – often qualifying this with requests for 'nice houses' with children's workers or specific support for children. Several South Asian children also made it clear that there was a need for more specific provision for Asian families (see Chapter 6).

LEAVING AND LOSSES

Much of the literature on children and domestic violence that addresses its impacts focuses on psychological factors – damage that may have consequences both for childhood and adulthood. However, these are not the issues that appear in children's accounts of the costs and consequences of living with domestic violence. Bearing in mind that this group of children were, in the main, no longer living with the abuser at the time of the interviews, the themes that dominated in their accounts were safety and loss of the familiar (though see also Chapter 8 for more detail of what the earlier violence had been like for them):

It's not better at the refuge but it's safer. Yes, it's safer – definitely safer. I still want to go home though … I have to get up very early and go by taxi to my school. I still go to the same school, but it is so far from here. And then I don't get back here until late. (8-year-old mixed-race boy)

He made me leave my home. He made me leave all my best friends. He made me leave all my things behind. (9-year-old white girl)

I felt sad leaving [my] home, school, friends, my birds. (8-year-old South Asian girl)

We weren't allowed to take a lot of stuff with us because the refuge woman said we would be moving around a lot. I had, like, one big rucksack on my back and one big handbag. My brother had one big bag and my mum had two black plastic bags and a big bag. (10-year-old black British girl)

I had to leave everything – leave all my stuff. We just had the clothes we stood up in, and we didn't come home for 15 months. I had 14 porcelain dolls and I had to leave it all behind – all my things … I was really upset because I had to leave Thumper behind. We had to leave him in the garden shed. I cried and cried because they don't have pets in the refuge. (12-year-old white girl)

Children hugely resented having had to leave their home, possessions, pets, friends – literally everything that gave their daily lives structure, meaning and consistency – in order to be safe. It also made an immense difference if the most significant losses – which for many children often included their pets – could be ameliorated. The child with the pet rabbit quoted above had been so distressed and concerned that the local refuge group had bent its rules about pets, allowing Thumper to be collected and housed in a shed in the garden.[2] He was proudly displayed to the researcher, performing his party trick of climbing a flight of stairs.

This entirely justified resentment – children rightly asking why they should have had to leave everything when they had done nothing wrong – expanded into anger and rage when the relative safety they had found, and the limited comfort of reconstructed daily routines, was disrupted yet again by the abusive man's actions:

I hate him. We've been in three refuges. When I was in the second one I liked it. One day, when I was coming home from school – he knew what school I was at – I turned round and I saw him following me … I went to this friend's house who lived down the road and he was still with me, but she wasn't in – well she *was* in but she wasn't allowed to open the door because she didn't know who it was. Then I just started taking him around, saying: 'I don't live around here, I live about two miles down somewhere.' (12-year-old white girl)

Despite this young woman's resourcefulness in attempting to evade her father and in ensuring that he did not find their new location, the encounter had been deemed to have compromised the family's – and the refuge's – safety, and they had been required to move from the one place she had managed to begin to feel 'at home' since leaving her own house.

Even going home again was not straightforward. Three children talked bitterly about the experience of having returned to their family home, either with an injunction or because the man had agreed to move out. Rather than this being a much anticipated reunion with place and possessions, however, it had turned into a further betrayal on discovering that the house had been neglected or even deliberately trashed by the perpetrator before leaving.

If we are to take children's views and needs seriously, this creates an urgent requirement to find ways of decreasing the losses currently incurred as a result of seeking safety from domestic violence. There are a range of implications here, from creating partnerships between formal agencies and informal networks that increase the possibility of women and children remaining in their own homes, to the necessity of public policy focusing more directly on controlling and sanctioning the actions of abusive men (see Chapter 9). When responding to breaches of protection orders, for example, all criminal justice personnel should take into account the repeated disruption to children's lives that this entails and the costs to children themselves, as well as to the public purse, of repeated relocations.

TAKING A TOLL

Both this study and previous research (Grotberg, 1997; Jaffe et al., 1990; McGee, 2000) have pointed to the extraordinary resourcefulness and resilience that children display in the face of repeated threats to their physical and emotional security (see also Chapter 5). Some children even manage to learn and value important things from what have been called their 'nightmare lessons'[3]:

> I had to stand by my mum because she was not in the wrong. That pulled us through and has made us stronger and better. We have been through a lot. We can feel for others and are better human beings. (14-year-old South Asian boy, also cited in Chapter 6)

The burden that some children carry, however, was graphically illustrated by one young woman who insisted on taking part in the research (which she had heard about through a friend), even though her parents were still together and on this basis she should have been excluded from the sample (see Chapter 2). She both wanted and needed to talk about what she was going through but, at the same time, she felt a conflict of loyalties:

> I can't bear it that he hits her. I feel so ashamed. I always worry that the neighbours will hear or that the teachers will find out at school … I felt really nervous about talking to you, and guilty because my mum and dad are wonderful – they are really good people and I don't want you or the researchers to think badly of them, because they are very good parents and they love me a lot and they have always done everything they can for me. They are really interesting people. It's not their fault, it's just the way it is with them. (14-year-old white girl)

Whilst it is important to pay detailed attention to children's own perceptions and understandings, they are not necessarily the best judges of the impacts and consequences for them over time of what they are going through. Another young woman of the same age appears resilient, if somewhat in denial, given the discrepancy between the vehemence of the first part of her comment and the nonchalance of the second:

> Well, I am not going to get married – never! It hasn't affected me really, I'm OK. (14-year-old white girl)

The refuge children's worker who had worked with this second young person, however, was extremely concerned about her future welfare, noting that she had been in five refuges, rehoused twice, and had not been attending school for over a year. Bravado and minimization can play a part in children's coping strategies so that they do not always reveal what they are really feeling. Another teenager makes clear why, for some children, talking is difficult, if not impossible:

> I don't really want to remember those times too much – they upset me. I used to feel I was bleeding inside. (15-year-old white girl)

Mothers in their interviews with us tended to place more emphasis on the psychological and behavioural impacts on children that have been reported elsewhere in the literature (Jaffe et al., 1990): becoming withdrawn; fearfulness and anxiety; nightmares and disturbed sleep; becoming overly compliant or aggressive (both seen by mothers as applying to boys *and* girls, and one teenaged girl said that both she and her brother tended to get angry very easily).

> Not exactly nightmares, she keeps dreaming about her dad – that we meet him, that we were hiding and came out and he was there and we had to run … it's always about running away from him. (White mother)

Many children also talked about problems in sleeping, either lying awake for hours or being woken from sleep by shouting and screaming. This, in turn, had caused headaches or problems in concentrating at school the next day. The two other major tolls on children that mothers reported were interruptions in education and more serious psychological and health effects such as speech and language problems (see Chapter 6), developmental delays and learning difficulties (Hague et al., 1996). Whilst these were the case for a minority of children in our sample, that they were reported in six families (24 per cent) suggests that domestic violence is implicated in these childhood difficulties. This supposition is supported by similar proportions of children with special needs being reported in the interim findings of an evaluation of children's programmes in refuges (called crisis centres) in Denmark (Berens, 2000). Notably, speech problems were particularly widely reported by South Asian mothers in our study (see Chapter 6).

The fact that many children appear to find coping strategies that limit the impacts on them of living with domestic violence (see Chapter 5) should not, then, give rise to an overly optimistic outlook. There are several reasons why not. First, the psychological and other problems that many continue to experience are real. Second, as the previous section outlined, children themselves are aware of the losses they have sustained and rightly regard them as unjust and unnecessary. Third, domestic violence constructs relationships between children and their parents (biological and social) in particular ways that are not desirable – themes we explore in subsequent chapters (see Chapters 7 and 8). Fourth, several children revealed that they were still struggling with feelings and confusions they did not know how to resolve:

> My mum is better, but I'm not. Can I say a bit about it? You know, how it made me feel? It affected me a lot. It gets me all muddled and weird … I think it has frozen me up a bit inside. (8-year-old mixed-race boy)

> Interviewer: What about things like sleep, do you sleep all right now?
> Young Person: No. I have to sleep watching two doors and with my back against the wall. (12-year-old white girl)

And, finally, a minority of children sustain extensive damage which may prove difficult, and perhaps impossible, to repair. There were five families (one in five) in our sample where the levels of harm to individuals and family connections had been extensive and severe – in each case there was some combination of at least one estranged sibling, histories of children in care, at least one child with significant developmental delays and/or educational difficulties, and a young adult with drug addiction problems or in trouble with the police. One mother also talked of an eldest daughter who, she said, had been so disabled by the violence that she had been in an institution for some years and did not recognize any of her family. In addition, two of the mothers in these families had serious problems with alcohol that were evident during the interviews. (In both cases, appropriate statutory agencies were involved.) We can only speculate whether earlier intervention to help these women and their children be safe might have prevented some of this catalogue of distress and damage.

It is important, of course, that we recognize survivors' strengths, as well as the risks and harm they have experienced, however extreme. Even within a small sample such as ours, for example, were two boys who had survived dire circumstances with resilience. They had been separated from their mother because the violence she had been experiencing from her new, drug-misusing partner had become so terrifying that their father had taken the boys away. The pain of this separation, especially for the older child, had been immense and was accentuated both by his mother's (to him) apparent disappearance (she was actually in a refuge but her whereabouts could not be revealed) and the fact that his father began hitting him, necessitating a further move to his aunt's. Despite these successive crises and disruptions, the woman and her children had eventually been reunited, and they were amongst the most open, honest and reflective families involved in the research. Whether the reunification of the family would have happened so successfully if the children had gone into the public care, rather than to other members of the family, is a matter of speculation. Either way, there is certainly a message here for professionals, not least about continuing to value the role of the non-abusing parent wherever possible and understanding why women are not always able to keep their children safe without help while they themselves are facing life-threatening danger.

Three elements appear to have played a part, probably in interaction, in the lives of the families in our study who had coped least well. These were frequent violence over a long period, severe depletion of the mothers' physical and emotional resources, and multiple moves. We know that repeated moves in the care system are related to the poorest outcomes after leaving care (Broad, 1997) to the point where the Government has made minimizing the number of moves for looked-after children a performance measure in its Quality Protects initiative. Much of the explanation has focused on the damage to attachments and the absence of consistency in caring. The experiences of children fleeing domestic violence are rather different from this. Usually, the primary attachment to an adult – the non-abusing parent – is not broken (although their relationship may well be affected, see Chapter 7), but the child's links with place, neighbourhood and home, in the sense of a familiar space filled with well loved objects, are cut. Also, each place that is left behind is likely to have been associated with other people who have provided support, including family members and 'best friends' at home, supportive peers and helpful adults encountered *en route* to safety. The thwarting of successive attempts to recreate a semblance of a settled life elsewhere does appear to have a cumulative impact on children, undermining their (and probably also their mothers') resilience and coping strategies (see Chapter 5).

There are particular challenges here for refuges, which have historically (at least in the UK) moved women and children within the network whenever there has been a threat to their safety. The findings from our study suggest that this policy is not one that benefits children. That said, to do otherwise would require investment in security measures for refuges far in excess of currently available resources. Reliable and consistent multi-agency protocols would also be needed, to ensure that anyone breaching the safety of refuges was dealt with speedily and seriously. There are countries in which women's shelters are able to become public addresses because the protective web surrounding them feels strong enough to repel unwanted intrusion (see Hague et al., 2001, for an example in London, Ontario). As well as preventing the multiple moves that result when abusers track down women and children, this surely sends a message that refuges should aspire not just to improve the chances of remaining unharmed – as a child quoted earlier astutely noted, a refuge is 'safer' but not safe – but literally to live up to their name. This aspiration can only be made real by the willingness of governments, private funders and local communities to invest in the security of those women and children whose lives are so unsafe, so desperate, that they choose to leave behind everything they have and seek sanctuary elsewhere. There is also a further challenge here to the civil and criminal justice system, and to local communities, to recognize the dangers of post-separation harassment and violence and to reinforce their efforts to tackle the behaviour of the most persistent domestic abusers. At present, it is still women and children who are paying the price of perpetrators' continued attempts to assert their power over others. There is a long way to go before the police and the courts, let alone attempts to change the behaviour of perpetrators (Mullender and Burton, 2001), can claim effectiveness in crime prevention in relation to domestic violence.

HOW SAFE IS SAFE?

Separation from the abuser does not guarantee safety for women or children. The small number of cases in our research where the abuser was still in the household (see Chapter 2) were certainly not the only instances where children continued to be, or to feel, under threat. Six children in the study who had contact with the abuser reported not feeling safe. This adds support to current scrutiny of child contact policy where domestic violence is concerned (see Chapters 8 and 9).

The majority of respondents reported feeling secure at the time of the interview:

> I feel safe. I know he can't kill us now. I used to really worry about it when he was at home. He used to frighten us all the time. He used to say he was going to put petrol in the house and burn it while we were asleep. (8-year-old Asian girl)

Nevertheless, for a third of this group, there was a strong qualification – they were safe so long as they were not found:

> I'm better than I was but I'm scared to go into the garden in the dark in case he jumps out. (12-year-old white girl)

Here, in the words of children and young people, lies the strongest possible message that society is not yet doing enough to control the behaviour of perpetrators. As a refuge children's worker remarked, for these children the bogeyman they fear in the bushes may not be a figment of their imaginations but may be really there.

It is a truly awful thing not to be able to tell children with honesty that they no longer have anything to worry about and that the adults around them can guarantee to keep them safe.

SIMILARITIES AND DIFFERENCES

Talking with children has led us to question some of the more simplistic accounts in earlier literature of the meanings and impacts of domestic violence in children's lives. Whilst a number of boys and young men were intensely worried, for instance, about 'repeating the patterns', the main examples we found of children who had themselves used violence were two who had physically intervened with the perpetrator (see above) and very young children whose actions, though clearly copied from what they had witnessed, could not be fairly adduced as evidence of 'growing up like it' since they were far too young to have formed unshifting patterns for their own relationships:

> He smacked me the other day, and I said, 'That's naughty.' He said, 'Daddy did.' He's not even three yet! (White mother)

Rather, we encountered sensitive and thoughtful boys who were concerned for the well-being of their mothers and siblings. They gave us far less cause for concern than did the apparently endemic toleration of violence by teenage boys in the general population that we saw in the last chapter. Nor did we encounter any single pattern or syndrome, or any obvious gender division in children's reactions. Indeed, we were more struck by the differences between children than by the similarities. Interviewing siblings, in particular, revealed fascinating variations in perceptions and understanding, even when they had lived through identical events. Some remembered similar incidents but most had widely divergent accounts, influenced by their age and incorporating their individual responses to the violence. Within the same family, for example, might be one child who was hyper-vigilant, trying to ensure his or her mother's safety and that of younger brothers and sisters, while, perhaps, the oldest child might have given up and be spending long periods of time outside the house. Children also varied in how afraid they were and in the degree to which they were dominated by abusive men, as well as in the extent to which they bonded with their mothers or siblings in a protective alliance. For some, the violence and control acted, rather, as a lightning fork – separating family members emotionally just at a time when they needed each other most.

Most importantly, children are actors in their own lives. Like adults, they draw on the information they have, their level of understanding, and their experiences to date – such as the frequency of the violence and apparent severity of the danger – to calculate the likely consequences of particular courses of action. As many of the quotes in this chapter have illustrated, children are daily involved in taking decisions about whether to speak or act, and in what context. And, again like adults, they need to find assurances that they can talk about issues outside their family and in confidence. Much as policy-makers and practitioners might wish it were otherwise, there is no simple, single story we can tell about living with domestic violence, and each child must be given the respect and space to tell their own story and to explore their personal issues, conflicts and questions.

The difference between children's accounts where accessible forms of support had been present for them and those for whom this had been lacking was marked. Children who had not had an aware and helpful social network talked regretfully and in a resigned way about this having been unavailable to them, despite adult relatives and friends having known about the violence. Those, on the other hand, who had been able to access such support spoke animatedly about its significance and often told stories to illustrate what difference it had made for them. Children learn to hide and disguise what is happening at home and, as they get older, this often involves lying to those they care about and then hating themselves for this betrayal of trust on their part. The fear of their friends and others finding out, linked with a sense that they will then cease to be considered worthy of care and support, silences many children and makes them discount the fact that others often know more than they admit. This conspiracy of silence traps children in a form of isolation which they may take to the extreme by limiting social contact that could otherwise provide much needed escape from anxiety and even valuable understanding and help. Just as victims of domestic violence need others to name abuse (Kelly, 1988), so children need permission to talk and reassurance that this is neither disloyal to their family nor a reflection on them or their worth. (See also Chapter 7.) South Asian children represented something of a variation at both extremes of this overall pattern, being both those who talked least with each other and the wider social network but also, in the exceptions, giving the most extensive accounts of ongoing and wider-ranging forms of support from grandparents, uncles and other relatives. This may be because their family and community can be both their chief source of help, if their mother is treated with sympathy and the abuser's behaviour is condemned, but also a route to ostracism and isolation if the violence leads instead to a loss of the woman's 'good standing'. (See Chapter 6 for a fuller account.)

As with responses to domestic violence generally, the role and significance of informal support have been neglected in research and public policy (Kelly, 1996; 2000), reflecting a tendency to over-emphasize the role of formal interventions both by state agencies and the voluntary sector (Kelly, 1998). A pilot project in Boston, USA, has moved the concept of children's advocate in a new direction, seeking to encourage members of informal networks to take seriously children's need for sanctuary and to enable children to dare to seek and ask for it (Thompson, 2000). In our research, informal supports topped children's list of what had helped, with specialist domestic violence services next in importance. There was a concurrence of opinion between children themselves, mothers and children's workers on the scope for refuges to provide discrete and sensitive services for children that are simultaneously linked to support for women, provided that children's work can be adequately resourced and not conflated with the needs that mothers also have (Hague et al., 1996). The statutory services were 'also-rans' for children, behind family, friends and specialist projects. Professionals sometimes got it badly wrong and appeared not even to notice that children were there, let alone giving them a chance to talk about what was happening to them.

VOICES OF HOPE

We end this chapter with messages of hope from children whose lives had changed markedly since being able to leave the violence. When asked how they felt now, some of the most encouraging and joyful responses were:

Safer, freer. (10-year-old white girl)

I used to be sad about it, now I feel better. (9-year-old white boy)

I feel safe now because I know no one can come and harm us. (9-year-old South Asian girl)

I feel I am part of the community now. Before, I was locked away. (16-year-old South Asian girl)

Things couldn't be better. I'm not seeing all the things I used to see that I didn't want to. I hated seeing those things. And I'm seeing Mum being happy instead, and laughing.

5   Children's Coping Strategies

This chapter moves on to explore how children cope with living with domestic violence, as well as their advice to other children on the basis of their own experiences. It once again draws on children's own words, as expressed in in-depth interviews with the research team. As we discussed in Chapter 1, far from being 'blank sheets', children adopt individual coping strategies and have their own particular perspectives on what is happening to them. We heard many examples of how children had tried to make sense of the events in their lives and the feelings these had aroused. Many had carefully thought about how they could relieve the situation and had chosen ways to be more passive or active, whichever they thought would help the most. Although such attempts had often been overlooked by the adults involved, children talked openly to us about feeling sad, worrying, formulating plans, and trying to take responsibility for their mothers and siblings. Overall, they told us about seeking out, and wanting to be part of, solutions to apparently impossible situations, both during the violence and in its aftermath:

> I'm doing everything I can to help her get more courageous. We could change it around to take out all the terrible memories for her. We've got all our friends there to help. We could get a guard dog. That's what I'd like to do – help her be stronger ... I want to make an effort to help her ... I want to help out with the washing-up. (8-year-old mixed-race boy)

Despite the distressing and often complex impacts of domestic violence that we saw in Chapter 4, the qualitative phase of the research frequently provided a sense of what can only be called inspiration in children's responsible, careful and painful efforts to make things better.

HOW CHILDREN COPE WITH DISTRESS AND TRAUMA

There is a considerable literature on coping strategies and resilience in general, in relation to adverse experiences of various kinds (Grotberg, 1997). There are also extensive sources both on childhood trauma and the specific ways in which children cope with it (Garmezy, 1983; Rutter, 1983) and also on children's adjustment and coping strategies in particular relation to marital discord, separation and divorce (Emery, 1982; Jouriles et al., 1989). This wide-ranging empirical and theoretical work can provide a useful framework within which to understand the real-life coping strategies used by the children with whom we talked, and to situate our discussion of these later in the chapter.

In most accounts the mechanisms that people of all ages use to cope with difficulties include the development of 'protective factors' (see, for example, Garmezy and Rutter, 1983; Kashani and Allen, 1998). Successful coping with adverse experiences of any type appears to depend not only on the strength of these, but also on their occurrence in some sort of combination rather than singly (as above, and see also Jaffe et al., 1990).

General preventative strategies, which are likely to assist both adults and children in coping well, include the presence of fewer life stressors apart from the causal trauma itself. In particular relation to children, for example, Rutter (1985) and others have suggested that the protective factors and behaviours that contribute to coping mechanisms include positive self-esteem, personality factors (being easy-going and humorous, for instance), secure attachment to a non-abusive parent or carer, the existence of networks of personal support, and supportive community and social frameworks (see Fonagy et al., 1994). In particular, self-esteem emerges as a critical element underlying children's ability to develop successful coping strategies (Cicchetti et al., 1993; Neighbors et al., 1993). However, the domestic violence literature tells us that it is often likely to be damaged in children who have lived with the shame and the undermining attitudes of the abusive man (e.g. McGee, 2000; Peled and Edleson, 1995). These children may therefore face a double obstacle in terms of coping.

Overall, in the general literature, two over-arching issues are highlighted in respect of both self-esteem and coping. First, most research accounts suggest that secure attachment to a non-violent parent or other significant carer is an important protective factor (Katsikas et al., 1996; Neighbors et al., 1993). Emery (1982), for example, has described how the existence of particularly warm relationships between children and their mothers or other non-abusive carers can mitigate trauma and distress. In specific relation to violence and abuse, strong relationships with mothers can play a protective role in terms of children's coping. In instances of domestic violence where a mother and her child share strong and supportive bonds, this can contribute creatively to the ability of them both to get through the experience. Despite the damage that domestic violence may cause to mother–child relationships and to women's ability to parent effectively (see Chapter 7), mothers (along with siblings) were named as the most common source of support by children and young people in our study. It is particularly worrying, therefore, that child protection practice appears sometimes to undermine mothers as key figures in their children's lives, accusing them of 'failure to protect' when they decline to adopt simplistic solutions such as leaving home in the face of threats to pursue and kill (Hague et al., 2000; Humphreys, 2000a). At the extreme, this can result in children being removed from the care of the person who is most able to help them survive emotionally. This should be borne in mind in risk assessments, with every effort being made to help the woman be safe with her children and to name and tackle the abuser's behaviour as the real site of the danger. Increased use of the exclusion orders that Schedule 7 of the Family Law Act 1996 introduced into the Children Act 1989, as a way of removing the perpetrator in emergency protection and interim care proceedings, would be one useful way forward, for example.

The second general issue that recurs repeatedly throughout the literature as an important element in coping is having someone to turn to for emotional support (Kashani and Allan, 1998; Watt et al., 1995). Clearly this overlaps with attachment issues but most accounts also emphasize the key role of wider social and community support structures and of supportive family relationships more generally (Valentine and Feinauer, 1993; Watt et al., 1995). Domestic abuse is likely to be particularly difficult to survive, then, since women and children who leave home as a result of the violence are forced to abandon the very fabric of their lives. For children, regular contact with grandmothers, other relatives and close friends may be lost just when they need it most, though siblings remain important throughout (see below).

Overall, then, it can be seen that coping with domestic violence may be additionally difficult when compared with other adverse situations, since key protective factors are likely to be missing or compromised. This conclusion has clear implications for housing policy in terms of the injustice and harmful effects of abused women and children being forced to flee their homes while perpetrators stay put. There are also lessons to be learnt by social workers and criminal justice professionals who may be involved in decisions about who stays and who leaves. (See Chapter 9 for more detail on policy and practice implications.)

Another key element in facing potential trauma of any kind involves being able to be directly involved in finding solutions. Grotberg (1997) suggests that children's resilience and ability to cope in the face of adverse circumstances can be encouraged by supportive interactions with adults which specifically foster autonomy, the development of personal communication skills, and a sense that they are important and will be listened to and taken seriously. These suggestions have resonance with our findings (discussed later in this chapter) about treating children with respect and giving their views and self-expression credibility.

In specific relationship to violence in the family, Kashani and Allan (1998) suggest that more research is needed on protective factors, to feed into the policy process on preventative work with children and more constructive agency responses. What are the specific strategies that children use to cope with violence and do they differ from the more general factors identified above? The evidence is that, overall, the same issues apply, but that the specific way they are manifested may vary. Our research contributes to the process of clarification, adding to the work of others (e.g. McGee, 2000) and building on insights from related fields such as child sexual abuse. Hall and Lloyd (1993), for example, have identified childhood survival strengths in relation to sexual assault and victimization as including minimizing, rationalizing, denying, forgetting, positive decision-making and hiding (either physically or emotionally). Even if not beneficial as long-term solutions, they suggest, these ways of coping may help the child not to be overwhelmed by the experience.

As regards domestic violence itself, Jaffe and his research and practitioner colleagues in London, Ontario, were among the first to identify and write about coping strategies. They showed in a number of early studies (Jaffe et al., 1985; Wolfe et al., 1986) that, when compared to control groups, some children have the ability to cope with and resist the debilitating impacts of witnessing the abuse of their mothers. They also demonstrated that protective factors and family relationships in such situations may be multi-dimensional and complex (Jaffe et al., 1990). While their findings remain key to our understanding, insights into the inventive and practical coping mechanisms used by children living with domestic violence have in fact been principally developed not within the academy or by professional agencies, but by the activist movement in many Western and other countries. Notably in the UK, since the 1970s, Women's Aid (and other women's and children's organizations more recently) has developed direct work with children to help them overcome the damage and distress caused by the violence (Debbonaire, 1994; Higgins, 1994; Mullender et al., 1998; Scottish Women's Aid, 1999). Childworkers explain that 'what we try to do is to build on children's strengths, find out what they can offer each other, and encourage that' (children's worker in a women's refuge, Hague et al., 1996).

HOW CHILDREN HAD COPED

The present study showed mixed results in relation to children's ability to survive difficult and violent situations. While the majority had clearly been adversely affected by living with the abuse of their mothers, others across the age range had been able to deal with its most negative impacts, as some told us in a group interview – without denying the seriousness of the situation:

> We all cope in all sorts of ways … but lots of children are good at it. Children don't necessarily get upset and in a state about it. They can do fine with it. Some do get upset and they need support and caring because it is such a big thing. It is definitely really a big thing for children. (Group interview with children of various ethnicities, aged 8 to 13 years)

This finding of many children being able to cope was echoed by a children's worker we interviewed in a women's refuge:

> Children have such resilience – lots of them become stronger quite quickly. Often they bounce back. It can make children more determined, more wise – special people. Their distress can have a short span – and they get stronger … Their experience stretches out their imagination and their minds. They can understand more because of their experiences and having to learn to cope. They become better at working out coping strategies of all sorts. (Refuge children's worker)

Since there has not as yet been any full-scale study in the UK of the longer-term outcomes of living with domestic violence on young people, and since we only got to know those we interviewed over a period of a year to 18 months, we must point out that even the more resilient amongst them could yet encounter problems in later life (though it seems most likely that their fortunes will continue to be as varied as their personalities and circumstances). Nor does some children's ability to survive apparently unscathed lessen the need to develop practice responses well beyond the currently patchy level of provision (Humphreys et al., 2000 and see Chapter 9). But we know enough already to say that it is wrong to stereotype all children as inevitably and permanently damaged by living with domestic violence or as sustaining only negatives from their experiences if they are able to come through with support. As the childworker above went on to comment, 'They can become wiser – growing up a stronger person. We should celebrate them.'

CHILDREN'S ACTIVE PARTICIPATION

Two issues emerged from our study as crucial to children's ability to cope. They were the importance of:

- being listened to and taken seriously as participants in the domestic violence situation; and
- being able to be actively involved in finding solutions and in helping to make decisions.

LISTENING TO WHAT CHILDREN HAVE TO SAY

Many children believed they would have coped better if they had been engaged by adults in talking about the issue. Where no one had listened to them, they felt doubly disadvantaged: 'Grown-ups don't realize sometimes because they are always going on about their stuff and they forget that the children might be hurting too' (group interview with children of various ethnicities, aged 8 to 13 years).

Children confirmed how badly many of them felt about the violence and about no one having talked or listened to them about it. The 15-year-old girl who, as we heard in Chapter 4, unusually in the study was living with both her mother and her abusive father at the time of some of the interviews, was resourceful and insightful about her situation. Her life decision had been to put herself on the line, constantly to 'guard' against the violence of her father. In this non-stop painful vigilance, she got no thanks or support from anyone, it seemed.

> Yes, that's what I do – I lie awake at night. I still do. I make myself be awake so that I can jump up when it's happening and get between them. I make myself be awake. Every night I do that. Usually it helps because I get between them and cry and try and stop them and my dad does, because he wouldn't want to hurt me and he gets embarrassed that I am seeing it and that I am awake, so I can stop them that way. So it's important that I don't go to sleep for my mum's sake. If I didn't get between them, I don't know what might happen. So I have to help my mum. So I jump up as soon as it sounds like it is getting bad. I just stay quiet and listen because they'd be upset if they thought I could hear. (15-year-old white girl)

This girl coped by exerting whatever protective influence she could without the adults concerned really knowing about it. She said that her life was dominated at all times by the domestic violence, in terms of dealing with it when it happened, trying to prevent it beforehand, and inventing strategies to deflect or lessen it.

These strategies were often effective but were never acknowledged by either of her parents. She was never able to talk with them about what she was going through. Nor was her social agency in the situation either acknowledged or validated.[1]

Like the young woman quoted above, many of the children and young people made it clear that they had wanted to be told what was going on by the adults in their lives, both family members and professional helpers, rather than being kept in the dark as a way of trying to protect them from upsetting knowledge. Obviously there are age differences here, and very young children may not be in a position to deal with information about violence. We chose not to interview children below the age of 8, partly on the advice of other children (see Chapter 2). We also found mothers to be particularly protective of their younger children, often refusing to allow them to be interviewed for fear of upsetting them. Researchers like Jaffe et al. (1990) have also noted age-related factors. However, there is consensus emerging in the literature that, where painful issues of abuse are discussed with children this can be helpful when it is done in an age-sensitive manner, and is conducted at the children's pace and led by their needs (see, for example, Hester et al., 2000). Indeed, McGee's (2000) research and children's groups in Canada (Hague et al., 2001) have extended downwards as far as 4 or 5 years of age and still found children able to talk about violence they had witnessed.

Children we talked to frequently described how they had known about the abuse even where their mothers thought they had not: 'Mum thought I didn't know much about it, but I did. We knew all about it all the time. She thought she was hiding it from us, but we knew' (14-year-old white boy). In this respect, our research confirms the findings of previous studies, from Jaffe et al. (1990) to McGee (2000). In interview, mothers told us they had been trying to protect their children from what they saw as 'adult business' or sometimes as their own mistakes and responsibility (see also Chapter 7). A few had done their best to explain, but had found it extremely difficult. Again, children were fully aware of this:

> Mum used to try to explain. When [abuser] went out, we'd all sit cuddled up together under the duvet and talk … Mum, [sibling] and I would sit on the settee and she'd try and explain it to us. (9-year-old white boy)

More frequently, women had tried to hide what was happening (see Chapter 7). As a result of their attempts to conceal the violence, and in some cases of similar efforts by the perpetrator, several children talked of having gone to great lengths to pretend that they did not know. They had done this because they had understood it to be what the adults wanted to believe. The consequence was that they had been doing their best to fulfil adult needs while receiving little help or support to meet their own. Ironically, the whole convoluted situation had arisen from what the adults thought was in the children's best interests. This points to important lessons for parents and practitioners (discussed more fully in Chapter 9) that can be derived from listening to children. In one set of interviews with two boys, both white and aged 9 and 15 years old, for example, their mother sat in on her children's sessions with everyone's agreement. She was stunned to find how much they had known and to hear completely accurate details of violent incidents, going back years, which they carefully related and which she thought had been hidden. In later contacts by phone and at subsequent interviews, all three members of the family (who by that stage had been living violence-free for many months and appeared to be a happy and settled unit) described how they had talked the issues through after the interviews and supported each other in dealing with the revelations.

WANTING TO BE INVOLVED AND TO HELP MAKE DECISIONS

Children and young people of both genders and all ethnicities in our sample spoke not only of wanting to talk and be listened to but also of wanting to be consulted about possible outcomes and to have their opinions – even their advice – considered. They said they wanted 'to be believed' or 'to be told what is going on' (group interview with children aged 8 to 13 years). Many suggested that children should be directly involved in decision-making about the situation and should certainly be told what was happening: 'People need to explain it to children in ways they can understand and be involved' (group interview). Unfortunately, they felt that this had not occurred and that their feelings and suggestions had been overlooked or ignored. They related incidents where their attempts to contribute had not even been noticed, and certainly not heeded, by the adults involved. McGee's study also found evidence of children's powerlessness in this respect and of their distress being aggravated by their 'absolute loss of control over the situation' (McGee, 2000: 107).

All the secondary school age children, and many of the younger ones, said they wanted to be involved in making actual decisions – for example, about leaving home and going to a refuge:

> We could help, we know what is going on and we could help. It would be better if they let us help. (12-year-old white girl)

A depressing but important message from interviewing children was that they said their opinions and wishes had often been overlooked, not only by the adults who were personally involved but also by the professionals who were trying to find solutions. For example, social workers had sometimes omitted to talk with the children, when intervening as a result of domestic violence, and had only talked to their mothers. Discussion and consultation with children about the violence they had lived through – or even acknowledgement that they had been affected – were slow in coming from most of the adult parties involved (with the exception of most refuge children's workers and a few of the mothers).

DETAILED COPING STRATEGIES

The detailed coping strategies the children and young people had used were wide-ranging and inevitably intertwined with the impact of the violence itself. (See also Chapters 4 and 6.) They could be roughly divided into two categories, namely:

- immediate: how the child or young person had coped during actual incidents of violence; and
- longer-term: coping with the situation both after the event and over time.

Within both there were physical and psychological elements (see also McGee, 2000), frequently intertwined, that could be positive or negative – the latter, for example, where children bottled up their feelings.

COPING IN THE IMMEDIATE SITUATION

In immediate situations of violence, children had utilized a wide range of short-term ways of coping physically and emotionally which did not appear to reveal particular gender divisions or stereotypes (although some older boys had taken particular responsibility for their mother's safety). These ways of coping had included: a) responses or frames of mind which had helped the child or young person deal with the actual incident; b) strategies to achieve safety or to summon help; c) ways both of supporting and being supported by siblings; and d) means of trying to protect their mothers and intervening in the violent situation.

Psychological reactions that had enabled children of both genders and diverse ethnicities to get through the experience had involved 'shaking', 'screaming and screaming' and 'getting angry'. Another said: 'I used to cry and cry.' Many immediate coping mechanisms had involved trying to pretend the violence was not happening. Children talked about 'trying to ignore it, not to hear it', 'pre-tending you are not there', 'I blank it out, block it', 'hiding it from everyone', 'not talking, being withdrawn'. One young girl said that throughout arguments and violent episodes she 'used to keep very still, I don't move at all, not a muscle'. Other children said: 'I put my head under the bedclothes'; 'I hide away in cupboards or under beds.' Hiding was, in fact, a frequent psychological coping strategy for children from all backgrounds and of all ages that also doubled as a practical mechanism for trying to stay safe.

Some children had preferred to keep themselves busy. They described how they had tried to keep occupied during abusive episodes, often in an activity which had generated some noise to block out the sound of the attack: 'watching TV, or playing on the PC, or playing music until it's over'. When hiding or keeping busy was ineffective, some children had tried to escape: 'climbing out of the window'; 'we'd climb onto a nearby roof'; 'running out into the street'.

Safety strategies during the immediate incident included trying to tell someone and to obtain assistance. Various children either alerted the police, or tried to. Many phoned or went to fetch a relative or friend, or otherwise attempted to get help. One girl suggested 'running to tell an adult – your grandma, a relative, family, a friend'. A 9-year-old boy advised other children to 'call the police or get another adult to do it because it is hard for children to do that sometimes'. As we will see in Chapter 6, children from minority ethnic backgrounds were more nervous of involving outside agencies for fear of a racist response.

Looking after or being with siblings emerged as a particularly important way of coping at the actual time when mothers were being assaulted. Interviewees spoke of 'cuddling up with brothers and sisters' during the violence. We found examples of children having gone to dangerous lengths to get to their siblings and moving stories of their support for each other at the moment of crisis. In the following quote, the boy who climbed out of the first-floor window was only 8 years old at the time and his older brother was 13:

> We would get together when T [abuser] and Mum were arguing, and cuddle up and put some music on in C's [brother's] room. When it started, I used to climb out of the window and climb back in [C's] window to get to C because I couldn't go out the door because they were arguing and shouting and he [abuser] was hitting and I was so frightened. Then we'd be together and we'd try to play music so we couldn't hear, but we'd still listen. Or we'd get on one of the outside roofs outside and crouch there together. And we'd stick together. Sometimes I'd cuddle up into his bed. Sometimes I'd go to sleep on the floor and then, early in the morning, before Mum woke up, I'd creep back into my own room. So no one ever knew we would do it ... We used to cry together about it. We're very close. He looked after me. (11-year-old white boy)

Trying to be helpful to and worrying about mothers was another key aspect of coping. Many researchers have found evidence of children intervening to protect their mothers (e.g. Abrahams, 1994; McGee, 2000). In our interviews, only a minority of the children we talked to said they had attempted to intervene directly in violent situations in the sense of 'trying to physically get between them'. At least half the sample, though, talked about a wider range of behaviours intended to try and assist their mothers, such as 'staying in the room to prevent it', or 'shouting at him to stop'.

> I run down the stairs to see what is happening ... I tried to help. I tried to guard my mum so he couldn't hurt her. I didn't talk about it with anyone. I used to run downstairs to see Mum was OK. (8-year-old mixed-race boy)

Almost all the mothers we interviewed talked about at least one of their children having attempted to help in one way or another. (See also Chapter 4.)

LONGER-TERM COPING STRATEGIES

Guarding mothers in this way emerged not only as a short-term strategy but also as a long-term one. In general, we found that longer-term mechanisms for coping often paralleled the more immediate reactions discussed above, but that they presented a more complex and varied picture over time.

Some authors on sexual abuse have claimed two types of long-term coping mechanisms. The first is defensive and leads to an ongoing 'accommodation' with the abuse situation. In such instances, the person concerned tries to protect themselves by adapting to what is going on. The second mechanism leads to 'resolution', with a re-framing or overcoming of the abuse so that the individual can move forward (Kelly and Radford, 1998; Koss and Burkhart, 1989). Applying this framework, we can see that most of the children and young people in our survey had adapted to the situation as best they could whilst it was happening. Some had achieved a degree of re-framing when growing up, or leaving the violence had given them enough perspective to see that the responsibility for the violence lay with the abuser and that there was the potential for a violence-free life.

Overall, there was no single pattern, with both individual differences and, importantly, cultural and class issues coming into play. To simplify the discussion, the longer-term coping strategies our interviewees used have been broadly divided into two main groups:

- 'outward-looking' or more social, 'external' strategies
- 'inward-turning' or more personal, emotional, 'internal' strategies.

Outward-looking strategies

Talking to someone   A common coping strategy used by the children was finding someone to turn to, both during the violence and in its aftermath, so that they could avoid keeping their distress bottled up inside:

> Have someone to talk to you can trust – someone to help you understand how you are feeling ... help you cope with the changes. (10-year-old African-Caribbean girl)

Mothers, siblings, grandparents figured prominently amongst people to confide in, and even perpetrators were mentioned. The general view was that 'having someone to talk to' was helpful and that young people had felt strengthened as a result.

In order to be able to turn routinely to a trusted adult, such as a grandparent or neighbour, some children had not told them the full truth. Just being able to go and see them was enough. Being safe and being able to talk about whatever came to mind, not necessarily about the violence, was what these children had found helpful.

Others, like the girl quoted above who had cried a great deal, had talked to no one at all – ever. However, even she said that: 'If people are not as nervous about it as me, it's good to talk about it. I just feel ashamed. But some others don't, I know. It's better like that (15-year-old white girl). Others had similarly told no one themselves, but said they had learned, as a result for example of meeting others in refuges, that this had probably been a mistake. This extended to talking directly to parents:

> Talk to your parents more. I didn't and, when I finally did, it made me feel better ... If you talk to your parents – sort it out in your mind – you'd feel a lot better ... I think it makes sense to sort out exactly why and not let it hang around in your mind, really. (16-year-old white boy)

Having a 'haven' to go to   Some children found ways to get out of the house with friends or had worked out somewhere special to go when things at home became fraught, as a conscious or unconscious escape mechanism. A 'haven' of this type could be a friend's house, or that of a relative or neighbour, where the young person knew they could just call in whenever they needed to get away and find some peace. Some confided at these times in someone special, as discussed above, but many just wanted somewhere calm and supportive to go, to be with other people not involved in the violence. A refuge worker described how:

Many find an old person. They pop round – a comfortable person – have a cup of tea. Like a grandparent figure. It could be a grandparent, but it doesn't have to be. Just someone they know. Maybe they don't tell them, they just enjoy going round there. Or perhaps they do tell them – but it needs to be someone they feel safe with. A special place for them, perhaps where they can be pampered, made to feel safe and secure and important. (Refuge children's worker)

Finding a safe private space   Some children had found a place to go to alone where they could be quiet on their own. It appeared that in the emotional complexity of living in a household characterized by domestic violence having one's own space away from the household was an effective way of coping:

> … because your life can just be tangled up with your parents and you are worrying about them all the time so it's good if you can get away and just be you. You feel free doing that and you can concentrate on your own life instead of having to always worry about theirs. (15-year-old white girl)

Safe, quiet places could be in the garden (if there was one) or a park, or just on the streets. Some children deliberately left for school early so they could have a few quiet minutes on their own, to think and gather themselves together.

> Even if it is raining, they tell me they shelter under the shed or something, but they just must have that time and space on their own. It's a wonderful idea to get some space just for yourself to compose yourself. (Refuge children's worker)

Seeking help and getting adults to take responsibility   Children and young people often used coping strategies, both longer-term and immediate, in which they tried to get adults to take the final responsibility, the 'weight' of the situation.

> Children may want someone to take responsibility for them, instead of them doing it … to take the weight off their shoulders. (Group interview with children)

In our study, children did not typically blame themselves for the abuse (see Chapters 6 and 7). Most understood that it was the perpetrator's responsibility, perhaps because most were no longer living with the violence and had had time to reflect and, in some cases, to talk things over with refuge workers.

Children also wanted adults to take responsibility for intervening and stopping the violence. A common coping strategy was calling the police, as noted earlier, and this could be on both an emergency and a longer-term, regular basis. In the latter instance, the officers contacted were frequently from specialist domestic violence or community safety units. Some respondents felt, however, that this could be too difficult for children to do and that they should get another adult to do it on their behalf or that there could be other complications:

> Try the police if it gets really bad. Get a grown-up to phone them if you don't feel able to. But remember the police can be more trouble than they are worth. If you are going to call the police … good to have talked about it with your mum first. (Group interview)

A few children had contacted social workers, teachers or other agencies when things got particularly bad. Even fewer mentioned a need for formal counselling, in addition to informal ways of talking and sharing. (See Chapter 9 for discussion of professional help that children want to see made available.)

As will be described more fully in Chapter 6, children from minority ethnic communities, and South Asian children in particular, had often been anxious that they might become isolated from their community if the violence had been acknowledged to outsiders. Such anxieties were critically compounded by fears of encountering a lack of cultural understanding from white people and organisations, together with bad, unsympathetic or ill-informed advice, which was ignorant of cultural issues:

> They may not know about 'izzat' [family pride] and shame and they can make you do things that bring shame to the family. (16-year-old South Asian girl, also cited in Chapter 6)

Hence, coping strategies used in terms of getting adults and agencies to help had been more complicated for children and young people from minority ethnic communities and had often had to be pursued more persistently than those used by their white counterparts. Dealing with domestic violence, which is traumatic enough on its own, is affected by racism and discrimination and it is hard to have to cope with all these distressing issues at once. Clearly, then, support needs to be culturally sensitive and attuned to difference and diversity in children's backgrounds.

In addition to talking about the help they had summoned for themselves, children gave the interviewers advice about what adult intervention other young people would require in their situation:

> They'll need support and, like, care. People will have to be friendly to them because they'd most probably be scared. (12-year-old mixed-race girl)

They were concerned that adults should be equally aware:

> [The adults] should think about this. (9-year-old South Asian girl)

Supporting mothers and siblings   Siblings had remained as important over time as at the point when the violence was occurring. Children identified strongly with siblings and had done their best both to protect younger members of the family and to obtain and offer support. They advised other groups of siblings to:

> Stick together and help each other – lots of cuddles. Keep thinking things will work out better in the future. (14-year-old South Asian boy)

Time and again, children had attempted to assist both their mothers and their siblings to deal with the emotional impact of domestic abuse. Particularly moving were those children who had helped their mother to find her emotional reserves.

> Try and help your mum be strong. Tell teachers so they can get help for your mum. Be there for your mum, talk to her about what's happening, keep your mum strong. (9-year-old white girl)

Another girl of the same age had the following down-to-earth advice to offer:

> Don't worry. Think about your mum, care for your mum. And if you've got brothers and sisters, make them feel better and then just forget it really. (9-year-old white girl)

Children also took responsibility in practical ways. They talked about 'always trying to get my mother out of the way', 'being frightened of going to school in case it happens while you are away', and 'taking responsibility, taking over, acting the adult'. Often, the adults had not known that the children were thinking or doing these things.

Being active and involved in finding solutions   These secret and responsible activities belied the fact that children do not (or are not expected to) know about the violence. As discussed earlier, children not only do know but also often prefer to be told about the situation (in age-appropriate ways). Some children in our study, particularly the older ones, had wanted so much to be active in coping with the difficulties that it appeared they might have been subjected to further unnecessary detrimental effects by being prevented from doing so. Where children had not been allowed to engage in concrete action, both the practical and the potentially therapeutic benefits had been denied them.

> Grown-ups think they should hide it and shouldn't tell us, but we want to know. We want to be involved and we want our mums to talk with us about what they are going to do – we could help make decisions. (Group interview)

Some considered taking matters into their own hands. A 17-year-old mixed-race girl talked about how she and her brother, two years younger, had planned many times to leave home together, although this had not actually happened.

Inward-looking strategies
Living with domestic violence is a long-term problem for children to cope with: 'It's like a nightmare and it goes on and on' (14-year-old white girl). To get through this awful experience over time, children and young people in the study had reacted not only through their actions but also emotionally and psychologically. All such 'internal' strategies had assisted children to get by and so are regarded here as aspects of coping, even though, to an outsider, they might be quite worrying and might make the child appear out of control. For example, frequent crying bouts over long periods of time could help release the fear and tension: 'cry and cry for hours ... eyes tight shut and swollen' (15-year-old white girl). Several mentioned being constantly on edge. The same girl described 'staying awake deliberately to stop it, stopping yourself sleeping'. An 8-year-old boy portrayed a situation in which he saw himself as guarding his mother at all times. They had both coped by being watchful. Others developed behaviour patterns that had got them into trouble at school or more generally. Some of the South Asian children virtually stopped speaking, for example (see Chapter 6).

Children had often learned to hide the violence (or the fact that they were living in a refuge) at all costs, developing skills in secrecy and concealment. Children's workers described how ways of coping for some children involved engaging in deception:

> It can really help you get through life when you need to hide things. Negative coping. And they've told me, lots of them, that they get upset because they're lying and they don't like themselves. (Refuge children's worker)

Some of the other emotional strategies that children used over time had included disassociating from the violence to pretend that it was not happening (see

Chapter 4). Sometimes children had withdrawn from other aspects of their lives as well, in order to distance themselves from painful events and memories. Others had lived a very private and perhaps lonely life – hiding their own responses from everyone, weeping in secret perhaps, but in all situations covering their own tracks: 'So I just stay really quiet so they don't know, and listen and check' (15-year-old white girl). For example, a childworker from a refuge described how some children wet the bed and then use complicated strategies to dry their bedlinen so that their carer never knows. They might go to extraordinary lengths to cope with this difficulty without ever having to tell anyone else.

There were examples both of withdrawn behaviour and of 'acting out' and, unlike the assumption adopted in the early research on the subject (see summary in Morley and Mullender, 1994), we did not find these reactions to be gender specific. Both sexes sometimes coped by expressing anger and aggression to release their feelings and sometimes their frustration at feeling impotent to do anything about the situation: 'getting the anger out' (16-year-old white boy). Other girls and boys became possessive of their mothers, attempting to be beside them at all times, like the 8-year-old boy mentioned above, or clinging to them. We came across only one example of a child coping by identifying with the abuser over time (more had accepted his view of the situation initially but had seen through it – see Chapter 7), although several children identified with other men in their mother's lives.

CONCLUSION

Overall, the protective factors identified in the literature that might be expected to help children cope with the distress of living with domestic violence are precisely those that tend to have been damaged or destroyed by the abuse: self-esteem, the presence of social and community support structures and of access to supportive family and friends. Interestingly, our youthful respondents had often tried to create equivalent forms of help for themselves when protective possibilities had been denied by others, such as finding new people to gain strength from or other ways of surviving.

Children had attempted, when they could, to build new social networks of support, to seek help from other family members or from those friends who might understand, and to access community frameworks. They had also often attempted to deepen their relationships with their mother, the non-abusing parent, and to take actions to protect her, their siblings and themselves. This activity, at the same time, had maintained or helped build their own sense of themselves and their self-esteem (and sometimes hers). While these attempts to help were not always successful, they do show children and young people rather bravely using all the resources at their disposal to deal with the abuse and violence they had been forced to live with. In terms of the loss of social support networks, children, both in refuges and elsewhere, frequently bonded together in solidarity with siblings or friends to assist each other. Some, though, found all this more difficult and tended to withdraw into themselves and their private worlds. Every child is unique, but virtually every child can communicate, given the right circumstances, about what they have experienced and the ways they have tried to cope with it.

NOTES

1. This young woman asked to participate in the research in order to have her say, although, strictly, she did not fit the sampling criteria because the abuse was ongoing. She adamantly opposed any intervention in her family by the researcher or her youth worker and was clear that she would stop attending the youth club (her main source of support) if this happened. The researcher, who had over 20 years' social work experience, discussed the situation with the youth worker and with the research team and agreed to take no action. The young woman herself was not felt to be in physical danger, although she was clearly distressed. She has since gone to university.

6   Barriers of Racism, Ethnicity and Culture

INTRODUCTION

A group of children who have continued to be silenced in the literature on children's experiences of domestic violence, even after children more generally have begun to be listened to (see Chapter 1), are those from black and minority ethnic communities living in Western societies. Only very few studies attempt to explore the additional issues and concerns they face or to identify the significance of racism and ethnicity in their lives (Fantuzzo and Lindquist, 1989; Stagg et al., 1989; Westra and Martin, 1981). Dupont-Smith's (1995) work on aboriginal Canadian children and Imam's (1994) important contribution on South Asian[1] children in the UK are the only references traced on children living with domestic violence in particular communities.

As stated earlier (see Chapter 2), the present study aimed to address this short-coming through the development of a sub-sample of black children. This chapter reports findings relating specifically to this sub-group, exploring those experiences and perceptions that differentiate them from their white counterparts. It also draws upon interviews with their mothers. Difference can only be explored in context. The chapter therefore examines the significance of racism, ethnicity and culture in women and children's lives and identifies the barriers these present for their processes of coping and help-seeking, as well as the supports they draw upon in surviving, and contextualizes these issues within broader experiences and meanings of life in South Asian communities in the UK.

THE SAMPLE OF CHILDREN FROM BLACK AND MINORITY ETHNIC COMMUNITIES

The qualitative aspect of our research was designed to include a sub-sample of children from black[2] and minority ethnic[3] communities who would be interviewed by black researchers. The original intention had been to include 25 to 30 children to be representative of all the major black and minority ethnic communities in the UK. We liaised over a two-year period with 35 black-run domestic violence agencies, including 20 specialist refuges, in an attempt to access a varied sample. However, a number of problems were encountered. First, there were unavoidable organizational obstacles. Specialist refuges and agencies working with minority ethnic women and children are small, under-funded and over-stretched. Since staff time must be devoted primarily to direct work with women and children, liaison with other professionals, including for research purposes, has to be given a lower priority. In several cases staff turnover was high owing to the pressures of the work, and negotiations for access could not be followed through after key people left. Several projects and refuges were very supportive and committed to the research but could not help as the children attending or resident at the time were below the age range required. Second, mothers' fears of the negative effects on children of recounting distressing events acted as a further barrier. Some mothers who were approached by agency or refuge workers and later by researchers were reluctant to 'put the children through re-living painful experiences' or felt that 'they have settled down after a long time and would be unsettled again' (quotes taken from research notes). This relates to a recurrent theme of this book, that children want to talk about what they have seen and heard – the interviews themselves having sometimes been quite cathartic. A related problem was the mobility of the women and children fleeing domestic violence. In a few cases, after initial contact had been made, families had to move to other parts of the country, for safety reasons, and were not therefore accessible to the researchers.

The 14 children who were eventually accessed and interviewed (a further boy, with considerable speech difficulties, did not want to speak, though his brothers participated) were mainly of South Asian descent (there were also two from south-east Asia) and were drawn from London and the north-east of England. Twelve children were Muslims and their families originated from Bangladesh (2), Pakistan (7) and Kenya (3). Half of the mothers in the sample were born in the UK, and the others in a variety of countries of origin. It is interesting to note that the majority of children from London interviewed in the rest of the sample were also black, self-identifying as African (3), Black British (5) and mixed race (7). This means that the black experience is well represented in the research as a whole. This chapter reports the findings only from the Asian sub-sample, however, drawing out diversity and difference within this sub-group of children as well as between them and the wider sample overall.

IDENTIFICATION WITH THE RESEARCHERS

One explanation for the bias towards South Asian children in the sub-sample could be that both the researchers were of South Asian descent. It is possible that women and children from these communities participated because they were able to identify with the researchers and had confidence in them to understand and represent their views accurately. They could feel comfortable in not having to explain or clarify terms or ideas and in knowing that cultural experiences and meanings would not be misconstrued. This was evident in the interview situation. Although the interviews were mainly conducted in English, children freely used terms from South Asian languages, such as the different titles for addressing maternal and paternal relatives, terms used for white people (*goray*) and their own communities (*apna*), and concepts like *izzat* (honour), *badnaami* (ill-repute) and so on.

The identification of the children with the researchers, as a result of shared ethnicity, emerged as significant. One of the researchers was of Indian origin and the other Pakistani. Between them they communicated in three South Asian languages. The children moved easily between the multiple contexts of their lives in the UK, communicating bilingually, talking freely about their fears of racism without having to consider the researchers' ethnicity or feelings, and not needing to be anxious about explaining unfamiliar cultural issues or experiences. The researchers were also aware that, in keeping with South Asian tradition, there would be a level of respect awarded to them in relation to their age and as adults. One illustration of this was that most of the children referred to them directly or indirectly as 'Auntie', as it is considered rude to address elders by their names in South Asian communities. In particular, this understanding of different role expectations was significant in the initial stages when children were giving consent to be interviewed. The researchers had to ensure that children did not feel obliged to accede to requests made by elders (refuge child workers or researchers) or their mothers, and that they consented freely. Some children demonstrated their collectivist thinking (see below) when discussing why they were willing to participate in the research. They commented that, although they recognized that the research would not help them personally, they would share their experiences and perceptions if it would help other children in similar situations. In particularly, they expressed the hope that this research would contribute to raising awareness among professionals and promote a more effective response to other children in similar situations.

Most of the mothers were interviewed in English since they had grown up in the UK or were confident in using the language. Those who were not very fluent in English and were more comfortable in their own languages were interviewed in Urdu or Punjabi by the researchers, and one was interviewed through a Bangladeshi interpreter. In the latter case it was essential to ensure the woman's confidence in the interpreter, both because of the sensitive nature of the discussion and because she had had earlier negative experiences of confidentiality being breached by professionals. On her recommendation a Bangladeshi community worker, and not a community interpreter, was chosen as someone she could trust.

Confidentiality emerged as a very distinctive concern for both the women and the children in the sub-sample, compared with the wider sample. Rai and Thiara (1997) report similar concerns being expressed by South Asian women in their research into the needs of Black women and children in refuges. In the present study, all the children in the sub-sample, in contrast with the rest of the children accessed, refused permission to the researchers for interviews to be tape-recorded, despite re-assurances that only the research team would hear them, not mothers or workers, and that the tapes would be destroyed after the study was complete. Nevertheless, the children were apprehensive. They felt their full stories would easily identify them in the small communities to which they belonged. A few had already had negative experiences of family or community members breaching confidentiality, with adverse consequences for family honour (see below). It was therefore agreed that the researchers would transcribe the responses which would later be checked for accuracy by the older children. In the case of younger children and those with learning difficulties, the researchers read out their records for the children to agree. Quoted material has been selected with permission and with particular care.

THE INTERCONNECTIONS BETWEEN RACISM, ETHNICITY AND CULTURE

South Asian communities are not homogeneous and include diverse people whose individual experiences are shaped by their class or caste, religion, cultural practices and traditions, and rural or urban origins.[4] They do, however, share similar patriarchal systems and traditions and the collective experience of colonialism and racism (Brah, 1992b). These were issues that emerged strongly in the in-depth interviews. This study revealed that the barriers that South Asian women and children face in coping with and surviving domestic violence operate on several levels. On the wider, societal level, the clash of Western and South Asian cultures and values creates dilemmas and distress, as, naturally, do institutional racism and racial harassment. At the intermediate level of family and community, it is religion, patriarchal cultural practices and the traditions of individual families that emerge as significant (Imam, 1999b). At the individual level, a child may benefit from, or struggle with, the impact of his or her ethnicity. Each of these three levels will be considered in turn in this chapter though, in real life, racism, ethnicity and culture converge in the lives of women and children, and interact with the patriarchal relations in British society (Brah, 1992a) and with the norms and traditions of particular families and communities, to compound the oppression of the domestic violence itself.

INTERCONNECTIONS ON THE WIDER, SOCIETAL LEVEL

CONFLICTING VALUE SYSTEMS: COLLECTIVIST VALUES AND EXPECTATIONS IN AN INDIVIDUALIST SOCIETAL CONTEXT

The present study revealed that the interface between South Asian collectivist structures and systems and the individualist structures and institutions of Western society complicate children's experiences. On the cultural level, the significant difference lies in the priority given to group interests or personal interests: the tendency to value interdependence, emotional closeness, group achievement and co-operation or to value independence, emotional detachment and competition (Triandis, 1995, cited in Smith and Schwartz, 1997). South Asian families and communities are collectivist, while the wider society in the UK is in the dominant Western mould, underpinned by its individualist values and traditions. The institutions and agencies to which women and children are referred or gain access, unless they are black- or Asian-run, operate from individualist perspectives. Their limited awareness of the connection with family and community in other cultures inhibits effective and appropriate intervention with children from non-Western communities.

South Asian children growing up in the UK are simultaneously socialized into both the collectivist values and traditions of their families and communities and the individualistic thinking of the wider society through their peers, schools and other institutions (Imam, 1999a). The relative significance of these, and the balance between them in individual lives, may depend on a range of variables, including age, gender, caste or class, education, rural or urban background and religion. Our research revealed that, although individualism and collectivism co-exist in South Asian children's experiences, the latter is clearly more influential in their thinking and expectations of the family. This finding is supported by other research indicating that South Asian young people wish to retain the core values of their families and communities (Anwar, 1998; Stopes-Roe and Cochrane, 1990). Inevitably, these collectivist values influence the children's perceptions and expectations of what help and support should be forthcoming and from where. In all the interviews conducted, the South Asian children had greater expectations of help from family and family friends than from professionals and agencies. This was to some extent true of all the children interviewed, in fact (see Chapter 4), but it was emphasized and also took distinctive forms in the accounts gathered from this sub-sample. In responding to the question as to who had been most helpful to their mothers and themselves, almost all the South Asian children mentioned members of the extended family. Within this, there was a particular expectation of assistance and support from the father's family and relatives, even though he was the abuser, because they would normally be looked to in this way. Where such help was not available, it was commented upon:

> They don't see any of their relatives. Their father's sister has never bothered with them since I became divorced. I feel very hurt about this and angry about this. The children are innocent, and need love; they are not responsible for what happened. She thinks if her brother doesn't bother with his children why should she. The children feel hurt about this too; they talk about it to their friends. (South Asian mother)

One of the other mothers felt that, in living with and coping with domestic violence, children needed:

> the support of other people in the family. I think especially the father's family. You know how close most of our Asian families are. His sisters have had problems with husbands and their in-laws have actually supported the daughter-in-law and children, but I did not get any support from them. (South Asian mother)

Responses to questions about who could have helped but failed to do so revealed the children's collectivist thinking and expectation of help and support from the extended family:

> Mum's family. They could have supported us more and told Mum, 'If you break up with him we will look after you.' But, this didn't happen. One uncle [maternal] really helped and looked after us. They were there for her and for us. We would get love and attention – no violence. (14-year-old South Asian boy)

His brother, aged 13, also expected more help and support from his father's family than was forthcoming:

> No one really tried to help my mum. My mum's family lived in [name of city] which was far away. No one locally tried to help. Maybe they tried to help a little bit but it didn't really work. My dad's brothers lived in the area. I think they tried to stop the fighting but they couldn't really do anything. (13-year-old South Asian boy)

If appropriate support and intervention are to be provided to children living with domestic violence, professionals and their agencies will need to address their traditional individualist bias. They need to acknowledge that the support needs and expectations of South Asian (and other black) children are different, and may require a more creative response. Rather than intervening in ways that cut across family and community structures, professionals need to liaise more closely with agencies that are working to raise awareness of gender inequalities and the abuse of women and children in minority ethnic communities. Inevitably, male dominance in indigenous communities can be obstructive and needs to be challenged, as it would be in the wider society. As one of the mothers suggested, there needs to be:

> more awareness-raising within Asian communities about the impact of domestic violence on children, so that extended families are more aware of this and their responsibilities to the children, even if they don't get along with the mums. (South Asian mother)

CULTURAL RACISM OR PROFESSIONAL IMPERIALISM?

Racism against people of South Asian descent has some commonalties with that experienced by other black communities, but it is distinctive in the exclusive focus on ethnicity and culture: 'cultural racism' (Ahmed, 1986). The responses of practitioners, policy makers and other professionals to South Asian women and children living with domestic violence are often coloured by popular social representations, based on myths and stereotypes. Shah's (1995) research on South Asian children with disabilities highlights the way in which these stereotypes and assumptions about South Asian families, and about South Asian women in particular, continue to inhibit the responses of social workers and other professionals. In the UK, the focus on the ethnicity of South Asian communities emphasizes the differences between the majority and the 'alien' minority. These differences are then attributed to the fixed culture of the minority. The stereotypes of 'cultural conflict' and the 'insularity' of 'Asian' communities are based on assumptions that cultural values are fixed, unlikely to adapt to a different context in Western society, and incapable of the fluid and continuous cultural change attributed to the majority (Woolett et al., 1994). There is also insufficient acknowledgement in policy and practice that young British Asians are successfully synthesizing British values with their traditional values or that, consequently, new cultural patterns are emerging (Anwar, 1998; Ghuman, 1999; Imam, 1999a) that need to be recognized and understood if intervention is to be effective and appropriate.

Our findings indicate that children's perceptions about this lack of sensitivity and understanding on the part of professionals influence their expectations of help and support:

> If you speak to adults, make sure they understand about your family and religion and they don't take things the wrong way. Like, sometimes, *goray* [white people] will not know about *izzat* and shame and they can make you do things which bring shame to the family. You are left without any help or support from the community, if they feel that you have gone against the religion. I don't say it is always right, but sometimes we have to sort things out in our own way – white people can never really do things in the same way if they don't understand. (16-year-old South Asian girl)

This example also highlights the dangers of extending colour-blind social welfare services to culturally diverse communities. Azmi (1997) points out the imperialistic nature of social work in the profession's inability to acknowledge its lack of knowledge and understanding of social and cultural diversity. One of the mothers we interviewed commented on these limitations:

> Workers should ask mothers how they are feeling if there are problems. Instead, workers label the women as a problem rather than providing more comprehensive support. Some of the problems are because the services are inadequate and insensitive – sometimes they are inappropriate too. (South Asian mother)

One disturbing example concerned a family who had taken the opportunity to flee to the UK from south-east Asia when the abuser was sent to prison. The elder boy was referred for counselling but, owing to the boy's lack of fluency in English, the counsellor thought the domestic violence was ongoing and made a child protection referral to social services. No one checked with the South Asian community worker who knew the family's circumstances and understood their cultural context. Thus the family's main source of support was undermined, the boy was left distrustful of all helping services, and the family was bewildered at the swiftness with which their problems were picked up on while their appeals for help and support had not led to any effective response. This case illustrates what has been evident from other research (Humphreys et al., 1999; Qureshi et al., 2000): that an incident-focused, insensitive and narrow approach to child protection issues tends to be taken with Asian families. It also confirms the limited provision of family support services to Asian communities, who frequently experience the punitive rather than the welfare aspects of social services (Ahmad, 1990; Qureshi et al., 2000). An illustration of insensitivity at best, or arguably racism at worst, was the way in which the South Asian worker was completely marginalized in the referral process, ignoring her ability to bridge between two cultures (Imam, 1999a). Yet it was she who continued to support the family after the other agencies had withdrawn.

RACIAL HARASSMENT

Fear of racial harassment and children's experiences of racial abuse emerge strongly from the interviews. There were specific implications in relation to fleeing abuse. Often the decision to move away from family and community had meant a choice between exchanging one form of violence, domestic violence, for another – racial harassment outside the home. Children also reported direct experiences of racial harassment:

> Sometimes people tease me and call me names, especially white people in the area … It makes me feel unsafe. Mum is trying to get me a transfer to another school. I am just worried about being teased by white people – they do it because they don't like black people and can cause problems and be violent so you can feel really unsafe. (10-year-old Asian boy)

In addition to the loss of familiar surroundings, friends and family, shared with all the other children in our sample (see Chapter 4), for South Asian children, moving away had also meant greater vulnerability and exposure to racism in new surroundings and new schools: 'the [secondary] school in the area is violent. My brother goes there and people are not nice. They call you names and don't like you because you are black' (10-year-old Asian boy). This vulnerability, and fear of racial abuse and violence, was echoed by a 9-year-old girl:

> Everything is OK now but sometimes I feel really scared now. That is not to do with my dad, because he is dead. I feel scared because English people call you by names – this happens more often in the street than in school. They do this because they don't like black people. I feel scared of that because they also set dogs on us. Sometimes I am scared because I think that what is happening in different countries can happen in England. People might start killing us because we are Muslims like the war in Kosovo … and there are so many murders which doesn't make you feel safe. Jill Dando [television presenter] got murdered, people just come and murder … even if you haven't done anything. (9-year-old South Asian girl)

Positive contact with the wider family appeared to be an important resource for children in coping with and surviving domestic violence. (See also Chapter 5 on coping strategies.) Where support within the community (through either the maternal or paternal family) was available, it was useful in developing a positive sense of self, in connection with the community, and an important resource in dealing with racism. Where children did not have this support, both they and their mothers were isolated and lonely, and felt more vulnerable to racism.

Importantly, most of the children in the specialist black sample talked to the black researchers about racism and racial abuse. Over half the children did so unsolicited. Consequently, the researchers raised this issue in the second contact with those who had not mentioned it previously. Clearly, the ethnicity of the interviewer was significant in children choosing to express their feelings and fears of racism. All the mothers in this sub-sample, in varying degrees, had also had negative experiences of racism from professionals and agencies, at both individual and institutional levels, as they struggled with their children to survive domestic violence. What is evident from our research is that experiences and fears of racism – together with insensitive and inappropriate treatment by individuals, agencies and institutions – engender women and children's suspicion and mistrust and hence present considerable barriers to seeking help and support in their struggles against domestic violence.

INTERCONNECTIONS AT THE INTERMEDIATE LEVEL OF FAMILY AND COMMUNITY: THE IMPACT OF PATRIARCHAL TRADITIONS AND PRACTICES

Although South Asian families and communities in the UK are extremely diverse and are differentiated on the basis of countries of origin, patterns of migration, class/caste, urban or rural origin, language, religion and distinctive cultural traditions, what they share in common, and with other black communities in the UK, are their collectivist family values and patriarchal traditions.

IZZAT AND BADNAAMI: FAMILY HONOUR AND SHAME

In order to be able to support South Asian women and children in making informed choices about dealing with abuse and violence, it is essential to be aware of specific cultural practices and traditions which may present barriers to the help-seeking process. In South Asian communities, women are controlled by the powerful concept of *izzat* – a patriarchal notion that may indicate honour, reputation, respectability or status (Southall Black Sisters, 1993) that is used to control women's behaviour (Bhopal, 1997; Choudry, 1996; Imam, 1994; Imam, 1999b). Although, theoretically, the concept applies to both sexes, women are held primarily responsible for upholding family honour. There are grave consequences for actions that bring the family into disrepute – often complete ostracism from the family and community group in order to preserve the honour of the other members.

Even though they live between two cultures, the majority of young South Asians in the UK still consider family and family honour sacrosanct and would not like to damage them through their own actions (Anwar, 1998). The present study similarly found that the children and young people interviewed were generally influenced by considerations of family honour. This not only limited choices for mothers, but also restricted children and young people's own actions. Interestingly, it was the girls who typically raised this as an issue, confirming the cultural bias towards women carrying responsibility for upholding family honour. In the case of the younger girls it was more by implication:

No, we didn't talk to anyone else because, if we did, then those people would talk to someone else [in the community] and everyone [in the community] would get to know about it. I think it is too private for anyone to know. (8-year-old South Asian girl).

Older girls were more explicit in their explanation of the reasons why their mothers stayed with abusive men:

He wanted to keep us under his control – that is why he terrorized us. Mum stayed so long because of us and because of *izzat*, you know. 'What will people say?' She hid it from her family – wouldn't tell them how bad things were for such a long time. (16-year-old South Asian girl)

She extended this to outlining why she herself was restrained in seeking help and talking about the abuse: 'It was our *izzat*. Our family is really big. Wherever you go, people would say: 'She told the authorities', 'Her dad's in trouble', '… brought shame to the family' (16-year-old South Asian girl).

As families and communities are close knit, it is implicit in children's fears that information would become common knowledge and bring dishonour. The repercussions for individuals deemed responsible would be total rejection by the family and community. If women are ostracized in this way, they become completely isolated. In extreme cases, the dishonour has resulted in honour killings, where women have paid with their lives for shaming the family. One practical consequence is that women may have to leave female children behind with husbands and in-laws when they flee violence, for fear of transferring their dishonour onto their daughters who would suffer adversely in the community and lose, for example, their opportunity to marry well (Imam, 1994). Girls themselves, of course, are conscious both of the responsibility they hold and of the serious sanctions they face if they contravene these social norms. Abusive men are equally conscious of the pressures on their wives and daughters and some use this as a way of exerting control. In the example given below, the young woman concerned demonstrated her awareness of her father manipulating herself and her mother, and trying to isolate them from their family and wider community by casting aspersions on their characters:

He has never liked me. He has always threatened me and said I will do *badnaami* [get a bad name] – bring shame to the family. He used to say that I slept around. Really, Auntie [to the researcher]! My own father! He also called my mum names. He wrote on the streets that my mum was sleeping with her brother. My mum had to pay someone to get it cleaned off the walls. It was so shameful – *badnaami*. (16-year-old South Asian girl)

In order to help this family, a professional would need a very clear understanding both of the power this man was exerting and of the social code he was using to do so. Children in the study showed themselves very aware, so practitioners would be well advised to listen to them.

PREFERENTIAL MARRIAGE SYSTEMS:
ARRANGED MARRIAGES

Arranged marriages are an important aspect of the collectivist South Asian social structure. They are not merely a contract between two individuals but bring about the union of families and are aimed at promoting financial and social interests (Anwar, 1998; Bhopal, 1997; Wilson, 1978). Parents and relatives who arrange these marriages make sure they remain intact, and there is social pressure on them to mediate if there are problems. There is a general preference for endogamy (marrying within the community and/or religious group) in South Asian communities, with some variations arising from religious traditions (Anwar, 1998). Amongst Muslims, cousin marriages are preferred. Sikh and Hindu traditions do not allow marriages between relatives; however, there is a preference for marriage within the same class or caste and occupational group. For young South Asians synthesizing traditional and Western values and choosing their own partners, there is pressure of a different and perhaps more intense kind to make the marriage work. If there is violence and abuse the customary mediation by family members may not be available, or the woman may be conscious of its implications of blaming her for her choice as well as her husband for his actions. One of the women we interviewed, who was born in the UK, explained why it had been difficult for her to seek help from her family when her husband had started abusing her:

> This was a love marriage. Isn't it strange? We both liked each other and wanted to get married. I was very young – I fell in love with him. My family is of higher status and well respected. I was a real catch for him and his family, but it was also my choice. There [must] be something wrong with me, attracted to such a violent man. He was really good to me in the beginning. I daren't tell my family at first because they would have killed him. I didn't want a lot of fighting between the families – I protected him from my family. My family really loved me and supported me. They [brothers] would have killed him. I had married him for better or worse. I felt that I should stick by him. (South Asian mother)

Although empirical evidence suggests that the majority of South Asian young people still favour arranged marriages in which they can exercise a degree of choice (Anwar, 1998; Gupta, 1999), the system may be used to abuse and control women, particularly through forced marriages undertaken for financial or communal benefits. It is also used by abusive men to control their daughters, even after separation or when the mothers have moved away, as recounted by the young girl below:

> I have started feeling a bit scared recently because Dad has started to come into the house a lot, sees Mum … I feel, sometimes, that they may get back together. I am really scared that this is because he wants to get me married off. That's why he is coming around. I want a job, I want to help Mum. He just wants to show his control by getting me married off. (16-year-old South Asian girl)

The young people in our sample expressed mixed views. Although many were not opposed to arranged marriages in principle, they had very clear views about what they wanted for themselves. There were distinct gender differences, with the girls more accepting than the boys (see below). Our findings also supported earlier empirical evidence that young people do not favour endogamy like the first generation of immigrants (Anwar, 1998; Ghuman, 1999). Some were also very clear that they would not marry partners from their families' countries of origin because they attributed the abuse and violence with which they had lived to irreconcilable differences in their parents' socio-cultural backgrounds.

All my experience, and Mum's, has really made me think. I know that I want to get married to someone from home – *apna* [from my own community] not *gora* [white] – but not someone from Pakistan. There is a lot of difference. You grow up in two different worlds. It is always difficult for men to be dependent on the wife. (16-year-old South Asian girl)

The latter comment refers to the fact that, under UK immigration legislation, the newly immigrant husband cannot have recourse to public funds and is entirely dependent on his wife until he finds employment. Another young boy stated: 'I will never have an arranged marriage.' He went on to explain:

I will not marry an Asian from an Asian country. My dad came from Pakistan. That was maybe why Mum and Dad were always fighting. I would marry an Asian from this country who lived here like us. An Asian marrying an English person [non-Muslim] also doesn't work because of the difference in religion. So it is not just arranged marriages that don't work. I might marry an English person who is Muslim or an Asian Muslim. (13-year-old South Asian boy)

His older brother similarly commented:

Always see that you have something in common. It should be a partnership. You don't get married because your parents say so. They were so different, like a dog getting married to a cat – nothing in common. Mum has been brought up in England, got married to a Pakistani. I would never get married like that – arranged marriage – because your parents say so. They were too different. (14-year-old South Asian boy)

Girls, meanwhile, had learnt important lessons from their own and their mothers' experiences and made their priorities clear to us:

I want to study and make something of my life. Marriage is not everything. I will marry when I think the time is right. People keep giving me *rishtay* [marriage proposals] but I don't really think Mum is serious now. She knows how I feel. I can trust her to wait for me – when I have made something of my life. I would want to be an equal partner. But if my husband acts funny, like Dad, I will leave him. She [mother] never did that. I think I know what children feel like. I will never put my children through this. But she was really very sick. What could she do? She stuck with him because of us. (16-year-old South Asian girl)

THE STIGMA OF LONE PARENTHOOD

Recent research indicates that a small number of South Asian families in the UK are lone parent families. Estimates vary from 8 per cent (Modood et al., 1997) to just over 10 per cent (Anwar, 1998), compared to 21 per cent of white and 45 per cent of African Caribbean families. This is significant because it is a fact not easily acknowledged within South Asian communities. There is a stigma attached to women living alone, outside the extended family. Invariably this group includes women who have left their husbands and families as a result of abuse and violence. Living on their own, such women are vulnerable to exploitation by men in their own community as well as from outside (Mullender and Morley, 1993) because they are not protected by family honour and are seen as 'fair game' and vulnerable. In our research, all the mothers were living separately by the time they were interviewed but most were still connected in some way to families and communities. Those who were not, or whose families and support structures were in different parts of the country or in the country of origin, found themselves extremely vulnerable and isolated:

> I went back every time because of the children. I wanted the children to be safe and comfortable in our own home. Why should I leave my home? Why can't he leave? I have more right to the house. Also, for security, I didn't want to tell the world that I am on my own. Even now I am on my own, it is not acceptable in society. People always treat you differently if you are a woman on your own. No partner. I have stopped meeting other people in the community – only a few friends that know me well. (South Asian mother)

One of the women in our study described the harassment of single women in the community and, alarmingly, the collusion of some professionals by taking sides:

> Also, this worker really harassed me because she worked in the [name of] Health Project and was supporting another family, a family that harassed me and made my life hell! Actually it was a man from the family who used to come knocking at my door, thinking I was alone and I would entertain men. I had to see a solicitor and get injunctions against this man. The worker then started harassing me because he was her client. (South Asian mother)

The woman involved felt that this South Asian worker had transgressed her professional role and breached professional confidentiality when she had discussed these private problems in communal settings.

COLLECTIVIST FAMILY VALUES

Unlike for the dominant majority, where nuclear families are the norm, in South Asian communities the family has primacy over the individual. It is the family, not the individual, that forms the basis of social structure and social cohesion. Policy and practice, undertaken from a Western perspective with little acknowledgement of the diversity of family structure and experience, will have limited relevance in this context.

The significance of the extended, 'transnational' family

The traditional family system in South Asian communities is the joint or extended family. It is a multigenerational kinship system, welded together by a complex set of mutual obligations and an in-built system of welfare for its members and for the family as a whole (Anwar, 1998; Bhopal, 1997). Other distinctive features are patriarchal authority, respect related to age, and preferential marriage patterns, which together ensure the cohesion and extension of the kinship system.

Although migration has changed and modified the structure, and members may not any longer live together, they maintain family obligations and hold together as a joint family. Income is usually pooled and expenditure controlled centrally. Geographical distance does not weaken these ties or familial obligations; continued contact and links with the extended family in the Indian sub-continent and in the diaspora make these families and communities transnational (Bhachu, 1996). The geographical distance involved and the interdependent nature of far-flung extended families may further complicate women and children's experiences of domestic violence. The extension of the family across national boundaries was experienced both positively and negatively by the children in the present study. Children experienced it as beneficial when they had been supported by the extended family. Some reported how they had been given respite from problems at home by a visit to the family in the Indian sub-continent: 'Grandad took me to Pakistan. I like the shops there. It was fun. Dad was angry. Grandad told my mum not to go back to Dad' (12-year-old South Asian boy). And his sister, who accompanied their mother to Pakistan to get away from the violence and abuse, also talked positively about her experiences:

> I went to Pakistan for a holiday with my mum. It was good. I haven't been anywhere, with my dad being [left behind] in the house, before. I would like to go to Pakistan again with my mum. I know we have lots of relatives and cousins there who I haven't seen before. I would like to see them. (8-year-old South Asian girl)

On the other hand, there were examples of the geographical distance being used by perpetrators, for example to punish women by distancing them from their children. One woman explained how her husband had forced a two-year separation and emotional distancing between her and her then 6-year-old son:

> ... he brought me back to England with S [daughter] but left my eldest son in Pakistan with his grandfather. I wanted to bring my son back with me but didn't have any money or his passport, so I went along with what my husband said. I just went along with him because he would have just caused trouble. When I returned to England, I tried to get my son back with the help of solicitors but my husband had told my son that I didn't love him or care about him. My son didn't like to come to me because his father told him I didn't really want him. That was hard for me. (South Asian mother)

The boy's sister also spoke about her feelings about being separated from her brother:

> I would like my big brother to be with us. He was in Pakistan for a long time and now he is with my dad ... [he] now lives with my dad just up the road – comes sometimes, but he doesn't like coming to see us because they all [grandmother and father] give him money not to come and see us. (12-year-old South Asian girl)

Such examples are not uncommon where men use their control of financial resources in the family and their connection with the extended family in their countries of origin to punish women by separating them from their children and by isolating and distancing children and women from the rest of the family and community.

Welfare of family members: support or barrier?
The role of the family is highly significant to women and children who live with domestic violence. Although in situations of domestic violence the family is generally the primary site for the domination and subordination of women, for women and children belonging to collectivist communities the situation is more complex since the family may also provide support and refuge from oppression, stemming both from outside the family and from within (Amos and Parmar, 1984; Anthias and Yuval-Davis, 1992; Brah, 1992b; hooks, 1991; Knowles and Mercer, 1990). It is the extended nature of the family that provides the possibilities for support and/or challenge to the abuser by one or more family members. There is thus potential for both support and abuse within South Asian families (Bhopal, 1997; Imam, 1994). This was reflected in the experiences of the children who participated in our research. Support is usually forthcoming from other members of the family who are concerned about the welfare of the woman and/or the children. This can result in positive intervention by families and communities, mediating to influence the actions of the male perpetrators (Mama, 1989). In most cases, we found that the maternal family had given some level of support. For example:

My *Nani* [maternal grandmother] and *Nana* [maternal grandfather] have helped my mum the most. Her parents and brothers have always been there for her and for us. They bought this house for us – paid the deposit. [They] bought Dad the taxi. (16-year-old South Asian girl)

And her sister commented that: 'My uncles and grandmother [maternal] also used to help. My uncle used to say he would kill my dad for what he was doing' (8-year-old South Asian girl).

One of the mothers we interviewed explained why it was vital that children were helped and supported by the wider family:

Someone should talk to the children about why Mum has left – help them to come to terms with the changes. If there are other men in the family who are not supporting the father, it is important for boys to see and be with them, as role models. They have to learn that violence is not the only way for men. (South Asian mother)

In families where the couple were also related prior to marriage, the extended family was sometimes influential in invoking mutual obligations and some level of resources following the breakdown of the marriage and continued violence against the woman. A 12-year-old girl explained how her maternal grandmother and uncle had influenced her father's family to provide independent accommodation after her mother had left home and escaped to a refuge. This influence was possible because the woman's mother-in-law was also her father's sister and because, despite the fact she had left her husband, the earlier familial ties and obligations were strong and could provide leverage in this situation:

My mum's brother brought us back from the refuge – he contacted Mum through her friend. We came back and lived with my *Nani* [maternal grandmother] for a little while and then went back to the white house. Dad then started fighting again. That is when we moved into this house. My *Nani* and uncle [maternal] told my uncle [paternal] to help us with housing and so we moved into this house. We have been living here two, three years. I live here with my mum and little brother. (12-year-old South Asian girl)

Often it is this support that women cannot give up while they continue to suffer abuse. Sometimes the unconditional support for children in extended families (though the mother may be facing considerable abuse and violence) constrains women from leaving the abuser. Another illustration of this is the example of Saeeda, cited elsewhere (Imam, 1994), who stayed with her violent husband because she wanted her children to remain in the family home where they could receive love and affection from grandparents and the extended family.

Maintenance of the family unit

When the maintenance of the family unit and the need to preserve harmonious relationships are given priority over the needs of individuals, the woman and children may find themselves subject either to the collusion of the wider family in the abuse or to the exertion of patriarchal authority against the abuse. Examples of both these phenomena were seen in one family. Initially, the father-in-law's authority and power were perceived to exert influence on the abuser:

My husband is also my cousin. After getting married we lived in [name of city] for two or three years. A [son] who is 14 years old now and S [daughter] were both born there. My husband was all right when we lived there. His father was very strict, so he was afraid of his father and behaved himself. He was scared of his father so he did behave himself for as long as he was alive. (South Asian mother)

Following her father-in-law's demise, this woman's mother-in law and husband both started abusing her, yet she was seen as being in the wrong:

Both S and N [daughter and son] didn't like their grandmother [paternal] swearing at me. She once started pulling my ears and hurt me badly so I called the police. But she didn't like that, so she called my father. My father just blamed me for causing problems. He said no matter what your mother-in-law does, you should not call the police. My father told the police they did not need to interfere – that it was a family matter. So the police left. My mother-in-law always held this against me. She didn't like it at all that I had called the police. (South Asian mother)

It is evident that, in collectivist families, the interests of the group as a whole will be prioritized. This may result in the interests of the individual woman or child being subordinated to that of the group in order to preserve harmonious relationships with the wider family or kinship networks. The only effective challenge to this would have to come from families and communities themselves, through the acknowledgement that the oppression of individuals within the collective is not acceptable and needs to be addressed by the collective itself. At the same time, outside agencies need to recognize both the strengths and the threats that the collective social system can pose. The police in the above example, for instance, could have offered the woman the opportunity to give her own account confidentially and safely, without shaming her (e.g. by sending a female officer to her home).

Respect related to age
The hierarchical structure of extended families compounds role expectations. A distinctive feature of this is the respect and power enjoyed by the older members of the family. As illustrated in the example above, older females in the family sometimes use their status to perpetrate both physical and emotional abuse against other women. Western assumptions of the 'masculinity' of abuse in relation to domestic violence have often been challenged by black and South Asian writers because of this (Ahmed, 1986; Bhopal, 1997; Guru, 1986; Mama, 1989). Nevertheless, women have only limited power and control in patriarchal systems because of their gender and are always less powerful than their male counterparts.

Another notable aspect of South Asian children's experience in relation to age in our sample was their perception of the cultural expectations of their relationship with their fathers. Whatever they felt about their father's actions or the way he had treated their mother, they felt that they had to *show* respect. Unlike their white peers, who they thought did not have to respect a father who abused their mother, the children in this sub-sample emphasized how giving respect to elders (including fathers), was distinctive of their experience because of their cultural and religious traditions:

> We go to his shop sometimes, go the movies. He is okay with us, Dad. I have to respect him, not for the violence [but] because he is my dad. It is against my religion [not to]. I have to respect my parents. If I was *gora* [white], I don't think I would have [to]. (14-year-old South Asian boy)

Sometimes, in children's thinking, this respect for parents and elders could impose additional restrictions on seeking help:

> In our family, you have to respect elders. Everyone would think that I had brought shame on the family if I had told people about him ... I could talk to the social worker [but] I couldn't tell her everything – at the end of the day he was still my father. (16-year-old South Asian girl).

INTERCONNECTIONS AT THE INDIVIDUAL LEVEL: THE SIGNIFICANCE OF ETHNICITY IN CHILDREN'S COPING STRATEGIES AND SURVIVAL

The wide variation in children's experiences and responses highlights the importance of exploring these at an individual level. Chapters 4 and 5 have examined in some depth the impact of domestic violence on all the children in our sample and their responses and strategies in coping with their situations. This section attempts to draw out the influence of ethnicity at the individual level for the children in the South Asian sub-sample.

ETHNICITY AS A PROTECTIVE FACTOR?

An important finding that emerged from this study relates to our understanding of the impact of domestic violence on children. Research and practice have identified guilt and self-blame as significant in children's experiences of living with the abuse of their mothers (e.g. Jaffe et al., 1990; Loosley et al., 1997). Children are said to feel responsible for what is happening in their family, perhaps particularly younger ones or those who have been implicated in the abuse in some way. In the present study, in the sample as a whole, the majority of children did not blame themselves but appeared to hold the adults responsible (see Chapter 7). Certainly, we can say that none of the children in the South Asian sub-sample blamed themselves for the violence. They seemed quite clear that the adults in the family were responsible, with some also identifying other adults in the extended family whom they perceived to be implicated in the violence or in failing to stop it from happening.

An important factor here may be the nature of non-Western ways of being and thinking. As discussed above, despite the fact that the children seemed to have synthesized both individualism and collectivism to varying degrees, collectivism was more evident in the ideas they expressed in interview. This perspective seemed to have provided a more objective perception of the situation in comparison to their Western counterparts, who may be more prone to individualize and personalize problems. Children in collectivist cultures are socialized from an early age to distinguish between different roles and social expectations in the wider family. As interdependence and collective responsibility are distinctive features of their experience, they may also be protective factors since perceptions of shared responsibilities leave the individual less vulnerable. This may also explain the finding in two North American studies that children from black families who experienced domestic violence were less likely to demonstrate both 'externalizing' and 'internalizing' behavioural difficulties (Stagg et al., 1989; Westra and Martin, 1981).

Religious beliefs also appear to help some children develop resilience. Despite the influence of Western values and society, religion remains the basis of ethnic identity for many South Asians, particularly for Muslims (Anwar, 1998). In our study the majority of children and young people identified themselves as Muslims. For some of the children, their religious beliefs had been an important resource in making sense of, coping with, and surviving the trauma of living with domestic violence:

My religion kept me going. We believe that your time on Earth is full of tests. Our life is full of tests. If you survive, your patience and strength will end your suffering. These are my tests. I had to stand by my mum because she was not in the wrong. That pulled us through and has made us stronger and better. We have been through a lot; we can feel for others and are better human beings. (14-year-old South Asian boy, also cited in Chapter 4)

Reflecting back on his own experiences and on what life was like now that they were no longer living with the abuser, his brother added:

Sometimes I feel sad about it all, but it is our destiny and we have to live our life. We were destined to have life like this so we have to get on with our life. (13-year-old South Asian boy)

This fatalistic attitude and their collectivist thinking helped the children in the sub-sample to cope with the violence by externalizing and rationalizing it to some extent.

A further plus point for the South Asian children, in comparison to children in the general sample, was that fewer had had to face repeated displacement and disruption. Although some had experienced multiple moves, most benefited from the stability of remaining either in familiar surroundings or connected to families and communities despite having moved to a new area. Some did comment on the separation from their father or paternal family where the latter had chosen to break contact and/or to reject the children but even those who had sustained extensive emotional damage were improving now that they were away from the abuser. None had experienced violence from more than one violent man or now faced any further change of surroundings because their mothers were not involved in other relationships following their separation or divorce from their abusive partners. Because of South Asian patriarchal norms and restrictions relating to women's sexual freedom and marriage and their close association with family honour (Abraham, 1999), none of the women seemed to be considering another relationship, even though some were divorced and one was widowed. One recounted how her two sons kept encouraging her to find a new partner and one of the boys told the interviewer:

She is lonely, she should find someone else. I am not saying it is easy, but she is still young. She needs to get on with her life just like we will – all of us. (14-year-old Asian boy)

SPEECH PROBLEMS

While it is already well known that abuse and neglect can result in speech and language problems (Culp et al., 1991), with direct maltreatment linked particularly with selective mutism (McGregor et al., 1994), little has been written about this in relation to living with domestic violence (though a delay in developing language was noted as common by a children's worker in a general refuge in Hague et al., 1996). The South Asian sub-sample in the present study appeared to present an unusually high incidence of such problems, including a number of children who had become very quiet, despite having had fluent speech in two languages before. While this was also an issue for some other children, for example a 12-year-old white, girl whose mother had thought she would be unable to participate in an interview, no fewer than four of the six South Asian families who participated had at least one child who had been formally assessed and was now receiving speech therapy. In one family, all three boys interviewed were experiencing difficulties. Their mother was extremely isolated from her extended family and community and all the children had witnessed abuse since birth. They had responded to the stress in their lives by not speaking for long periods and were still monosyllabic at best. Other mothers noted similar concerns that, in one case, had lasted for two years. In interview the researchers fell back on using mother tongues when the children would not speak in English. In one case, they also switched to an interview schedule aimed at a lower age group and surprised the mother of the 12-year-old boy concerned by managing to get him to talk in whole sentences.

There would seem to be a strong case for more work to be conducted in this area. Perhaps children who are facing the additional task of communicating in two languages find it all too much. Or perhaps there is a connection with the imperative placed on children of not talking outside the home (the domain of English) about matters that are going on within. In families where the abuse has been very bad, and where leaving it has left the family isolated and the woman depressed, it may be that no one has been able to spend time talking to the children so that they have withdrawn into themselves. We can only speculate. Crucially, though numbers were small and, clearly, more work is needed in this area, we had the impression that, after moving away from the abuser, progress with communication had improved in children who were supported by families and building new lives. For children who had only limited support in the family and community, on the other hand, mothers continued to be concerned about their development and its educational implications. Still, though, they tended to feel that the children did not have underlying problems and that it was an emotional problem rather than a generalized learning difficulty that was manifesting itself. Schools did not always understand this, falling into an assumption that South Asian children could not understand English:

> Teachers keep contacting me and constantly keep saying the children need help, but they don't really specify what sort of help they need. I feel the children have been affected mentally and that their minds or brains are not working normally ... I don't speak very much English so I don't always understand what the school is trying to say about their problems. The children are not stupid but they have been affected, maybe by all the fights and arguments. My daughter is all right and the boys' behaviour is OK, but their development and education have been affected. They don't speak very much. The school also complains about this – they say maybe they don't understand. (South Asian mother)

One of the women reported how she had challenged the decision of the local authority to place her son in a 'special needs' school because it had had a negative influence on his development and behaviour. She reported that, following his reinstatement in mainstream education, he was making significant progress in communication. This would seem to reinforce the message to medical, psychological and therapeutic services that it is vital to include children's experiences of living with domestic violence in any response and also to be aware that insititutional racism could be playing a part in jumping too readily to conclusions about generalized problems. Failure to do so may result in an incorrect assessment and in attaching a label to the child that merely creates additonal problems. At the same time, children do need to receive prompt and appropriate help and not an assumption, in a kind of 'reverse racism', that 'It's just part of their culture'.

WHAT HAD HELPED

British Asian children's experiences of domestic violence are complicated by the multiple contexts of their lives in the UK. In negotiating conflicting values and systems, they struggle with a more complex set of meanings and understandings than do white children. It is important to consider their experiences of success-fully negotiating these different contexts if we are to offer more appropriate and effective intervention and support. Both children and their mothers expressed their concerns about the lack of awareness they had encountered amongst most professionals and their agencies, but were appreciative of the help and support received from specialist refuges and from others with a good understanding of South Asian communities who were able to play a useful intermediary role.

SPECIALIST REFUGES

Specialist refuges, which serve the needs of particular groups of mainly minority ethnic women and children, were established in the UK in the 1980s as a consequence of two parallel developments. First, black women's challenges to the concept of 'universal sisterhood', which they felt ignored differentiation on the basis of ethnicity, and to the dominance of white women in the early refuge movement, were crucial. Second, the funding and development of a range of black-led women's organizations and self-help groups resulted in the autonomous organizing of specialist services. A further important consequence of black women's activism was a strong anti-racist commitment in the Women's Aid movement to provide a safe environment for all women, irrespective of skin colour or country of origin. In the last 20 years there has been a gradual development of specialist provision, accompanied by an increasing involvement of black women in general refuge provision (Mama, 1989). In a study commissioned by Women's Aid, it is reported that, of the 240 or so refuges in England, there are over 40 catering for black and minority ethnic communities (Rai and Thiara, 1997), with a majority specifically for South Asian women and children. Specialist refuges are important because they provide:

- a safe space for women and children fleeing domestic violence, free of the racism and discrimination sometimes experienced in mainstream provision despite anti-racist policies;
- responses and services that are racially, linguistically and culturally sensitive and appropriate;
- workers who have a good understanding of the issues facing minority ethnic women and children and who are well placed to challenge both the racism

of outside agencies and organizations and the sexism within South Asian families and communities.

The women and children in our study who had come into contact with specialist refuges commented positively on their experiences. Those who had previously experienced racism in a mixed refuge particularly commended the specialist service. One mother explained what children need in moving away from abuse, on the basis of her own experience of both kinds of provision:

> Children need more refuges. Yes, it would be helpful to children if there were more refuges – not English refuges. English refuges are not suitable for Asian children. There is lot of prejudice in English refuges. They don't understand about the Asian way of life, so are not helpful. (South Asian mother)

Another woman commented on how the absence of specialist provision had inhibited her initial decision to leave her abusive husband:

> One friend really helped. She told me about refuges, took me for a drive once to see the one in [name of city]. It was so crowded and so white. I didn't think the workers would have a clue about me. Also, it was too far away from the children's schools. I didn't want to change things too much for them. (South Asian mother)

Our evidence suggests that specialist refuges were amongst the few agencies that provided effective and appropriate help to South Asian women and children. This does not obviate the need, however, for other agencies to take heed of the comments in this chapter and to provide a better informed and more sensitive response.

CONCLUSION

Children's perspectives on their own needs and support structures should inform the development of appropriate policy and practice where children have lived with domestic violence. Their mothers are also able to throw light on what constitutes an effective response.

On a wider social and institutional level, the cultural racism that tarnishes much of the response to South Asian women and children needs to be addressed. Support agencies appear to continue with a largely colour-blind approach, showing only limited awareness and understanding of the needs of South Asian women and children. There is little awareness of the imperialistic nature of social welfare intervention in South Asian communities in Britain and a lack of acknowledgement of alternative ideologies. Agencies and professionals need to develop a better understanding of the interconnections between racism, sexism, ethnicity, religion and culture in the lives of children. Only specialist refuges are 'getting it right' as far as South Asian women and children are concerned. More resources are needed to promote community-based intervention for women and children living with domestic violence. Diversity and difference in South Asian families and communities needs to be acknowledged and addressed in policy and practice, both in these specific settings and, more broadly, right across social welfare provision.

At the communal level, South Asian professionals and activists need to recognize and challenge the role of male power and control in supporting and condoning domestic violence in the family and the community. Awareness of the ways that patriarchal sexism and racism impact on the lives of women and children should be promoted within communities. Harmful practices and traditions that sustain the subservience and abuse of women and children in South Asian communities should be challenged. At the same time, assistance and resources need to be designed in ways that can help women and children without necessarily cutting them off from wider support systems in their own families and communities. This can only happen if Western ideologies of welfare are not perpetuated as the sole basis of policy and practice responses.

Children who are growing up in the context of South Asian families in the UK are handling the meeting of two cultures in quite sophisticated and complex ways (Ghuman, 1999; Imam, 1999a). They are planning to make life choices that combine the best of both sides of their experience. Living with domestic violence sharpens their awareness of the importance of these choices, particularly for girls who face restricted options and the threat of social sanctions. Professional and policy makers who fail to recognize the fine line that young people are walking, and whose attempts at support are inappropriate or crass in comparison, will not be experienced as helpful. And worse, they may further restrict options and choices if they force young people towards solutions they deeply feel to be shameful or inappropriate because they ignore obligations of family honour, gender roles and respect for elders. This is not to say that women and children should ever be left in danger. It does mean that policy and practice should, wherever possible, harness and collaborate with support systems within the family and community if we are to be effective and adequate in meeting the needs of culturally diverse groups.

NOTES

1. The terms *South Asian* and the more recent *British Asian* are used specifically to refer to people of Indian, Pakistani and Bangladeshi descent who have originated from the Indian sub-continent, including those who have come via east and south Africa. *Asian* is used in a wider sense to include all people of Asian origin; for example, Arab, Afghan, Chinese, Iranian, Malaysian and Vietnamese people, as well as those from Bangladesh, India and Pakistan.

2. *Black* is used from a British perspective to include all non-white people who suffer oppression and discrimination in the UK on the basis of skin colour, language and/or culture. Increasingly it is argued that the term 'black' is no longer relevant and has been rejected by some South Asians themselves as it denies cultural diversity and ethnic identity (Brah, 1992a). Although the limitations of the term are recognized, it continues to be used as a term of 'political description and cultural counter-assertion' (Cambridge, 1996: 163).

3. *Minority ethnic* is a term used to refer to people who are differentiated from the dominant white majority by their physical appearance, language, and distinctive cultural and religious traditions. Although most professionals working in the social welfare field

continue to use the term 'black', increasingly 'ethnic minority' and 'British Asian' are terms commonly used to refer to people of South Asian origin. *Ethnicity* is a term currently used synonymously with cultural identity. Its usage is disputed due to its origins and negative connotations (Thompson, 1993). In Britain the analysis of ethnicity began with the study of New Commonwealth immigrants in the 1980s and has consequently been entwined with racism. It is argued that everyone has an ethnicity, therefore to use the term only in relation to minorities demonstrates its ethnocentrism (Hall, 1992).

4. There are at least 3 million black and minority ethnic people living in the UK, comprising 5.5 per cent of the total population. Of these, over 50 per cent are of South Asian descent (Office of Population Censuses and Surveys, 1993) and over 95 per cent of the children and young people were born in the UK (Ghuman, 1994). The South Asian population is, on average, much younger than the white population, with 36 per cent aged under 16 years. The proportion of children in relation to the population is double that of the white population, and among Bangladeshis it is three times greater (Owen, 1993). This made it particularly important to include South Asian young people in the present study. The majority of South Asian people in the UK originate from Bangladesh, India and Pakistan following large-scale male migration due to the labour shortage in the UK after the Second World War. Migration from the Indian sub-continent was predominantly from rural, agricultural areas, while those who came via Africa were business people, mainly middle class and of urban origin. Unlike the United States, where skilled and professional individuals migrated (Gupta, 1999), distinctive to the nature of migration to the UK was the large-scale, localized migration of large numbers of people from the same region (Shah, 1995). The nature of migration has established strong extended family and kinship networks of South Asian people in the UK. Cultural traditions and norms are, consequently, more zealously protected and promoted through communal settings. For example, the concept of *izzat* assumes greater power and significance in close-knit families and communities than where the influence of families and kinship systems is distant or removed.

Patterns of migration are significant because they determine the extent to which South Asian women have been able to negotiate and control their lives in Britain (Bhachu, 1996). Indian women were the first nationality to arrive, in the 1950s – some of them in their own right, others accompanying husbands. They came when there was a need for labour and very many were able to enter the labour force and developed knowledge, skills and experience which are important resources to draw upon in time of need. Although the jobs available were at the lowest end of the labour market, they nevertheless contributed to confidence and a sense of self-efficacy. Pakistani women joined their husbands much later, in the 1970s, when world-wide recession meant that they had fewer opportunities to work, and were therefore confined to the home. This is rarely acknowledged, popular assumptions about their lack of participation in the labour market being attributed to their cultural and religious traditions. Bangladeshi women have been the latest arrivals, joining husbands in the 1980s, and migrating at a time of economic decline, recession and stringent immigration regulations. Peach (1992) points out that the Bangladeshi community rose from a population of 16,000 in 1981 to 116,000 in 1987. As primary immigration had been curtailed by legislation in 1971, most of those who arrived came as dependants. Abused women in these communities, who have migrated to the UK later, some in the last decade, have faced more limited choices in dealing with their situation. They are less settled and more dependent on husbands and partners, both financially and socially. Being recent immigrants, they have limited knowledge of the structures in place to provide support and help in times of crisis, as well as limited skills in communicating in English. For these women and their children there is greater alienation and isolation if they face abuse in the home, which is otherwise their refuge from the unfamiliar and sometimes hostile surroundings in which they live (Imam, 1994).

7 The Influence of Domestic Violence on Relationships between Children and Their Mothers

> The worst part of it is that my children are involved. If it was only me I feel I could endure it for the sake of the kids, but the kids are also involved. (African mother)

In the last three chapters, we heard accounts from and about children living with domestic violence, putting their experiences in context, and considered how children react and survive. In this chapter and the next, we look at issues concerning children's relationships with their parents, first mothers and then fathers, both from children's own perspectives and also drawing on the interviews with 24 mothers in our sample.

As we have seen, children witness and overhear the abuse suffered by their mothers. They sometimes act as protectors, intervening in a range of ways to disrupt assaults (see Chapter 4), and older children may become confidants or advisors. Mothers may turn to their children for support but also do their best to try and protect their children from the knowledge and sight of violence, and from direct assaults. They invest in creating 'good times' with the children as compensation for the bad (Bilinkoff, 1995). Our interviews with mothers and children revealed that both sides are involved in negotiating emotional minefields, with patterns of avoidance and protection existing alongside openness, honesty and challenge. There were variations between mothers and between children, and over time for the same individuals, in how they picked their way through dangerous territory. In this chapter, we interweave children's and mothers' accounts to ensure that some of the complexities involved are made visible. Six key themes are explored: the desperate straits women found themselves in and how domestic violence altered the contours of mothering; the extent to which children were deliberately used by abusive men to hurt and control women; children's complex thinking in assessing who was at fault and why their mothers had not left the violence sooner; the ways children affected women's decisions to stay or leave; how protective actions could create unhelpful silences; and conflicting needs and perceptions between some mothers and their children. The chapter returns, finally, to the theme of giving children the chance to talk, concluding with a section highlighting the power of openness and honesty, both in situations of continuing domestic violence and in its aftermath. Before engaging directly with the interview data, however, a brief overview of perspectives on mothering and motherhood will set the discussion in a wider context.

RHETORICS AND REALITIES OF MOTHERHOOD

There is an extensive rhetoric of 'good enough' parenting within social policy and social work (spanning Winnicott, 1964, to, for example, Boushel et al., 2000). At the same time, repeated research projects show that mothers are constantly judged as failing this ostensibly minimal test, especially where abuse or violence occurs in the household (Hooper, 1992; Humphreys, 2000a; O'Hagan and Dillenburger, 1995). Feminist analyses of motherhood have pointed to the impossibility of being a 'good' mother; the way motherhood is socially constructed means that women are doomed to fail, however much they may care about their children (Nicolson, 1993; Rich, 1985; Richardson, 1993). Women are considered responsible for the well-being and safety of their children and for mediating relationships between children and fathers (see Chapter 8), but these responsibilities have to be exercised in a context of relative powerlessness in terms of adult familial relationships. The conditions in which women parent either facilitate or limit the extent to which they can fulfil their own and others' expectations of them. Those who have few economic resources cannot always ensure their children's well-being. Those whose physical and emotional resources are depleted, for whatever reason, will find it even more difficult to cope with the needs and demands of children, and those whose children face additional hurdles due to disability or racism will be less able to protect them from discrimination by others. Abused women share these contexts with non-abused women, but their frequent conjunction within domestic violence creates an environment deeply unconducive to achieving even 'good enough' mothering. That so many women do resolve this impossible conundrum is testimony to their spirit, endurance and determination. That many are unable to surmount the obstacles constantly and consistently should surprise no one.

Children grow up expecting their mothers to fulfil their needs, care for and protect them. They may not understand, in the context of domestic violence, why their mothers are unable to do this. Some of the children we interviewed were, in fact, remarkably insightful, reflecting afterwards not only on what their mothers had gone through but also on ways in which their own behaviour, including after leaving the violent man, had not been easy to deal with. This young man, for example, recognized the ways his hurt and pain and sense of responsibility had been directed towards his mother:

When we were at the refuge, I used to have a go at Mum quite often. I think it was pent-up rage that I did not know how to deal with, probably because of my dad. My dad wasn't there, so I took it out on my mum instead. I think maybe I thought it was my mum's fault for a while. Probably just the anger clouding the issue really ... I can remember being angry quite a lot when I was at the refuge ... [now] I am older, I understand the situation. I can see – because he still, now, is like he has always been. If he doesn't get his way, he argues and so on. I can see why Mum didn't cope before, because he's more of the same, if not worse. But, being the age I was, I didn't see it as anything other than normal behaviour, I suppose. (16-year-old white boy)

The impossibility of being a 'good' mother while experiencing domestic violence is a key aspect of women's dilemmas. Their typical role of being the emotional sponge in the family, managing and mopping up conflict and distress, becomes impossible when they are being used as a physical and emotional punchbag. They may be in no position to give the level of care they would wish (see section on 'Desperate straits', below). The sense of 'failure' becomes even more pronounced when women are in touch with statutory agencies. They become reluctant to contact social services, for example, in the fear that concerns for the children's safety will dominate and that they will lose their children (Hester et al., 2000; Kelly, 1994b), meanwhile remaining unprotected themselves. They know the perpetrator will make all sorts of accusations against them, often appearing far more credible than they do:

He's so bloody clever that they are going to believe him. (White mother)

and that they will come over in a bad light. As later sections of this chapter will demonstrate, from the standpoint of hindsight after having separated, women are often able to reflect on the damage children have sustained – to see what outsiders may have seen at the time. But professionals also need to be able to look and think from the 'inside', to see how, within the logic of living and coping with domestic violence, women often believe that they are protecting their children. And, within the limited frame of reference of their daily existence and absence of other options, they may be well be right. Protection here may involve shielding children from harsher treatment by the man by taking on the role of disciplinarian themselves, or remaining in the relationship so that children do not lose their home and standard of living and pay a price through disruption to schooling and social networks (see Chapter 4).

A sense of failure and guilt is probably the most common feeling reported by all mothers (Rich, 1985; Richardson, 1993). Domestic violence accentuates this, with women often aware, at some level, that all is not well with the children despite their best efforts (Hester et al., 2000). But it is not women who are responsible for creating this impossible household context and, as the next two sections demonstrate, many abusive men impede women's ability to parent and deliberately involve children in the abuse, completely removing women's options for protecting their children either from knowledge of the violence or from witnessing it directly.

DESPERATE STRAITS

Women's relationships with their children, and their ability to mother, are deeply affected by having to cope with domestic violence. Even in conducive contexts, we know that most women, whilst finding fulfilment and pleasure in mothering, also experience it as hugely challenging and demanding (Somerville, 2000). Children's needs for reassurance, attention and support are accentuated in situations of domestic violence, at the same time as the resources of their mothers to meet them are taxed to the limit and invariably depleted. It is not an accident that abusive men attack women's abilities to mother; they know that this represents a source of positive identity, the thing above all else that abused women try to preserve, and also that it is an area of vulnerability. Thus, undermining a woman in this respect gives the man the potential to assert his power to define and diminish her. But the situation need not reach this extreme for women's mothering capacity to be affected.

Every one of the women interviewed in this project, when asked if the abuse had affected her parenting, said she believed that it had (cf. Hester et al., 2000, for a summary, and Levendosky et al., 2000). The most common theme here was that anxiety – constantly being on guard – coupled with the violent episodes, had meant that she was exhausted, and hence had had very limited energy to devote to her children. The next most common issue to arise was that children had been a flashpoint around which violence might erupt. As a consequence, how women mothered had been orientated not around what they felt and believed was good for children but around efforts to limit further harm to themselves or their children. This 'externally controlled' motherhood had included elements such as insisting that children keep quiet so as not to anger the man; keeping toys and children's possessions invisible when he was at home; sending children to bed early so that they were not targeted for criticism or worse; and hitting and shouting at children before the man did, since the harm would be less.

> I didn't have the same patience with the children when he was there, because I think I was frightened he was going to lose his temper. I was much more calm when he wasn't there. (White mother)

> They were never allowed to talk, they were never allowed to play, they had to be quiet. My son did not talk until a year after we left the refuge, because that's what they had to do at home. He [the father] always slept on the settee in the daytime ... We used to have to keep it very, very quiet. They knew what he was like, I never had to say anything. Sometimes I made excuses. (White mother)

> I was so hooked into placating him that I emotionally neglected the kids. (White mother)

> I mean, if you've been, like, punched in the face – It's, like, I was getting really bad headaches and I couldn't get up. But I was thinking, 'I've got to feed the kids.' I'd be walking around all dazed and bruised and that. (Black British mother)

Often, women and children had lived in a double reality where there were times of freedom and fun when it was just them, and not just the times of control, anxiety and watchfulness when the violent partner was present:

> As soon as he went out, we'd do stuff – tidy up, cook, talk, do all the normal things that we couldn't do when he was there. (11-year-old white boy)

> I would plan something for the kids. Every year, say: Well, I am going to take them to Butlin's – something to do with them. You are just generally too dominated by this man to cater for them. (Black British mother)

But such compromises were not always possible – the partner might have been unemployed and hence present for much of the time, or mothers and children might not have dared do things even in his absence, or might not have felt able to sustain two worlds in the same place. The ever present threat of violence, and men's intolerance of children's presence, meant that many women were driven to restrict their children's lives in order to avert, contain or conceal abuse.

Some mothers were remarkably honest about the extent to which repeated abuse, and especially the belittlement and confused or depressed mental state that accompanied it, had undermined them and had meant that their mothering was severely compromised, even though they loved their children dearly and had been well able to care for them in better times:

> I was always fearful, upset, and did not concentrate on them and their needs. I was physically weak – having to go for days without food. (South Asian mother)

> It did, it did so much [the violence affected her parenting]. Because, initially, I'd do the homework with them – everything. But when the load was too much for me, I'd just come in, prepare their dinner, not even eat with them, or make sure if they do eat their food. I'd just go into my room and sit down there. Maybe in the middle of the night I go down and start the washing, you know, doing the housework. I didn't really care about the children. I think I felt I was helpless, and that I thought my whole world revolved around him. That's how stupid I was, most of the time I forgot things. One day I woke up and thought I was going crazy. (African mother)

> Yes, the violence did affect me quite badly ... I felt suicidal all the time. I was really depressed ... I couldn't really look after them properly. (South Asian mother)

> Well, I cared for them as far as their health was concerned – their food, their clothes and everything like that. But, obviously, mentally – I was so mentally confused. Well, I didn't think I was a fit mother. I know I loved them dearly, and I would have died for them. But I couldn't see things that were happening to them because I was in too much of a state myself. (White mother)

These are the kinds of desperate straits that some women had had to contend with when living with men who lashed out unpredictably and where the woman could not find any strategies that protected herself or her children. Children were aware of the impacts the violence had had on their mothers, and of the pain and desperation that had resulted:

> My mum used to cry a lot. She tried to commit suicide once with pills. We thought she was drunk because she was falling around and acting really strange. (13-year-old African girl)

Whilst separation removes the dynamics that compromise women's capacity to parent, it is not always a simple process to change the patterns of interaction that have developed within this constraining context. This mother discusses her 9-year-old daughter's concerns about her after they had left and how hard it had been to enable her to let go of this burden:

> I have actually put on two and half stone, but I was very thin and she was worried that I was virtually wasting away. It's taken me quite a while to get this from her. I knew she was worried about something. (White mother)

In the research interviews, several women discussed continuing problems in their relationships with their children, making clear that the impacts of domestic violence on themselves and their children were still evident. For some, the problems had proved insoluble – two women had older sons who had themselves become violent, and with whom they no longer lived. (It should be noted, lest this be taken as evidence of a deterministic 'cycle of abuse', that there were many more young men in the sample who displayed an understanding and awareness of the costs and consequences of violence, which they and their mothers believed would prevent them ever using it in personal relationships.) For other women, it was the pressures of single parenthood, but with an additional twist, that lay at the root of persistent problems:

> I find it very difficult. My nerves have really been affected. If they don't listen to me, I am quite short-tempered – fly off the handle … They have seen me be treated as subordinate, inferior, and that must have had an effect on how they think about roles in the family. (South Asian mother)

For children who have seen their mothers demeaned and treated as a 'thing', even if they reject this view of her, some damage is likely to have been done in terms of respect. As the later section of this chapter on communication illustrates, this can only be overcome through openness. Whilst much research documents the extent to which domestic violence undermines women's sense of self (Kelly, 1988; Mullender, 1996, for a summary), the ways that this is reflected in children's perceptions of women and mothers have received less attention. But these are the issues that many women and children struggle with after violence has ended, and they represent some of the more subtle damage of living with abuse.

USING CHILDREN TO ABUSE WOMEN

When asked 'Did he ever use the children against you or as a way to abuse you?', only two women in the study's in-depth interviews were uncertain whether this had happened and, even they, after initially saying no, on reflection thought that it had indeed happened. What varied in women's accounts was the extent to which children had been implicated and used, and the forms that this had taken. At one end of the spectrum were women who thought that this was integral to their abuse – it had happened 'all the time'. At the other were those whose abuser had begun threatening to harm the children, or not to let women have them, when it had become clear that the relationship was over. The ways men had used children, then, fitted into these two broad categories: implicating and involving children in their mother's abuse, and controlling women through threats towards, and mistreatment of, the children. This is a crucially important area for professionals to understand if they are to challenge men's behaviour in ways that protect children. It is relevant to the roles of the abusing and non-abusing parent in child care cases, to contact and residence disputes between parents where there has been violence, and to work in perpetrators' programmes and on men's parenting following domestic violence (Mullender and Burton, 2001).

The most common way in which children had been made parties to the abuse involved men deliberately and systematically forcing them to witness the abuse and/or compelling them to listen to accusations about, and the demeaning of, their mothers. In the latter case this could either be in front of the woman, or in a covert attempt to create an alliance with the child against the mother; this had also often been combined with treating children differently from each other:

> Oh, every time he wants to start abusing me he makes sure the children see, are there. He sits them down and tells them lots of rubbish: 'Your mother is a slag. Once she drops you off at school, she goes after men'… He was using the children – trying to turn them against me … Fortunately, when the children were growing up, they had seen things for themselves. (African mother)

> Well, as I said, he could turn us against each other. He was very jealous of my oldest son, or of me doing anything with the children. That's partly why I let them go to my ex-husband's [not the abuser]. I thought they'd be safe there and it would stop the trouble a bit. It was so hard – I hated them going, but I didn't know what to do. (White mother)

One mother talked of how she had been assaulted if she had tried to protect or defend her child, and that she had had to deal with instructions such as 'You'd better smack him before I do'. This child was also persuaded by the father not to act as a witness in a court case against him. In several instances, in fact, fathers (and it was only fathers who had done this) had placed their children in invidious positions – asking them to intercede and persuade their mothers not to leave or not to get a divorce.

Many studies on domestic violence note that children are often used to control women, awareness undoubtedly having been raised by the inclusion of this as one of the elements in the 'power and control wheel' developed by the Domestic Abuse Intervention Project in Duluth, Minnesota, in the late 1980s (see Pence and Paymer, 1990; Shepard and Pence, 1999). This had most frequently occurred in our sample through men deliberately picking on children in order to 'get at' the woman, typically at the point that women had found some ability to resist strategies that had previously assured men of the control they sought. The most extreme examples in our interviews involved accounts of children having been systematically deprived of food while the abuse was going on and of one child who had been locked in her room for a year whenever she was in the house (she had been allowed to go to school). Another common ploy was to criticize women's parenting:

> He certainly used her at times when she wasn't there, telling me, you know, that I was an unfit mother. It was all down to me. It seems to me now that this 'unfit mother' title – that seems to be standard, doesn't it. They question your abilities as an attractive woman and your abilities as a mother – the two things that do seem to work, as well. (White mother)

Again, professionals need to be fully aware of this ploy because women's low self-esteem and feelings of failure may make it difficult for them to refute their partners' allegations in cases where social services or the Family Court are involved.

Being prevented from leaving, either by the man controlling access to one of the children, or by his threatening to report the woman to social services, was also a repeated story:

> He tried a few times – when I left this last time – he's tried in the past to make sure she was blocked between, to keep me in the house. There were times I couldn't get her, because he'd sort of managed to manipulate to get her upstairs. This last time I left, we were having a big row in the road and he just grabbed hold of her and said, 'Well, you've got to come home now because I've got her.' (White mother)

These turned out not to have been idle threats for several of the mothers in our sample, who had lost their children to their ex-partner, been denied access to them, or had had to leave them behind (see also Chapter 6 for transnational variations on this theme):

> I haven't been able to see my son for three months because, the last time, I got a beating from my husband. And if I meet my son, I'm frightened he will tell his father where I am, because he will get it out of him. So, at the moment, I am not able to contact my son. (White mother)

In the case of older boys, not taking them when women left had sometimes been because the children themselves had refused to leave or because they had been above the upper age limit allowed in refuges. And one mother even talked of how her ex-partner had turned her adult children against her by telling lies about why she had left and what she was doing now.

Thus, in many households, children had not just witnessed or overheard, but had been directly implicated in their mother's abuse. This blatant disregard for children's feelings, let alone their rights, illustrates the single-minded pursuit of power and control that some abusive men exhibit. It is this behaviour that both women and children find perplexing and impossible to cope with or explain:

> One night he were proper bugging me, asking me all these questions about her: 'Was she this?', 'Did she that?' And he got really angry and jumped out of bed and slapped my mum really badly. I was crying and crying. He beat her up with me crying my eyes out! (16-year-old white boy)

Whilst some women and children had been able to see this behaviour for what it was at the time, many had not. The deliberate attempts to destroy or damage connections between women and children had had an impact. It is not surprising, therefore, that relationships between mothers and children within and after domestic violence are complex and varied – affected by the ways in which children have been used and by their level of understanding of the events in their household. Also, the few examples we came across of children wondering whether they had been in part to blame for the violence were always where the abuser had implicated them in some way: for example, by picking an argument involving them or their behaviour, being jealous of attention or possessions they had been given (which he sometimes took for himself), or, in one case, asking the child to try and prevent the woman from going for a divorce. (The child concerned, a mixed-race 15-year-old boy, blamed himself for not really wanting to do this.) More typically, children were quite clear that: 'It definitely wasn't *my* fault' (11-year-old white boy).

WHEN EFFORTS TO PROTECT HAVE
UNINTENDED CONSEQUENCES

Just over half our sample of mothers believed that they had made considerable efforts to protect their children, both from knowledge of the abuse and by trying to minimise the amount of violence that occurred:

> Yes, I did everything I could to prevent [their knowing] – never argued back, never retaliated when the children were there. (White mother)

> Yes [I tried to protect them], because I never provoked him. Even when I was on my own, I didn't get out of line. I did exactly what I was supposed to do and that way things kept calm. I had to do things I didn't want to do, just so he didn't start shouting, screaming and throwing things. (White mother)

A slightly smaller number argued that, whilst they had wished to do this, it had simply not been possible:

> I couldn't protect her, although he never touched her. I couldn't hide it – it was too severe. So I would try and talk to her. (White mother)

Clearly whilst the above strategies might at times have limited the violence they did not prevent it and the consequence for mothers (in addition to possibly increased emotional and sexual abuse) was that their children, especially older ones, might have perceived them as weak and defeated. Thus, in trying to act protectively, women diminished themselves and hence perhaps affected their relationship with the children in other ways.

It is important that the complexities of the situation are recognized. Social workers persist in attributing to abused women the allegation of 'failure to protect', yet women who reported in interview with us that they had been unable to protect their children from seeing the abuse attributed this to the actions of the man – their partners either did not care or had deliberately chosen to abuse them in front of the children, and even other adults. Thus it was the behaviour of the abusive man that ultimately determined what children did and did not witness:

> It would depend on where the situation was going on. I mean, it could be in the front room and he wouldn't care if people were there. My brother's been there, my friends, and he'll pick things up and throw them. (White mother)

He couldn't care less whether the children were there or not. I spent my whole life with him trying to gauge his emotion. If I felt the tension rising, I would try and placate him. Actually went to the doctor and said, 'Can you take half my brain away?' – that's how crazy I became. 'Can you take half my brain away because I just want to be a shadow on the wall.' Because I could breathe wrong, or move wrong – didn't care where. (Black British mother)

South Asian women especially said this about their husbands, whilst South Asian children talked less about seeing violence. This paradox is partly explained by the coping strategies that children adopted, many South Asian children discussing having found ways to cut off or disappear – either out of the room, or into themselves (see Chapter 5).

Mothers who believed that their children had at least been protected from extensive knowledge were, in fact, unaware of the extent of their children's awareness: 'Oh, I always did know, but I wouldn't – I don't say it to her' (12-year-old white girl). There is an analogy with the notion of 'behind closed doors' which presumes that domestic violence is hidden from those outside the household when in fact others, especially neighbours, are often aware. In most cases, all parties choose to say nothing, preserving an illusion of lack of knowledge. A similar process appeared to have come into play with respect to children where, for example, if the violence had taken place when children were in their bedrooms, mothers had presumed they were asleep, and children had chosen not to shatter the illusion:

Interviewer:	So were you aware of it?
Child:	Oh, all the time. Although my mum did used to try and hide it from us at night, after we had gone to bed. (11-year-old white boy)

The desire to protect often meant that women we interviewed had forgotten incidents where children had been present. Exchanges similar to this one, in terms of mothers not remembering what children could recall, took place in most of the interviews in which children asked their mothers to be present:

Young Person:	No I didn't see it much. But I did see it with my brother and I tried to stop that, didn't I, Mum? I tried to stop it, and then I fell across the room and banged my head on the table, and I had a cut. Don't you remember that?
Mother:	No, I don't remember. Are you sure? I don't remember that at all. They always say that children remember better than adults.
Young Person:	Yes I did. I can't believe that you don't remember that. (12-year-old white girl)

We asked women if they had talked to their children whilst living with the violence. Only two said they had talked a lot and tried to explain everything. The largest group were women who spoke of talking sometimes, either to reassure the children or to make excuses for the man:

Things accelerated, so then I talked to her so she knew the whole process. She could see he was getting worse. She knew that he was into drugs now and all those things were more out in the open. (White mother)

A bit, but they were so little. I thought the best thing was to give them a lot of cuddles – loving security. (White mother)

I told them their father was ill … it helped pull me through. That is what I thought it was. I wanted to stand by him, but now I know he was manipulating it all. The doctors don't think he is ill. (South Asian mother)

About a third said they had never talked to the children at the time. This was both about protecting children and also their own coping strategies of not focusing on the violence as well as the sheer difficulty of doing so:

No, I couldn't explain really. I didn't know how to. (Mixed-race mother)

No, because I used to, like, after each incident, put it to the back of my mind and, like, pretend it never happened. I didn't think – I didn't realize what effect it was having on the children, to be honest with you … Deep down, a bit of me was saying, you know, I wonder if the children are picking up on it, because of their behaviour … Now I look back and I could kick myself why I didn't pick up on all this. You just, like, put every incident out of your mind because you think it's not going to happen again, because you're told it's not going to and you start believing that. (White mother)

One woman talked about being explicitly threatened with violence if she had talked to her children, and another that the children had been prevented from talking with her. It took most of women's energy to get through each day. Attempts to protect the children from finding out, and not knowing what to say, acted as further barriers to talking and explaining. Many women had not had ways of making sense of what was happening to themselves, let alone anyone else.

This use of silence as a form of protection continued for some families after separation, and could represent choices made by mothers and also children, like the one quoted below, that they understood as protective:

Child: She [mother] doesn't really talk to me about it.
Interviwer: Do you want her to?
Child: No, not really, because I don't want her to think about what happened to her. I know already, and I don't really want her to explain it to me because I think it will hurt her. (9-year-old white girl)

As a consequence, some children were still unclear about all that had happened or why, and certainly had only a vague sense of the extent to which their mothers had been hurt and undermined:

I don't know why it was happening. I know we had to go to a refuge ... Mum got a friend to take her. Mum didn't explain to me where or why we were going. No one told me anything. No – I didn't ask any questions. (12-year-old South Asian girl)

He didn't do bad things, but every time we wanted him to go he wouldn't stay away, or he wouldn't leave ... He just caused rows and that. (13-year-old South Asian boy)

The consequences of these protective silences were starkly evident in the several mothers who were visibly upset and profoundly shocked by what their children told them and us in the research interviews. In all the study examples where children chose to be interviewed with their mothers, revelations by children about the extent of their awareness at the time, and specific memories that continued to hold immense significance for them, took women by surprise. This was the case even for one family in which a huge amount of prior discussion had gone into making sense of what had taken place.

The linked processes of self-protection and protection of others combine for both children and women to create contexts in which silence had appeared the best, or at least the safest, option. But silence, in turn, had meant that it was possible to misread and misunderstand each other's knowledge, needs and motivations. Women had stayed because of the children, whilst the children had been desperately wishing they would separate. Children had suspected that their mothers were trying to look after their best interests, and had seen how depressed and hurt they were, so had chosen not to say anything, whilst their mothers thought they were leaving the children in happy ignorance. We will return below to the themes of separation and of communication.

IT WASN'T HER FAULT, BUT ...

We asked children whose fault they had thought it was when the violence began, and what they thought now. Most children were clear that the abuse was not their mother's fault, and the majority, especially those aged under 12, attributed the responsibility to the abuser (see also Chapter 6, and Chapter 8 for a fuller account of blaming the abuser), but they moved through quite complex territory to reach this conclusion and were sometimes critical of their mothers too. When the violence had first begun, children had been more likely to see what was happening as fighting and arguing, especially where physical violence was not brutal from the outset. Fighting and arguing can appear, and may even have been at times, mutual. Given that domestic violence often arises from contexts where men seek to assert power and women resist this imposition (Kelly, 1988), children sometimes interpreted their mother's refusal to be subservient as meaning that she bore some responsibility for particular incidents: 'I used to tell my mum just to leave it' (10-year-old mixed-race girl). This child, however, went on to reflect in the interview that, even when her mother had 'left it', it had made no difference.

Whilst we did not ask children explicitly whether the man had attempted to enlist them on his side, through blaming their mother or other strategies, a number of children recounted examples of this. Many of these accounts resonated with the archetypal sibling arguments about 'who started it', but with the additional layer here of torn loyalties to parents and fear of losing their affection:

> I don't know [whose fault it was]. My dad used to say it was my mum's. I don't know why, but I believed him, and then I didn't know who to believe. If I believed my mum that it was my dad's fault, then my dad wouldn't love me. And if I believed my dad that it was my mum's fault, then mum wouldn't love me. I didn't know who to choose. But I think it is my dad's fault really. (12-year-old African boy)

As they get older, children see through the 'tit for tat' arguments and understand that men are capable of disproportionate force:

> I ask him sometimes, when I see him, why he hit Mum. He always says that she hit him first and she started it, but she didn't. But I say to him that he was a boxer, so that makes it different. (12-year-old white girl)

And most can see clearly that their mothers were not to blame for the violence:

> Interviewer: When all this was going on, whose fault do you think it was?
> Young Person: Not my mum's because sometimes I'd go into the kitchen and he'll start on me for no specific reason. (17-year-old girl)

> Interviewer: Whose fault do you think it was?
> Child: I don't know whose fault it was. It wasn't my mum's fault. (8-year-old mixed-race boy)

The children we interviewed tended to be clearer about responsibility for the abuse than about whose fault it was that the situation had continued. About a third of our sample expressed some uncertainty. Older children whose lives had been disrupted on more than one occasion did tend to see their mothers as carrying some responsibility for staying or returning, even when they placed the blame for the violence squarely on their fathers:

> It was Dad's fault because he was violent. He should have talked it over instead of hitting, shouting ... Like, if Mum was in the wrong, you don't use violence. But I still think the same, that it was her fault for going back to him. She was just doing it for us, but she should have finished it. (14-year-old South Asian boy)

Several demonstrated sophisticated understandings of their mothers' motivations, knowing that they had returned for the children, whilst at the same time expressing a strong opinion that they should not have done so. It is difficult to know how much of this was being wise after the event, since many of the mothers themselves expressed similar doubts in retrospect and, in their advice to other mothers, were as unequivocal as most of the children that women should leave sooner rather than later. Yet this had not felt possible at the time, for a whole range of practical and emotional reasons (see section, below, on staying and leaving). The one young woman in the sample who was still living with ongoing abuse gave an account that had no benefit of hindsight and was riven with ambivalence – she loved both her parents, could not bear the violence and conflict, thought they should separate, but at the same time would have preferred an outcome where they remained a household. Revealingly, the only route to peace she could imagine was for her mother to accede to her father's control:

> Yes she often does [leave] but she always comes back within half an hour and she says that we are a family. But I think they *should* separate, but they won't. They need each other, I suppose, but they hate each other. My mum is scared of him, but she stands up to him. I wouldn't. I tell her to give in and just smooth it over, but she won't. I say it won't be any harm to her just to agree with him, but she won't – I beg and beg her. (15-year-old white girl)

Another young woman began her response by assuming that we expected her to say it was her father's fault. After being encouraged to say what she really thought, she continued:

> Oh well, all right. I thought it was both their faults because she was always depressed and tearful – but he was a bastard. He's mad. He's off his head. Really, you should meet him. I think he did too many drugs in the '70s! (15-year-old white girl)

These two responses reveal a 'Catch 22' for women. If they resist what they regard as illegitimate demands and expectations by their male partner, they risk their children (and others) viewing them as in some way culpable for sustaining the context in which violence occurs. If, on the other hand, they choose to cope by accommodation, and as a consequence become depressed, this may be interpreted by children (and especially adolescent girls) as weakness – letting themselves be victimized. What is also evident in these accounts from children is that they take the violent behaviour by the man for granted; it is a factual reality that cannot, in their opinion, be changed. 'If a man hits a woman, then they ain't gonna change' (10-year-old white girl).

In this context, therefore, only their mothers can make a difference – either by adapting their behaviour to control or limit his outbursts or by leaving. This lack of belief in men's ability (or motivation) to change is not just the outcome of children's experiential knowledge, but is also a reflection of the cultural expectations of men and women within families. These same constructions of masculinity and femininity also come into play when agencies intervene; they, too, tend to take men's abuse for granted, with far too few programmes designed to change perpetrators' behaviour (Mullender and Burton, 2001), and to focus on the woman – her actions, mental state and options to protect herself and her children (Humphreys, 2000a).

STAYING AND LEAVING FOR THE CHILDREN

It is widely recognized that women have traditionally remained in violent relationships for the sake of the children (see Hague and Wilson, 1996, for a historical perspective, and Mullender, 1996), and that this factor weighs heavily, alongside the practical necessity of finding somewhere safe to go.[1] Familial ideology makes women responsible, not just for the well-being of children, but also for the good functioning of the family. Familiarist discourse is widely evident in the media and party politics, with stress increasingly placed on children's needs for stability and relationships with both biological parents (see, for example, Department of Health, 1999; Somerville, 2000). Such messages place considerable pressure on women to 'make the best of a bad job.' In addition, few women are unaware of the costs to themselves and their children of leaving, the potentially dire consequences of having to cope as single parents with reduced economic, social and cultural resources. A recent unpublished study in Australia, for example, demonstrates that single mothers who separate because of violence fare worse on every measure employed than women whose single parenthood is not connected to matters of physical safety (MacInnes, 2001). Women who have been abused receive less favourable property settlements, are less likely to receive maintenance payments, and get less support with child care from the other parent and from their kinship network. This wider context combines with the woman's continuing hope that the violence will end, and with coping strategies that focus on living from day to day and dwelling only on the good times (Kelly, 1988), into a lethal cocktail which implies that remaining, even in a bad relationship, is better for children.

Within the interviews were some examples – though not many – of women's decision to return having been influenced by children's desire to do so:

> She wanted to go home. We had started seeing him in bits. There wasn't much help at the refuge – the staff were never there, and all the other women were already going back to their husbands and things. It just became like a pressure, and I missed everything. We'd started to see him, I'd tried to talk and made the mistake of taking her a few times. Then she started missing him. She wanted to go back. So it was her as well, but that wasn't the deciding factor. (White mother)

More often, what had made up many women's minds to leave was a dawning awareness of the extent to which children were suffering within the family, or that the violence was being directed at them:

> That's the reason why I left, really, because then it was affecting the children. Because, up until then, I'd just thought … it was affecting me and not them … I didn't want to take my children away from their father. (Mixed-race mother)

> After the birth of the children, he used to be violent in front of the children – in fact, the children also became targets. He started to hit and abuse the children. It was because [of this] that I decided to leave him. That's why I left home – I had to protect the children from all this. (South Asian mother)

Sometimes, the decision to stay against her better judgement was due to the woman's taking seriously threats the abuser had made to harm or snatch the children:

> You've had everything threatened – 'You won't have your children' – and you stay. Because he *has* threatened that. (White mother)

On occasion, explicit threats had been made to kill the children or to remove them to another country. Here, mothers had been placed in intolerable and impossible situations where leaving might literally have put their children's lives at risk. Deciding to leave in this context was a little like exercising the judgement of Solomon, and could not be contemplated unless safety could be assured.

The barriers to communication between mothers and children explored earlier (see section on efforts to protect, see pp. 164–7) had meant that awareness of the impacts on children often took longer to become evident to women than might otherwise have been the case. Many women were able, with hindsight, to see that their decisions had not necessarily been for the best, despite this intention on their part:

> I should have left much earlier. We may think that they do not understand ... if it is behind closed doors. But now I know that they do, and they are affected by it. (South Asian mother)

> Looking back on it now, I feel so amazingly, unbelievably, almost unbearably guilty about the one thing that never entered my head – and that's not leaving sooner. I'll carry this burden of guilt for the damage done to my kids. (White mother)

Had communication been possible earlier, children might have been able to tell their mothers that they did not want them to stay for their sake. South Asian boys – whom one might (wrongly) have presumed to be the least supportive of separation, given the overriding value of the family in their cultural context – were adamant that staying for the sake of children was an illusion. This young man is responding to a question about what he would like to say to mothers:

> Think about your children – they are being affected by what they are living with. You are not helping them by staying, even if you think you are, because the fighting will go on. (14-year-old South Asian boy)

There was considerable irony in the number of quite young children whose advice to mothers was to leave immediately when the violence began. If their mothers had acted in this way, most of these children would not have been born.

The silences between women and children are a direct outcome of the dynamics of domestic violence, coupled with cultural constructions of mother-hood and childhood. Both women and children's coping strategies, and their desire to protect each other, militate against openness. But this may be precisely what would enable earlier exit from dangerous households. Early intervention strategies need to be sensitive to the complex dynamics between women and children, and could usefully foster ways to enable them to talk to one another more readily.

CONFLICTING NEEDS AND PERCEPTIONS

The over-riding theme in this chapter has been that women and children have shared interests but that these may be distorted by the dynamics of abuse, or not obvious because women and children are unable to communicate openly.

This is not the whole story, however. There were examples in the interviews where women's and children's needs and perceptions had been incompatible. In just two cases, women had arguably prejudiced their children's safety in order to protect their own, though they had undoubtedly been terrified and terrorized, had been reacting in a moment of imminent violence, and had made an instantaneous judgement that their husbands would injure them but not the children:

> I used to ... [send the children into another room] but they used to get more scared that way. He used to beat me up in front of them. I then began to keep the children with me to protect myself. I used to put them in front of me, against me as a shield, so that he would not beat me up. (South Asian mother).

> I'd run off with her, and he caught up with us in the road and just knocked me out in the road. She was already crying and screaming then ... Well, he took her. He basically said to me, when he knocked me out, he said: 'That's it, you're dead' ... and I knew he meant it at that time. There was just no way that I was going to go into that house [to fetch her]. I knew he wouldn't hurt her, it may seem selfish now to say it, but at the time I was feared of my life. I had to get away. (White mother)

This was exceptional. More commonly, though still in only a small number of cases, the conflict of interests had taken the form of women choosing to prioritize a new partner over their children and pouring everything into 'making this relationship work'. There were instances in which this had resulted in children living longer with the violence, experiencing multiple moves, spending periods of time away from their mothers with other relatives or, in one case, being looked after by the local authority. One child talked (as did his older brother) about the involvement of his mother with a man who misused drugs, and the fact that he had spent time living with his grandmother and later his father because his mother had found it so hard to make the break:

> He tried to hang my mum once with ropes. She jumped down and she fell. We jumped out of the back window and someone – not us – got the police. He was taken away. One time, we went to Grandma's and we had to climb back in the window to get some clothes. We went back the next day – we went back to the house. He had locked it up to stop us. After a while, my mum went to see him and we went back. It went on and

on. He was violent all the time. Finally, I went to stay with Dad and then, eventually, I came down here. (11-year-old white boy)

Alternatively, how separation is resolved can itself produce competing interests. One young boy explored his current conflict with the interviewer: he desperately wanted to return, without the abuser, to the family home, but his mother did not (she had been sexually assaulted there). His awareness of their conflicting needs and wishes is both remarkable and poignant. (This is the same boy we also quoted in Chapter 5, struggling to imagine how the dilemma might be resolved by getting a guard dog and by his helping more in the house, for example by doing the washing-up.) His struggle to imagine how the conundrum might be resolved is as remarkable as it is distressing in such a young child:

> If you are a child, think what your mum is going through. When I think about it, it makes my head all weird inside. I can't bear it. I do want to stay in the old house, but get things to change. We could change it all around, change the furniture, and start again. But my mum doesn't want to. I'm trying to help her get a little bit stronger and braver so she can face it. She just needs to be a bit stronger ... She said she really loved him, and she's crying all the time. It's really hard on kids. (8-year-old mixed-race boy)

Our interviews with children's workers involved with these families also revealed accounts of their having to cope with women deciding to return home when both the worker and the woman knew the children were opposed to this. The most poignant example was an 8-year-old boy whose mother was involved in prostitution. He had begun to open up in the refuge:

> He couldn't understand his mother, but he loved her desperately ... He was desperate not to go back if her boyfriend was there – he hated him. He'd suffered so much ... Every day he would implore her and she'd lie to him. I spent a lot of time getting her not to lie. (Refuge children's worker)

These kinds of situations are the ones that cause children and children's advocates the most pain and difficulty, since they are aware that the relationship has little to recommend it and that the outcome will be more abuse and more damage. That children have little if any power to influence their mother's decision-making, but at the same time seldom want to be separated from her, leaves children's workers (and other professionals with child protection responsibilities) in invidious situations. How do they assess the 'best interests' of children in such contexts? And, perhaps more crucially, are there strategies for working with women that might enable them to make different decisions? This is especially relevant with respect to early intervention and pro-active responses since at this point it is unlikely that women and children will have shared their perceptions and the impacts on children may not be apparent. Drawing on the reflections of both women and children in this work, within a practice that endeavours to support both parties to move out of protective silence, may provide a new route to speedier ending of domestic violence in individual cases. Over and above all this, of course, hangs the need for a societal response to tackle violent men more effectively, including through civil and criminal justice responses, so that women and children will not remain trapped in impossible situations where their needs and interests may conflict.

SUPPORTING EACH OTHER THROUGH OPENNESS

As we have demonstrated in the preceding section, we do not see women's and children's interests as always, or necessarily, coinciding. Within our interviews, however, there were many more examples of women and children discovering ways to support one another through honesty and openness – and even examples of conflicting interests being resolved – than there were of them pulling in opposite directions. This is a key message we would want to convey to child care professionals: that they can often work in partnership with the woman because, typically, she has a good relationship with her children despite everything, and does have their interests at heart. This is a strength that can be built on.

Several women gave detailed accounts of the ways they had been able to create communication with their children within the violent relationships:

> I told them everything. I even showed them the reports – what he had said, what I had said – so they knew exactly what was going on. (White mother)

> We did discuss it. They just used to say, 'Why don't you leave him, Mum.' (White mother)

Talking with and consulting children is not always a source of clarity. One mother recalled talking with her then young child about the need to leave home:

> I did actually go up to his bedroom one night and say we are going to go. He begged me – begged me not to. I didn't realize until years later that he thought I was going to leave him. That actually stopped me leaving on several occasions. (White mother)

More common, though, were stories of children having dared to tell the truth whilst living with abuse, thus strengthening their mother's resolve to separate, and stories of painful and difficult exchanges in the aftermath of abuse that shored up women's decision to make it on their own:

Interviewer:	So did you at any point say to your mum, 'What's going on?'
Young Person:	I did, when my mum was – before she wanted to go for the divorce she was thinking about it. She said, 'I don't think I can live with this man anymore.' And I was kind of encouraging her, telling her that – because I knew what was going on – that I knew it was really serious. I told her that he was too dangerous. (13-year-old African girl)

Her mother also recalled these exchanges, but suggests that they were rather more difficult and explicit:

> She said, can't I see that this man doesn't even like me, he does not talk of loving me, all this rubbish he had told her. I have never asked her to this day because I don't want to hear any more ... but she said there were lots of things he had said. There was a little she mentioned. [He had been seeing other women.] So when she said this, all I did was cry and promise her that I was going to leave him, no matter what. (African mother)

This is not the only example of children being rather brutally honest with their mothers. The young man speaking below was communicating with his mother during the research interview. They had discussed the same issues before, but only in retrospect. While they were still living in the violent situation, all their interactions had been dominated by secrecy, silence and fear.

> But, Mum, *if* he had kept his cool, *if* Dad didn't keep coming around and starting arguments, *if* there weren't any drugs ... if all those things, Mum, you'd still be with him, wouldn't you, Mum? I know you would. You've only been talking like this for the last few weeks. You'd still be with him, Mum. It's no use pretending you wouldn't. (16-year-old white boy)

Legacies of secrecy and of protecting one another from painful knowledge may be hard patterns to break. It was often the involvement of others – children's workers and, in a couple of cases, counsellors – that enabled women and children to find new forms of communication:

> It [counselling] was brilliant. She talked through things she couldn't talk to me [about], even though I stayed in the room most of the time, because she wanted me to ... I could cuddle her, I could love her, but I couldn't discuss the things that were hurting her ... and she couldn't discuss that with me, because she didn't want to hurt me. (White mother)

This extract from our field notes illustrates the same process, although in this instance facilitated by the research process itself:

> She [a 12-year-old girl] was really reluctant when I first arrived. Having told her mum that she wanted to do it, she then changed her mind just before I got there and said she wanted to go out. I briefly spoke to her and her sister – said quite clearly that I wouldn't push either of them to talk about anything they didn't want to. I was quite concerned about her and how she would cope, because in fact she did talk quite freely and never refused to answer at all. After the interview, her mum rang and said, for the first time ever, a dialogue had opened between them about feelings towards both her mother and father – also about a range of other things. She had started this process of communicating by writing a letter to her mum. The mother was absolutely delighted. (Researcher's field notes)

Research on the take-up of support services for children within a US domestic violence intervention project suggests that many mothers do not think their children need this kind of help (usually because they presume children have seen and heard very little) but, at the same time, have not talked openly with children about the reality they have shared (Peled and Edleson, 1999). Some mothers do not feel that they have enough resources to cope with distress the children might express. Thus, the silences continue to affect relationships between mothers and children, even where support is a possibility. Efforts to provide assistance to children may need to be more mindful of the emotional minefields that women and children still inhabit. A tentative finding from initial analysis of data from a national evaluation of children's services in women's crisis centres in Denmark offers some insight here. Increasing support for mothers appears to decrease the burden that children carry, and children fare even better where work also focuses on fostering and developing mother and child relationships (Berens, 2000). But, whilst some children are ready and can cope with support, many others remain trapped within a desire to help and protect their mothers, who in turn are desperate that no further harm be sustained by their children. Working within this reality – recognizing the fear of breaking the silence (Peled and Edleson, 1995), whilst knowing it will be ultimately beneficial – is the practice preferred by many children's workers in refuges and community-based support services.

CONCLUSION

This chapter has argued that relationships between women and their children are profoundly affected by living with domestic violence, and that women are aware that their ability to fulfil the mandates of motherhood are compromised. Women are acutely aware how, within the ideology of motherhood and the family, they have failed, but they believe that within the acutely constraining context of domestic violence they have protected their children both from extensive knowledge of the violence and from premature loss of their family and home. Simultaneously, children try to protect their mothers from awareness of how much they know and of how unhappy they are. The consequent silence means that women are living with the illusion that they are staying for the sake of the children, whereas children live with the burden of secretly wishing that their parents would separate. Finding ways to enable more open and honest communication between mothers and children is, therefore, an important element of any attempt at intervention and might be a better strategy for social workers to try, for example, than simply insisting women should leave if they want to keep their children. (Removing the man rather than expecting the women and children to leave their home is another, much under-used solution, of course.)

The importance of openness and honesty was reinforced in both women and children's responses to questions about what they would want to say to women currently trapped in violent relationships. Children's advice was unequivocal: leave when the children are young, do not wait (although a minority spoke about women needing to control the abuse and resolve it in the relationship), and, also, talk to your children. Many mothers echoed their children's advice:

I'd say to mothers: 'Get out! It's not going to change. Get out as soon as you can ... Don't stay for the sake of the children.' (White mother)

Go – just leave. Leave when they are young – don't leave it, like me. If you leave the first or second time, don't go back. (White mother)

Don't stay – make a break. And try and love yourself and find respect for yourself, even though it is hard. Women can become strong and live on and make something new. (White mother)

NOTES

1. Whilst not the topic of this study, it is important to note that every one of the mothers interviewed gave examples of statutory services that had failed to protect them or to offer them the option of either a refuge or other safe temporary housing. These are not accounts of service provision in the 1970s or 1980s, but in the 1990s, by which time police, social workers, housing departments should all have had policies in place on domestic violence. There remain gaps in this, in fact (Humphreys et al., 2000) and it remains the case, too, that policy on paper is one thing, while the practice that women and children encounter in crisis is something rather different. This absence of consistent response is a further reason why it is unjust to hold women to account for 'failure to protect'. Direct service providers continue to fail to protect women and children on a daily basis, yet it is not they who are made the subject of case conferences or legal action.

8   Life with a Violent Father

It is not surprising that the in-depth phase of our research revealed very difficult relationships between children and their fathers or their mothers' partners – on a level quite different from the problems we saw in the last chapter between some children and their mothers. Yet only the specialist literature on domestic violence and some elements of that on child abuse tend to reveal the issues involved with violent men as fathers. The more general research on fatherhood has other preoccupations.

CONTEMPORARY FATHERHOOD

The literature on fatherhood and fathering has burgeoned since the 1980s (at least in the English-speaking industrialized countries). This has been largely a product of concern about rising divorce rates, births outside marriage and the increase in lone motherhood, but it has taken place in the wider context of an examination of concepts of masculinity as a consequence of the challenge of feminism since the 1970s and of a felt need to change men's roles in families:

> We need data, especially, about men (and women) in egalitarian marriages to discover how these relationships flourish and survive ... But above all we need to know how much and why men ... value being husbands and fathers because this is the ultimate and crucial examination of the social glue that binds men to their families. (Lewis and Salt, 1986, writing in the USA)

Much of the research on fathers and 'fathering' has concentrated on the absence of fathers (Marsiglio, 1995). This can be either physical, if they are non-resident or orientated more towards the workplace, or emotional, in terms of the distancing effect of 'traditional' fathering and the contemporary encouragement of new patterns of engagement at the level of feelings (see, for example, Burgess, 1997). There appears to have been a reluctance to look at problematic aspects of fathers' 'presence' – clearly a major concern to those of us who focus on the impact of men's violence. Even when touching on negative aspects of fathering or of heterosexual relationships, studies of men and fathers tend to steer away from examining in any detail patriarchal, authoritarian attitudes or abuse of either partners or children. These are occasionally mentioned in passing (see for example Buunk, 1986; Daly, 1995) but are generally not allowed to slip into the 'good dad/ bad dad' dichotomy of earlier imagery of non-resident fathers (Furstenberg, 1988).

The literature on fathers and fathering can be viewed as falling into three categories: exploration of changing and innovatory patterns of fathering;

investigation of current social patterns; and defence of the 'traditional family' and of paternal authority (the latter group often based less on research than polemic). Each will be briefly examined in turn below, followed by a broader consideration of theorizing on masculinity, men's violence and violent men as fathers.

The research on changing ideas and practices of fathering, 'new fatherhood', often concentrates on interviewing younger married or cohabiting men to discover whether they take a more nurturing attitude and carry out a more equal role in the work associated with parenting than did previous generations (Lewis and O'Brien, 1987; Lupton and Barclay, 1997). These studies, though valuable and interesting, sometimes create the impression that authoritarian fatherhood is all but defunct. An implicit or explicit 'progressivist' framework tends to assume generational change rather than exploring how far traditional attitudes to parenting, sexual relationships and the division of labour and power within the home may still exist, especially where hegemonic heterosexual attitudes give rise to violent and controlling behaviour. The influential collection edited by Marsiglio (1995), for example, has no discussion of the use of physical punishment and no index entries for abuse, aggression, discipline, punishment, sanctions or violence. Those studies that do explore the persistence of more controlling attitudes tend to assume structural barriers to equal parenting and rarely touch on the possibly abusive consequences of fathers' own attitudes and behaviour towards women and children. In general, the same is true of work on separation and divorce, even where it is concerned with the effects on children (Bronstein and Cowan, 1998; Burgess and Ruxton, undated).

The second type of study, social policy-oriented research (for example, Burghes et al., 1997; Joseph Rowntree Foundation Findings, 1996a, 1996b, 1997, 1999; Warin et al., 1999), often concentrates on quantitative survey material on families and households – drawing out, for example, who fathers are, the proportion of them who live apart from their children, and the degree of contact and support that exists when this is the case or where working patterns impinge on family life. This approach provides a valuable corrective both to the view that fathers are wholly 'absent' in some segments of society and to the suggestion that 'new fatherhood' prevails. Often missing, though, is any discussion of issues arising from ethnic, cultural and religious difference and diversity. Even where studies do include material on minority ethnic (black, Latin-American, Mexican-American, Chicano) fathers (Connor, 1986; McAdoo, 1986, 1988; Mirande, 1988), they are mainly concerned to explode some of the more stereotyped racist myths about their difference from white fathers, so, like the studies of white fathers, they tend not to explore dimensions that impinge on domestic violence. Overall, because the policy literature is attempting either to demonstrate objectivity or to counteract gloomy prognostications about the state of 'the family' (Burghes et al., 1997; Utting, 1995), like the research on 'new fatherhood' it fails to explore the problematic side of persistent paternal control and abuse. Men's abuse of power in the family is, of course, acknowledged in specialized policy and practice studies focusing on children and domestic violence (for example, Abrahams, 1994; Hague et al., 1996; McGee, 2000), but these are not centrally about men or fathering.

The third and rather polemical type of literature on fatherhood and the family (Green, 1976; Morgan, 1995) is of little help in elucidating the problems inherent in children's relationships with their fathers where there is domestic violence. However, much of this literature does illuminate some of the core attitudes of men who, like those described in the present study, find it difficult even to begin to consider the needs of other adults – let alone children – for affection and respect in a non-authoritarian framework. (For a discussion of contradictions between the egalitarian rhetoric and more private attitudes of such groups in the United States, see Bertoia and Drakich, 1995.)

VIOLENT MEN AS FATHERS

From the late 1980s onwards, studies of violent men began to arise out of the critical study of masculinity (Fawcett et al., 1996, Hearn, 1996; 1998; Morgan, 1987; Thorne-Finch, 1992). They were given impetus by the development of pro-feminist perpetrators' programmes, initially in North America (Pence and Paymar, 1996; Shepard and Pence, 1999) and more recently in Britain (Morran and Wilson, 1997; see also Mullender and Burton, 2001 for a summary). A picture recurs of men who regard their own needs and feelings as paramount and themselves as having a superior legitimacy; they find it difficult to see others as separate individuals with their own needs. Perhaps not surprisingly, then, they appear to reflect very little on their role as fathers.

One of the first of these studies developed an overview of the origins of male violence against women in hegemonic concepts of masculinity and of the kinds of interventions needed to tackle it (Thorne-Finch, 1992). The focus of the book is on male violence against women in general, rather than within the context of close personal and sexual relationships. The impact on children and on their relationship with the offender is only touched upon. Indeed, there is more concern with the perpetrator's own childhood than with his role as a father, and even child protection concerns are mentioned only in passing. Despite a growing concern about the effects on children of living with domestic violence (see Hester et al., 2000; Mullender, 2001, for useful summaries), it remains rare for studies of violent men to ask questions about men's understandings (if any) of the impact of their violence on their children, even where it is clear that many of them are fathers. In a recent report on a US study of men's accounts of their abuse of female partners (Anderson and Umberson, 2001), for example, the authors fail to comment on the fact that one of the reported violent incidents is directed towards a daughter, despite this being clear from the extract itself.

Significantly, the most intensive British study of men's violence to known women does comment on the almost complete absence of any understanding of the impact of their behaviour on children amongst the men interviewed: 'Almost all ... did not appear to see violence towards women as child abuse, or vice versa' (Hearn, 1998: 93). The two examples Hearn records of men referring to children witnessing or being involved in the violence are described as 'unusual' because, otherwise, men did not talk about children being present. Yet we know from the research where women and sometimes children are the informants that the opposite is true; children typically *are* present in the house during violent attacks (see summary in Hester et al., 2000). Also, both accounts closely resemble stories we heard from women and children in our own research interviews and so are unlikely to be isolated instances. One describes an incident in which the man had 'grabbed the baby off her' before knocking the woman down in the street and beginning to walk away with the child (see Chapter 7 for a similar snatching of a young child). The other example clearly shows the man's apparent lack of awareness of any possible adverse impact of his own behaviour on his young son or of the little boy's distress and confusion; although he observed them, he completely minimized the seriousness of the child's reactions. The child may well have been clinging rather than hugging:

> There's been times when obviously I've pulled her hair or slapped her or something while he's been there. Because there's been a number of times when I can actually remember when he's had a little cry over it. He's too confused. He's probably hugged me or hugged his mother. Like, if I hit her, he'd probably hug me because he didn't understand. (Hearn, 1998: 93)

Again, Chapter 7 contains accounts of abuse carried out in front of children (as does this chapter) and this whole volume records its deleterious effects.

Latterly there has begun to be an interest in violent men as fathers. This relates chiefly to practice with perpetrators of domestic violence (see Mullender and Burton, 2001, for a summary) and in child protection practice where domestic violence is present – the latter leading to some useful discussion of social services' failure to engage with dangerous men and a tendency, as a result, to leave both women and children at greater risk (Farmer and Owen, 1995; Humphreys, 2000a). There is also the beginning of a more general literature on working with fathers in social and health care practice that acknowledges that their behaviour may be abusive or problematic (Daniel and Taylor, 2001). Post-separation violence and child contact arrangements give rise to particular concerns which will be dealt with in a separate section later in this chapter. Only one study has been traced that looks particularly at fathering in this context (Harne, forthcoming).

Concern for children has always been present as a background issue in work with perpetrators, 'using children' (in the abuse) having been included as one segment of the 'power and control' wheel developed in the pioneering groupwork programme in Duluth (as we noted in Chapter 7) to analyse and graphically portray the pattern of men's violence against their partners and 'responsible parenting' as an aim to be worked towards in the group (Pence and Paymar, 1990). Consequently, this concern is also evident to some extent in spin-off work in the UK, with the manual from the influential CHANGE project in Scotland, for example, mentioning children in two of its case studies as witnessing or being implicated in violent incidents (Morran and Wilson, 1997). In the commonly accepted minimum standards of practice for work in perpetrators' programmes in this country (Respect, 2000), children's safety is incorporated as a routine and urgent concern though, in practice, groups do not always have even a child protection policy in place

(Mullender and Burton, 2001). Most recently, work on men's parenting has begun to feature in some UK perpetrators' programmes (Mullender, 2001) while, in the USA, men are sometimes required to graduate from a group dealing with violence to a whole further programme where their need to improve their parenting skills becomes the main focus (Mathews, 1995). Interestingly, there is a suggestion that African American and other minority ethnic men may be effectively motivated to change their behaviour by an appeal to their cultural investment in family and community values (Healey and Smith, 1998; Williams, 1994; 1999), particularly if they can discuss this in separate groups without fear of racial stereotyping or abuse. This has resonances with the importance of family in many minority ethnic communities in Britain (see Chapter 6), though this has yet to be worked through into practice with violent men here in any noticeable way.

In view of the particular sensitivity of the question, we decided not to ask the children we interviewed (or their mothers) direct questions about their feelings toward their father or father figure. Instead, we focused on what they knew of what had happened, who they thought was responsible (see also Chapter 7), and whether they still saw the man now. The rich information emerging from their answers illuminated the emotions and relationships involved between children and their fathers. Given the key role that mothers play in mediating these relationships (see Backett, 1987, and discussion by Silva and Smart, 1999), we have also turned to mothers' accounts to fill out the picture. Reading the transcripts together sometimes explained the background to the children's accounts or supplemented them with mothers' observations on the impact of violence on the whole family. Mothers talked, too, about their partners' views on discipline, or about disagreements they had had concerning parenting practices, which were often matters of which the children would have been unaware except as part of the general fabric of their everyday lives. Consequently, as in earlier chapters, we have woven the two sets of accounts together.

HOW VIOLENT FATHERS HAD BEHAVED: WHAT CHILDREN HAD LIVED WITH

Some children could not remember particulars about life with the violent man, either because they had been very young or because they had not been physically present during the attacks. For others, the violence had been so diffused throughout their lives, or had taken such similar and recurring patterns, that it had simply become part of what life was like for them and specific incidents were hard for them to recall. Taken as a whole, however, children's interviews did cover virtually all aspects of what is normally recognized as a pattern of domestic violence, including physical and emotional abuse, jealousy and sexual possessiveness, financial abuse, and overlaps with direct child abuse. Only sexual abuse of the partner was not referred to by children, although at least two mothers mentioned marital rape, including one South Asian woman who revealed to the interviewer that her husband had raped her whilst her then 7-year-old child was in the bed with her. The child did not make any reference to this incident in her interview but whether this was because she had been unaware of it, had not understood it, had blocked it out, or was too embarrassed to mention it, we cannot say.

PHYSICAL VIOLENCE

A good number of the children were able to describe violent attacks by the man that they had witnessed or in which he had involved them in some way. The following is a typically graphic description, illustrating that the girl concerned had been present in the house, well aware of the violence and very scared by it, though perhaps 'out of sight and out of mind' to the abuser:

> When it started, the day before we left, I was up in the bathroom running a bath. And then I heard this massive wallop. Mum had been hit from here [demonstrating] all the way over here [demonstrating] – right over to the fireplace. I came running down. Mum was lying on the floor. I got ice and put it on her eye ... I was very frightened. He went upstairs and Mum had to go to hospital. I was very frightened. And the next day we left. (12-year-old white girl)

Often, more than one child had been present, involved in different ways: 'He was grabbing her by the hair and trying to push her down the stairs ... I was scared ... N [12 years old] was there and he tried to stop my dad from smacking my mum' (9-year-old South Asian boy). The physical violence with which children had lived had often been quite horrendous and persistent. One child mentioned seeing the heavily bloodstained bed after a night of violence; another saw bloodstains on the walls that were painted over after the perpetrator had gone. More than one child had been in the house during an attempted killing (for example, the noose incident in Chapter 7 and the bleach in Chapter 4) and others had been subject to threats to kill the children as well:

> He used to say he was going to put petrol in the house and burn it while we were asleep. We were always frightened he might do that. (8-year-old Asian girl)

EMOTIONAL ABUSE

Though less commonly recognized as domestic violence than physical attacks, and harder to take action against through the police and the courts, men's emotional abuse and verbal denigration of their mothers are as frightening for children as they are intolerable for women. A 13-year-old white girl with Down's Syndrome had been woken up by 'swearing and shouting' that scared her so much she was physically sick (see fuller account below). Frequently, this had been combined with violence in what children had seen and heard:

> He was just hitting her with his hands and shouting and swearing at her – saying that she's horrible, she's wicked and that she's not a very good mummy. Just saying all horrible things to her and really hurting her, making her cry, and Mum couldn't do anything. I just called the police. (12-year-old white girl)

Some children particularly remembered the periods of aggressive shouting by the perpetrator, or other kinds of overpowering and controlling behaviour. These could create a constant tension – an atmosphere of everyday brutality that was often described in more detail by mothers, recalling it as modifying every aspect of life with the violent man. Children remembered intimidation – like the threat to burn the house down – and they were conscious of domestic violence extending beyond individual attacks into constant fear and unease:

> ... he had violent behaviour, everything. He was throwing the pushchair around; all these objects were just flying around the house ... The room had been nicely painted and he painted it black, floorboards, everything. So, when you're little, you don't normally see houses with black floorboards and I think it was from that age when I started having worries – spiders and everything in the house – so I didn't feel comfortable ... it's like you can get a bad fear, I think, but I can't really explain it. (17-year-old mixed-race girl)

Once the threat of violence had become real, intimidation and fear pervaded the context of children's home life.

JEALOUSY AND SEXUAL JEALOUSY

Some men were jealous of their own children:

> ... [W]hen it was my birthday my mum bought me some clothes and stickers and he wasn't there when I was opening them and he threw the table and bashed her head on the unit. (10-year-old mixed-race girl)

> They were arguing about my horse-riding money. (10-year-old white girl)

There is a sub-theme in a number of both the children's and mothers accounts where the man, whether he is the children's own father or not, wants to be the centre of attention and is literally jealous of any care given to the children or to others, including other members of the family:

> Interviwer: When you were going through it ... was it making it difficult for you to look after the children?
> Mother: I think, mentally, yes. Mentally, to take time with him ... You are just generally [too] dominated by this man to cater for them ... He dominated, dominated ... If you like or love someone [like that], you avoid what is your main responsibility. My main responsibility is my children. (Black British mother)

In another family, the man had returned home, apparently contrite about his previous violence so that his stepdaughter now felt able to trust him, yet, during the research interview with her mother, he was in the house intrusively demanding his wife's attention. She talked of this as an intrinsic part of his behaviour:

[I]f I'm downstairs, talking to the kids, guaranteed he'll be calling my name every couple of seconds or banging on the floor because it's like he needs attention ... I'm sure he's jealous because of my time ... When he went to prison in February, he was there for three months and me and my kids got on like that [gesture signifying closeness] ... Especially me and V, because she's even said to me, 'When he's about you're all miserable, and you're moany and moody.' When he ain't about ... I can relax, enjoy myself. I'm not stressed. (Black British mother of four children)

This theme of jealousy of the children comes out far more clearly from listening to children and mothers than it does in more general accounts in the literature where sexual possessiveness perhaps predominates. Certainly, the latter had also been present and, again, children as well as women were aware of it:

My mum wasn't even allowed to hang washed clothes outside because he would say she was going out so she could look at other men in the front street. (8-year-old South Asian girl)

He would ask the children if any man had visited while he was out. (South Asian mother)

Indeed, sexual jealousy is arguably all of a piece with the man craving attention and insisting on being the centre of importance. One girl explained a violent attack by her father as the consequence of his jealousy:

When my mum went out [with her women friends on her birthday], I reckon Dad was jealous because Mum was having a good time and I don't think he liked it. (10-year-old white girl, also cited in Chapter 4)

Older girls may begin to be pulled into the same morbid fantasies:

[H]e said he knew what I was up to – I was a slut, I had taken after my mother, I was sleeping around ... he hit me hard on my head – banged against the wall. He then shut me in the toilet. (16-year-old South Asian girl)

This young woman's mother screamed out at such a slur on her daughter's reputation, knowing it would ruin her life and her marriage chances should it be voiced beyond the family. Yet the girl so retained her sense of her family's honour that, feeling obliged to continue respecting her elders, she told her teacher next day that her brother, rather than her father, had caused the cut on her face.

FINANCIAL ABUSE

Perhaps again because they are selfish and believe they rule the roost, abusive men tend to keep their families permanently short of money. This extends beyond not giving their partners enough to live on, to taking money from them and their children:

He also stole some of our money. It was about £80. (14-year-old east Asian boy)

... he was threatening me ... I signed the money away ... If I hadn't given him the money he would have killed one of us ... He did have an axe. We were so scared. I signed only because I thought, if I didn't, he would surely kill me. (16-year-old South Asian girl)

Children also resented how perpetrators left them and their mothers with nothing after separation:

[H]e's not giving us money. (13-year-old African girl)

I feel so sorry for my mum because she has to get all the money to buy all new things for our new house, like beds and kitchen stuff and cookers, and they are so expensive ... he's got a house and he's got the money, sort of thing. But we haven't got anything. (9-year-old white girl)

Mum ... worries sometimes about money, bills. She has nothing left. Left home without anything. (8-year-old South Asian girl)

Having no money reduces women's options, making it harder both to leave the violence and to survive afterwards. Hence, like much in domestic violence, financial abuse doubly serves men's purposes – giving them an easier life while keeping their family constrained and often trapped. Having broken free, this older girl philosophizes that you cannot put a price on safety:

He always made Mum pay for everything. All that he had – house, taxi – my grand-parents helped him to get ... He may have taken our money but money is not everything. I would have gladly given it up to get rid of him. (16-year-old South Asian girl)

OVERLAPS WITH CHILD ABUSE

Several children described having been attacked by the abusive man themselves, or having seen this happen to siblings:

He was lashing out at everyone for no reason. He's hit me before ... He was using his fists on me. (12-year-old African boy)

I have seen him hit all the members of the family at least once. (17-year-old mixed-race girl)

Some had observed a differentiated pattern of violence where, as well as the mother, one particular child, or more than one, was either an object of the man's violence or an exempted favourite:

[He] didn't like my mum or my sister ... He used to shout ... He threw hot coffee on my sister, he used to bang her head on the floor and on the wall (8-year-old South Asian girl).

J used to be Dad's favourite. He never really treated her the same way he treated me and D. (16-year-old South Asian girl)

Not uncommonly, men who perpetrated domestic violence over-chastised the children or punished them inappropriately, to a point that might well be considered abusive:

> [W]hen you think back ... they were, well, like, withdrawn. It was, like, 'What's Daddy going to say now? Watch out, is he going to shout?' He did used to smack them, like, around their heads ... He said that's how children should be punished. (White mother)

One white mother described her husband dragging one of his small sons out of the room by his hair when the boy got over-excited at his fifth birthday party, despite the man's own father's protests. Her daughter also remembered this incident, and recalled attempts by her grandfather and paternal aunt to intervene. This same mother would attempt to avert her husband's brutal chastisement of the children by lighter physical punishment, but this did not always work and, if she defended her children, this would also lead to later violence against herself, when the day was over and the children in bed. It is clear that, even if successful in averting violence, such measures were disruptive of a shared family social life, especially when the father was present, and sometimes it was precisely on occasions like birthday parties or present-giving that violence could erupt, either against the mother or the children. Sometimes such incidents made the children wonder for a while whether what had happened was their fault, but, in the main, it heightened their perception that the man's behaviour was unreasonable because their sense of natural justice was affronted if they could not even have their presents. Men also exercised excessive control over the lives of teenage children:

> Well, if I gave D some freedom – I would say she could go some place – He would say she couldn't go. Even when she was a teenager, she couldn't have gone. Then he'd shout at me and he would say I'd have her ruined – she shouldn't be going here and she shouldn't be going there, and that. So there was arguments all the time, over everything. I didn't feel that they should be deprived just because of his ideas and that. So I covered up a lot. (White mother)

CHILDREN'S FEELINGS ABOUT THEIR FATHERS

Only a minority of the children spoke directly about their feelings for their fathers or their mother's partners, as distinct from their feelings about the violence. It was quite common for emotional content to be embedded in an account of remembered violence or vice versa – sometimes a vivid memory emerged from a child trying to describe their feelings about what had happened, or a child trying to explain the violence was put back in touch with the sadness, fear and confusion it had evoked. A few said that they hated the man, although this normally came out as part of a response to other questions, such as whether they saw him now or wanted to do so. One 11-year-old white boy, for example, said that his advice to violent fathers would be: 'Go and die in a gutter.' It sometimes appeared easier for a child with mainly negative feelings about a stepfather or cohabitee, rather than a biological father, to choose to express this condemnation, perhaps because there was less of an issue of conflicting loyalties involved. Others, most notably when the abusive man was their own father, avoided talking about him and their feelings for him altogether.

Children spoke most often about having been made to feel upset and frightened by what the man had done. As we saw in Chapter 3, sadness is an emotion that children recognize in themselves and other children in relation to traumatic events, even though it may not be the one that adults most readily anticipate. It certainly cropped up in children's accounts of what they had gone through, in the second example below tied in with unexplained somatic symptoms:

> Because, if they were like me, sometimes … I'm really sad. I need someone to talk to. (9-year-old white girl)

> I'd be really miserable. I used to have these pains – people said they were stress, or something. I stopped breathing … I used to get really upset and cry a lot. (13-year-old African girl)

Even more commonly, when asked to say what had changed since leaving the violent man, children talked about now being happy, in implied contrast with how they had felt before:

> I'm happier. (8-year-old African girl)

> I am very happy. I feel very comfortable and happy. (14-year-old east Asian boy)

> They [younger brother and sister] are happier now. (14-year-old Asian boy)

More predictably for adults, perhaps, children talked about being 'scared and frightened' and about having had nightmares. A 16-year-old Asian girl explained that this made it impossible to concentrate at school and that it was not fair to put children through this. This disabled girl's fear becomes quite tangible:

> I was scared in case somebody came and got me … I always woke up … and I was sick … I was feeling it on the pillow … The door was open and I stayed in bed … Then I put the light on and saw him kicking Mum's head. My sister phoned the police and then I was crying and I wet myself. Then I went down to the police station. (13-year-old white girl with Down's Syndrome)

Especially where children had directly witnessed violent events, they would sometimes talk of anger rather than fear:

> When my dad started all of this, right, I would really get angry and start shouting at him, telling him off. I didn't hold anything back. (12-year-old mixed-race girl)

Interviewer:	Can you remember what you were feeling then?
Child:	Just angry … Angry at him.

And, where they had themselves been abused, this anger seemed unlikely to abate:

> [For] M, it goes much deeper because my dad used to beat him so he does have this resentment for my dad. He doesn't trust him at all. (13-year-old African girl talking about her 12-year-old brother)

Others talked about finding aspects of the situation, such as having had to change schools and make new friends, 'annoying' or 'irritating.' One teenaged white boy said all his unanswered questions made him 'moody.' A 17-year-old mixed-race girl considered that she and her 9-year-old brother both lost their tempers more readily than in the past and that she had lost some of her ability to take a joke. A few children turned their anger inwards and felt guilty in case they had contributed to the problems at home or, in one case, for talking about them to the interviewer (though consent to have the interview included was reconfirmed).

Some spoke of loss of respect, or of later forgiveness if they felt their father had begun to reflect on his behaviour or had actually been able to move on:

> He's changed now. He's sorted himself out and got a job and now I respect him. (12-year-old mixed-race girl)

In contrast to other children in the interview sample, South Asian children were less likely to see respect as an individual attribute to be won or lost and more likely to see it as a necessary attribute of inter-generational relations (see Chapter 6). Similarly, South Asian children perceived a reciprocal moral dimension to parents' obligations to their children which was contradicted by domestic violence:

> Tell them they should be looking after you instead of fighting with each other. Tell your parents that you should be the most important things to them in the world, rather than fighting. (9-year-old South Asian girl)

While some children, as we have seen, spoke of their early love for their fathers or of their fear of losing his love if they took their mother's side (see Chapter 7), only one girl, who was around 9 years old at the time of leaving and 10 at first interview, spoke directly of her sorrow at having left her father and even she was able to let her head rule her heart:

> I was a bit upset for my dad, leaving my dad. But then I thought, 'No, it's for my mum's safety.' (10-year-old white girl)

Some others spoke of being sad, upset or angry about having to leave home (where that was what had happened) but were glad to get away from the violence.

Some children revealed a complex of emotions – including shame, anger, longing for the violence to end – embedded within narratives about the pain and sorrow associated with living through the abuse. Over time, the only aspect left of fatherhood was often paternal authority exercised in the form of naked power and it seems that, progressively, this killed any feelings the children might otherwise have had for the man, just as happens eventually for women. Mothers' accounts, though, show that this did not happen before children had made real attempts to draw love and affection from men who appeared incapable of returning it, or even of understanding that parenting consists of this and not purely of discipline. This mother, having earlier spoken of her husband's harshness towards the children, also talked about how all three behaved towards him, including the two younger children, boys aged 6 and 3, who were not interviewed. After their little brother had gone to bed, the older boy and his 10-year-old sister were described as almost desperately vying for their father's love and attention, including in the midst of coping with the violence:

> They all, like, tried for P's affections, you know. After tea, they'd have their baths and they'd come down – I mean, obviously not T because … he didn't have much time for T … [but] J and K, they used to, like, see who could get his attentions – more so, they'd be all over him and that, and I think it was too much … And J would be very, um, 'stick up for his mum', like, if P shouted at me or anything. 'Don't you shout at my mum' and K'd be, like – 'Come on now, J. Come on, leave Mummy and Daddy alone.' She knew. She's a lot older than 10 in her ways. She knew, but J – he's a little man, you know. But then he'd get shouted at and he knew, then. But, every time, he'd walk away and he'd cry and he'd go, 'Horrible to my mummy you are.' But, then, he'd be cuddling him and all that, and 'I love you, Daddy.' You know, it was sad really. (White mother)

This 6-year-old still did not understand and was giving his father unconditional love. K, the 10-year-old, had moved onto conflicted feelings. She was the girl who, we saw above, felt sorrow at leaving her father whilst also recognizing the need for her mother to leave the relationship. One of the other white mothers perceived a distinction between liking and loving:

> I knew they didn't particularly like him, but they still loved him. (White mother)

and deep ambivalences about relationships would be hardly surprising, given the kinds of experiences these children had been through. Eventually, though, after many years of living with domestic violence, it seems that older children may become aware that expecting affection is hopeless and simply substitute avoidance of their father:

> They would sit in this window [living room at the front of the house] and run upstairs when they saw his taxi coming. Never watched TV downstairs. They recognized the sound of the car engine coming down the road. (South Asian mother talking about her teenaged children)

Children also frequently described physical effects of the emotional stress, particularly disturbed sleep but also including headaches, sickness and diarrhoea, wetting the bed and lack of concentration. One girl, aged 10 at the time of the interviews, had pretended to feel ill at school so that she could go home and see if everything was all right. In the main, these problems had disappeared or receded once children felt safe but they are a reminder to health professionals that what presents in the form of physical symptoms can turn out to have causes rooted in home life if the right questions are asked (see Chapter 9).

WHETHER CHILDREN BLAMED THEIR FATHERS

In some cases, children – including some of the youngest in the sample – had very clear ideas about the abusive man being responsible for his own violence:

Interviewer: Whose fault did you think it was?
Young Person: My dad's … I hate him. (12-year-old white girl)

I know it was my dad's fault. I know my mum did not want to fight. She wanted peace and quiet. (9-year-old South Asian girl)

[Fathers] have no right to hit women – if they want to hit someone, they should go into boxing. (12-year-old white girl)

For some, this recognition had always been part of how they viewed the situation:

Interviewer: When you first found out what was happening, whose fault did you think it was?
Child: My dad's.
Interviewer: Do you still think the same now?
Child: Yes. It wasn't right that he was fighting. (9-year-old South Asian boy)

For others, awareness of the significance of what had been happening had dawned only gradually:

At first, I thought it was just verbal abuse, just saying things – I didn't think. Now he just got more vicious. I think it's really life-threatening now, that he's really serious and means to do real harm to us I just thought before that he was just – really he hated my mum, they didn't get along. But now it's just so much worse. (13-year-old African girl, describing the past two years, including continuing contact with her father)

Similar narratives of the violence having been laughed off or obscured by references to the woman's clumsiness, or of her resultant depression being minimized by the man dismissing it as 'grumpiness', for example, were also present in mothers' accounts. For the children, this nexus of rather puzzling events had sometimes meant that they took longer to realize who bore the responsibility. This was also part of getting older and being able to make more sense of what was happening:

> I was very young when this all used to happen. I think it was my dad's fault ... I felt then it was my dad's fault but now I feel sure it was my dad's fault. (8-year-old South Asian girl)

This could involve a real conflict of loyalties – even 'changing sides' from a previously much loved father as a consequence of his violence:

> I had no idea it was going to be this bad ... Up until then ... from when I was a little baby, I always wanted my dad. Then, when I started to go with my mum he started getting angry ... M [her 12-year-old brother] preferred my mum to my dad, and my dad would beat him for no reason. (13-year-old African girl)

One boy described how his father had tried to 'buy' his allegiance but it had not worked, although the young man would not withdraw every last vestige of respect to an elder. When asked whose fault he thought the violence had been, he replied:

> Dad's, because he was violent. Should have talked it over instead of hitting, shouting. He was unfair. The person who hits is in the wrong. They don't have the right to hit others. Dad got us loads of presents. [I] still didn't like what he was doing to Mum. [I] don't hate him. (14-year-old South Asian boy)

Children's strong sense of fair play is relevant here. Sometimes the conviction that their father's behaviour was wrong had been reinforced by situations in which the children had also been attacked:

> I just thought my dad was just generally trying to ruin us ... He was lashing out at everyone for no reason. He's hit me before. He's hit my mum. He shouted at my mum. He was using his fists on me. (12-year-old African boy)

Conversely, where children are the occasion or direct target of arguments or violence, and where men are jealous of them, it can leave the child feeling to blame in some way:

> A couple of times I used to think it was my fault, because I used to be in the middle of it a few times; when the argument was going on or when, just before my mum divorced him, he was asking me to try and talk to my mum about it. Because I didn't really want to, I thought it was my fault that they fell out in the end. (15-year-old mixed-race boy)

> I blamed myself when they were arguing about my horse-riding money ... and I thought it was my fault for having money ... but people keep telling me it isn't my fault for anything. (10-year-old white girl)

> Sometimes I feel it was my fault a bit, because I was always there and I couldn't stop it ... And I would make it worse by being there because he was so jealous that he'd make a scene if Mum made a fuss of me instead of him ... he wanted all the attention. (15-year-old white boy)

Self-blame can also arise when no one explains to a child why a divorce is happening, as a 16-year-old white boy told us. Others, though, as we saw in the last chapter, were equally clear throughout that they were not to blame: '[I]t wasn't my fault. It definitely wasn't *my* fault' (11-year-old white boy). Some children, particularly younger ones, wondered whether their mothers were partly to blame for the violence, or particularly for not leaving sooner (as we saw in Chapter 7), and, very occasionally, a sibling was implicated, though not to the exclusion of understanding the abuser's responsibility for his own behaviour:

Young Person: Well, I don't want to be horrible, but it was a bit of everyone. It was a bit M's fault. Because my dad used to give him a lot of money and, when he didn't give J so much, so it caused problems and arguments.
Interviewer: So whose fault do you think it is if someone is violent to someone else?
Young Person: It is the fault of the person who is violent, I think. (12-year-old white girl)

In the longer term, children's view of the abuser's behaviour, and feelings towards him, were governed by whether or not he showed himself able to change:

Interviewer: Do you think the same now?
Young Person: No ... He hasn't done it for a really long time now. I think I respect him now. I didn't use to respect him when he used to hit my mum, but I do now. (12-year-old mixed race girl)

POST-SEPARATION CONTACT WITH FATHERS

Where men's behaviour had not changed for the better, the question of contact with fathers after separation raised many difficult issues, both for the women and the children we talked to. There is a vexed social policy and civil law background to this.

There has been some sympathy in the media for abused women whose violent husbands have gone as far as to abduct the children, particularly to countries where paternal rights are legally dominant and there is little chance of getting the children back. Short of this extreme, however, the assumption has prevailed in the UK that continued contact with their father is always in children's best interests. Any woman who has opposed it has risked being regarded as pursuing a personal agenda against her ex-partner and preventing him from being involved with his children (Harne, forthcoming). Even women's attempts to mention in court violence against themselves or dangers to their children have been taken as evidence of this kind of vendetta and have not, in the past, been accepted as relevant to the determination of future residence or contact arrangements (Humphreys, 1999). The main notions exercising the courts and the Lord Chancellor's Department, in the period since the Children Act 1989 introduced the principle of shared parental responsibility, have been their perception of mothers' assumed 'implacable hostility' to direct contact with fathers and belief that contact needs to be enforced (Advisory Board on Family Law, Children Act Sub-committee, 2001b). Hence, despite the requirement of the Act that children's wishes and feelings must be taken into account and that decisions must be based on their best interests and not those of their fathers (or mothers), even in cases where children have expressed the view that they do not want to see their father or are frightened of him it has been assumed that these words have been put into their mouths by their mothers. Courts have been unaware until very recently of the adverse impact on children of living with domestic violence (Sturge and Glaser, 2000). The present study, then, may add an important voice for children to a growing debate.

Until very recently, there has been no effective way for women or children to demonstrate the reasonableness of their opposition to contact where separation has taken place because of domestic violence and where they have continued to be in danger. Lawyers have even advised against mentioning it for fear of being labelled 'hostile' by the courts. Meanwhile, a body of research evidence has built up indicating that women and children are frequently unsafe during contact visits and particularly at hand-over points (Hester and Radford, 1996; Radford et al., 1999; Saunders, 2001). Intense campaigning has finally led to a degree of awareness, though only in Northern Ireland has this gone, to date, as far as legislative change. In 2000, the Court of Appeal attempted to improve court practice in England and Wales by passing down judgement in four test cases where violent fathers were appealing against decisions denying them direct (i.e. face-to-face) contact (Re L, V, M and H. [Contact: Domestic Violence] [2000] 2FLR 334). A government consultation exercise over the same period led to good practice guidelines (Advisory Board on Family Law, Children Act Sub-committee, 2001a). Yet, also in 2001, the same sub-committee issued a general consultation paper on enforcing contact that barely mentioned domestic violence (Advisory Board on Family Law, Children Act Sub-committee, 2001b), leading to the inference that official concern about post-separation violence was either short-lived or peripheral (Saunders, 2001). Most recently, there is a proposal in the Adoption and Children Bill to amend the definition of 'harm' in section 31(9) of the Children Act 1989 to encompass 'impairment suffered from seeing or hearing the ill-treatment of another'.

Our own research was conducted shortly before any of these changes took place and, not untypically, only a minority of the families had experienced contested court proceedings. Nevertheless, the interviews are important in casting light on children's experiences of different patterns of contact and non-contact with fathers and 'father figures' and on their perceptions and understandings, thoughts and feelings about this. Most of the women and children interviewed were managing contact on their own, a minority having already ended it.

A variety of situations prevailed. Contact was not always an issue for the children we talked to. One father was dead and another was in prison. The violent man was not always the father of any of the children, or not of the ones old enough to be interviewed. In a small number of households the perpetrator was once again living with the family. In another instance he was now a frequent visitor to the house, so that he could see and take out the younger children who were his, but was no longer regarded as a danger by either his ex-partner or older stepson – though they would have been happier without his visits.

There was still scope for considerable variety in the examples we did find of direct post-separation contact, which was happening for a majority of families in the sample overall. It ranged from formalized arrangements (sometimes through the courts) – for example, this 9-year-old white boy: 'Yes, we go on weekends. It's all right. It's better then when he was here' – to completely informal contact when the children visited other members of their father's family, as happened for two South Asian teenage boys and their 8-year-old sister. Contact varied in frequency, success and in the reactions it elicited in all those involved. For children and young people mixed feelings were not uncommon. One 15-year-old white girl said, for example, that she saw her father 'occasionally' and liked seeing him 'now we are away from him', but her opinion of his character remained very low.

Where there was no direct contact there was sometimes indirect contact by telephone and mobile phones proved particularly useful where safety was still an issue because they did not reveal as much about the family's whereabouts as landlines. Such considerations could be very important, as in one example where a man had paid some other women to kill his wife (a white woman with two daughters) in her own home, but they had stopped short at kicking her unconscious in front of the children. After an unsuccessful attempt at reinstating contact at the request of one of the girls, their mother has gone back to court and, meanwhile, was limiting them to regular Sunday phone calls to their father from a number he could not trace.

CHILDREN WITH NO DIRECT CONTACT

Some children did not see their fathers:

> We don't see my dad now and don't want to see him. I am happy about not seeing him. (8-year-old South Asian girl)

> I don't want to see him because he makes me upset. (9-year-old South Asian boy)

Contact, especially of the face-to-face variety, was most clearly unwanted by those children who said they hated their father (or mother's ex-partner) or resented his behaviour and the long-term effects it had on their lives:

> No. What he did to my mum – I don't really want to see him. I don't forgive him. (9-year-old white boy).

One child, a 13-year-old South Asian boy, refused even to talk about the issue. For several, the predominant emotion was continuing fear rather than hatred, particularly where the woman and children had had to flee the violence and go to undisclosed whereabouts. A 12-year-old white girl talked of constant nightmares about being found by her father, while another of the same age reported having to be able to watch two doors and have her back against the wall before she could sleep (quoted in full in Chapter 4). Children who were still this frightened naturally did not want contact to resume and discussed this as a safety issue when asked what advice they would give to other children or their mothers if violence were happening in their house:

> Move somewhere where your dad don't know [where you are]. (12-year-old mixed-race boy)

> Try and persuade Mum to get help, see someone. Try and get away before it is too late. Like the young woman [from the local community who] has just been stabbed to death by her husband. My mum would have been in that situation if she hadn't been strong enough to leave and get help from a friend. (14-year-old South Asian boy)

For children who feared their fathers this much, the main feelings about being separated from him were often relief that they were able to feel safe. For some, not seeing their father, or doing so only within the protection of family and community, brought not just relief but a strong positive sense of freedom, a literal release:

> I feel really different. I can sleep without any fear. I can really live like any other young person in the community ... Now he is not around to terrorize me I can get on with my studies. (16-year-old South Asian girl)

Although they had not been direct targets of the violence in the same way as she had, neither this young woman's 8-year-old sister nor her 12-year-old brother wanted to see their father, although the latter said his 2-year-old brother did:

> Some things have changed for us now. I get on better with my mum now. I can do a lot more things too ... My school is better now too. I can concentrate more on work and don't have to worry about home all the time. I sleep well now I know no one is going to kill me while I am sleeping or burn the house down. (8-year-old South Asian girl)

> Now we are happy. He comes here, wants to see us. We don't want to see him. Shouts at us ... J [2 years old] still likes Dad, wants him. (12-year-old South Asian boy)

Both the younger children in this family who were interviewed said their advice to children in situations of domestic violence would be to tell their mothers to move away and get help from other people. Their older sister had actually been driven to seek help outside her community, despite her fears of shame and isolation (see Chapter 6). Again, though, there is an issue here of a child too young to have known what had happened or to understand why he could not see his father. This can lead to contact being reinitiated in ways that are dangerous for other family members.

At the other extreme, contact had sometimes stopped at the children's own insistence because of further violence or aggression either towards them or their mother:

We used to [see him]. Up until around ten months ago. He started getting violent with me and my sister which he'd never done before ... He started doing that and it was getting worrying because he was quite violent so we haven't really seen him since. (16-year-old white boy, speaking about himself and his 11-year-old sister.)

I used to visit a lot, but then my mum just ran into my dad not long ago and her hit her and that. He tried to smash a bottle round her face or something. She wouldn't tell the police ... I told her to get the police. Then she did because he – all the men were trying to hold him back and he was – he beat up quite a few men. Then my mum went to the police station and they asked her to do something. I'm not sure, but I think it was so that he could get arrested, but my mum didn't want to because she was too scared. I had a big row with her about it. We're OK now, though. (12-year-old white girl, who said she now hated her father and was afraid of seeing him)

Other situations in which contact was dangerous for the child included one in which medication was withheld by a father whose faith prohibited medical intervention and another in which the man had offered drugs, including cocaine, to his 14-year-old daughter. After this latter incident, both the girl and her mother agreed that contact should cease.

In a number of cases where there was little or no face-to-face contact, there was still telephone contact or the children could have coped with that:

I wouldn't mind talking to him, right? But seeing him face to face – I'm not sure that I'm ready for that yet. I still have to get myself collected. (13-year-old African girl)

Even phone contact could cause strain, however. This girl's brother, a year younger, and her 8-year-old sister, when asked, also said they did not want to see their father, although he did occasionally see them. Though all three of them were willing to speak to him on the phone, it was clearly a form of contact initiated and controlled by him and it faced them with difficulties because of their fear of angering him and the pressure he exerted on them that the family should get back together:

Usually he starts off with 'How are you? I love you. I'm your dad' ... Usually when he calls, my mum's at work so I have to lie and tell him she's gone shopping. [The abuser did not allow his partner to work.] If he finds out that she's working, I'm not sure, but I know things would get worse. I don't know what we'd do [otherwise] because he's not giving us money. But we just keep that secret for now. Then he starts – recently he starts asking if we're getting ready to go back to Africa because he thinks we're going back [as a family]. (8-year-old African girl)

[H]e's saying that I should go back home, back to Nigeria, all the time – that I should pack my bags and go back with him. (12-year-old African boy)

AMBIVALENCE ABOUT CONTACT

While fear meant that some children were clear they did not wish to see their father, others were more ambivalent. One boy who no longer saw his father thought he would 'probably' see him again and was unsure whether, on the one hand, he minded not seeing him or, on the other, would feel unsafe if he did. The 16-year-old boy we saw above, although he and his sister had ended contact because of their father's aggressive and overbearing behaviour on their visits which the boy said he had got 'sick of', resumed it on his own initiative between the first and second research interview and seemed to have become more accepting of how his father acted towards him. His mother linked this with a resurgence of the boy's own aggression, which both touched on in talking to the researcher. Even a degree of contempt was not always incompatible with wanting to maintain direct links. This young woman was able to articulate her feelings clearly and to separate out the different elements of what she was going through:

Young Person: I like to see him now we're away from him. Mum doesn't see him though. Thank goodness … He doesn't admit it [his behaviour] or even think about it, I don't think. He thinks he's the king.
Interviewer: And what do you think?
Young Person: I think he's an arsehole most of the time – excuse me – but I do kind of love him too, because he's my father. So I don't want to lose touch with him. (15-year-old white girl)

The same strain we saw above in relation to phone contact could also happen if men used visits by their children to exert pressure:

Yes, I see him every week. It's all right now, but I get upset if he pumps me for information … It worries me if he keeps on at me about Mum. (12-year-old white girl)

Mothers also had good reason to be ambivalent about contact. One woman had been attacked in the street the last time she had bumped into her ex-partner and he had also tried to follow her daughter home in order to find her mother. Despite this, she still believed the children should see their father and found it hard to admit that the situation was too dangerous:

I just don't like to deprive him of seeing them, you know. I suppose I want everything to be friendly – friendly, you know. (White mother)

Indeed, what was remarkable in our study was the extent to which mothers were willing to maintain a variety of forms of contact between the children and their fathers, making judgements more on the basis of the children's wishes and interests than their own safety. This finding is consistent with that in earlier studies (Abrahams, 1994; Hester and Radford, 1996), thus demonstrating a pattern in women's decisions about contact that is at odds with what the courts frequently assume.

RELUCTANT CONTACT

However, some children who still had contact were unhappy that they had to see the man at all and felt resentful of legal and other intervention. The Christian denomination concerned in the following example took an ultra-conservative attitude to the sanctity of marriage and put added pressure on the woman and children to return to the violent man:

> I don't want to go, always, but I have to go because the law people said we had to … I like to stay with my mum. I don't like it at my dad's sometimes. We go to [church] meetings and that. (8-year-old white boy).

We came across only one instance where it was the child's mother who insisted on contact for reasons other than believing that children should see their father, albeit for reasons she felt were beyond her control:

> The children don't want to see him at all. S does go now and again – actually I send her once a week to collect money from him but she hates going to see him. I don't really want them to have any contact with their father, but I have no choice but to send S. (South Asian mother)

Her daughter told us:

> Yes, I see my dad. I have to go and see him on Sunday to get money from him … They don't take me out or talk to me when I go to see him [at a relative's house] … I don't like to visit him but I have to go. (12-year-old South Asian girl)

Some unavoidable meetings with the perpetrator happened when he had contact with his own children in the family and the older child was present in the house. Whether this was tolerable was entirely reliant on the behaviour of the former abuser:

> I don't like him being here but, as long as he don't tell us what to do or anything, I'm not bothered … he comes to see the two boys, really. Mostly. (13-year-old white boy, talking about his two half-brothers, aged 2 and 4)

Equally, it could be the woman who reluctantly had to be present at hand-over time, here with 8- and 10-year-old children who still wanted to see their father 'now and again':

> We go out together and then he brings us back but he doesn't talk to my mum. They don't talk now. He's got a girlfriend now. (10-year-old white girl)

ACCIDENTAL CONTACT

Some children found it hard to avoid their fathers in the course of visits to friends or other relatives.

> My friend, she lives a few doors down from him and, every time I go round there, he said I can't go round there unless I see him. So I have to sneak round there. I just came back from her house today. I can't go out in case he sees me or that. (12-year-old white girl)

> We would meet him by chance if he were visiting his brother. (14-year-old South Asian boy)

Meeting by chance at a relatives' home was more likely for the South Asian children, but not exclusively so. Mothers were not always happy about it, but in none of our interview sample had it caused real problems for the children or the women or led to a cessation of visits to other members of the family. For other children who were trying to avoid contact but still living in the same neighbourhood, there was always the chance of an accidental meeting. Children found this very frightening:

> I could bump into him. He was at [South Asian fair] – kept looking at me with his awful eyes, scaring me … I never want to see him again if I can help it … he was calling me names again. His own family told him he should not do that. (16-year-old South Asian boy)

> I saw him … [in town] when I was getting my hair cut. He was smoking. He saw me and I just turned my head the other way … My heart was beating fast. (9-year-old Asian boy)

> There was one time on the train I thought I saw him. I was shaking so much … then, a couple of weeks later, my mum thought she saw someone exactly like him get off the same stop. Mum was so scared that she phoned the police to report that in case he might come. (17-year-old mixed-race girl)

Some families had had to curtail their social lives considerably in order to avoid these inadvertent meetings with the perpetrator. One girl was afraid to go to see her father because of threats he had made about forcing her to stay with him and a fear that he would follow her home, as he had previously tried to do (see Chapter 4):

> No, I think about going to see him but I'm not sure. I'm just scared because I remember he said to someone that he's going to get me because he wants me to live with him. Someone I know – this boy, he's my best friend – his mum died. My mum wanted to go to the funeral and so did I, but my dad was [going to be] there. He was only there because he was looking to see if my mum was there, and that. They said that, when they got to the reception, he was – he kept looking to see if my mum was coming. He was watching for my mum, and that. So we can never go anywhere unless we know he's not going to be there.

She clarified the extent of her fears:

> I'm scared that he'll follow me home or if he'll just lock me in the house. I don't know what he'll do. (12-year-old white girl)

For others, the risk of seeing the abusive man was the one thing marring an otherwise improved situation: 'I don't feel completely safe because my dad could turn up at any time' (13-year-old African girl).

MEN'S UNRELIABILITY IN CONTACT

Whilst women have an undeservedly bad reputation in the courts as regards contact, the picture emerging from practice and research is more often one of women struggling against the odds, and in the face of continuing danger and distress, to continue giving their children the opportunity of contact with their father while men fail to keep to any aspect of their part of the bargain (see, for example, Simpson et al., 1995; Hester and Radford, 1996).

One woman, despite having been attacked with life-threatening intent post-separation, had reluctantly agreed to a resumption of monthly direct contact, and at Christmas and their daughters' birthdays, because one of her daughters wished to see her father who had moved to Scotland. The situation turned sour, however, when the man's new partner became abusive on the telephone and when he failed to turn up for arranged visits at Christmas and on one of the girls' birthdays. He also came to their home, although that was not part of the arrangement, reviving the woman's fears of a return to his former violence. She subsequently curtailed the visits on her solicitor's advice, and, at the time of the last interview, was applying to set up supervised contact through a court order.

COURT-ORDERED CONTACT

Although the majority of contact was organized informally, a small number of families had experienced court intervention and the mother mentioned above was contemplating this at the time of the interviews, to try and substitute a more formalized process for the rather arbitrary situation that prevailed for her children. However, as another example demonstrates, court-regulated contact did not necessarily prove more satisfactory than informal arrangements:

> Interviewer: Does your mum know you don't want to go?
> Child: Yes, and she's talking to the law people. (8-year-old white boy)

In another case where a court had been involved in determining the question of contact, the 15-year-old boy concerned was very unhappy about the way he had felt pressured by a series of court welfare officers' interviews to say he wanted contact when the opposite was the case. The repeated questioning caused him distress and, as we saw in Chapter 4, made it difficult for him to answer the questions:

> I don't think most of them believed me. I thought that saying it once would be enough. But it happened again about six times. Each time, the main question was if I wanted to see him again. (15-year-old mixed-race boy)

The woman mentioned above whose ex-partner had moved to Scotland eventually decided to apply through the courts for an order for supervised contact because he had proved so unreliable and the level of threat he had posed had been so great in the past. We only came across one child, a 12-year-old South Asian boy who had witnessed his father attempting to kill his mother, who had had direct experience of attending a contact centre. He remembered having had supervised access in the past, 'a long time ago', and having felt safe there, although he was not sure that he would still feel safe now. According to his mother, the arrangement, which had been set up as a result of her husband's application for contact, had broken down when he failed to attend for the arranged session:

> [S]o I told the workers that I wasn't going to waste my time by taking the children. The worker wrote to his [the perpetrator's] solicitor informing him of this. I am divorced from him now and have no contact with him. The children also have no contact now. (South Asian mother)

POST-SEPARATION VIOLENCE AND ABUSE

Too often, contact was an occasion for further abuse or aggression, either against the children or their mother:

> Of course, he wasn't married to my mum any more, who he always used to have a go at … he had a grudge against me and my sister. (16-year-old white boy who ceased contact for a time, as we saw above)

This post-separation violence could be life-threatening. One man, for example, used contact arrangements to insinuate himself back into the home as a visitor. On one such occasion, his daughter, K, was witness to the following incident: 'I heard my dad swearing and I saw him grab my mum's throat and push her against the door and, later, I saw him push her over the sink' (10-year-old white girl). Her mother, when we talked to her, said that what K had actually seen was K's father holding a knife to her (his ex-wife's) throat. K ran to an adult friend in a nearby house who called the police. Although this had led to a court case, completed just before the first research interview, the charge had been lowered to Actual Bodily Harm because her father had convinced K that he had only accidentally picked up the knife and persuaded her not to give evidence against him. Before the separation, K talked about having been sent upstairs or outside before the violence began but the post-separation situation had escalated. K was very young at the time and remained ambivalent in her feelings about her father, perhaps because she had directly witnessed rather little of what went on and because he had been able to play on her confused loyalties to minimize and deny the truth of his behaviour. She was one of the children who was most ambivalent about her feelings towards her father, saying she was sad about having had to leave him while being quite clear that they had had to leave for her mother's protection (as we saw above).

Men also used contact as an opportunity to continue exerting pressure on the family to behave in certain ways or to get back together (see above). Sometimes, both mothers and children had to negotiate difficult situations involving new partners and/or the latter's children, including rivalry, verbal abuse and difficulty in children getting any time alone with their father.

CONFLICTS OF INTEREST BETWEEN WOMEN AND CHILDREN

With contact, as with parenting issues more generally (as we saw in Chapter 7), there were a few instances of women's and children's interests conflicting. Usually, women considered contact important and let it go ahead despite their own fears or reluctance: 'She is never happy about us seeing Dad' (8-year-old South Asian girl). Children sensed their mothers' concerns and distress, and sometimes had to witness continuing emotional or other abuse as a result of contact. This affected their own weighing-up of a complex situation, as did the awareness of older children of what their fathers had done to their mothers:

> ... want to see more of him but my mum suffers, so it is up to her ... He is really happy to see us – forgets what he did to Mum ... Sometimes she gets upset when she thinks about all that has happened. (14-year-old South Asian boy)

So these situations, in the sample, reached a compromise resolution in which the children were able to retain at least some contact with their fathers where they wanted to.

There were no examples in the sample of mothers denying their children's wish to have contact with their fathers where this would have been practicable. Even a boy whose father had been imprisoned for his violent attacks on their mother had been taken by her to see him 'whenever I started to miss him' (14-year-old east Asian boy), until the point when they had moved to the UK. He said he thought he would like to see his father again, and expected to do so when he grew up and returned to his home country.

CONCLUSION

As we have seen, children in the study, though it often was not easy for them to do so, expressed complex and varied emotions about their fathers, including sadness, fear, hatred, love and bewilderment. In some cases, mostly with those who were older, they differentiated between love on the one hand, and respect and trust on the other. One 14-year-old South Asian boy wanted perpetrators to know that their children could love them and be frightened of them at the same time and that this was why violence set a bad example and was no way to solve problems. What had turned some children against their fathers, and left others confused and distressed as well as deeply concerned for their mothers, had been living with every kind of abuse and violence, often over a protracted period of time. The pattern of domestic violence had been played out in their own homes, by controlling and dangerous men whose behaviour had damaged their own relationships with their children as well as the children's relationships with their mothers, though in different and often quite complex ways, as we saw in this and the previous chapter. Children were largely quite clear that the abusive man was responsible for his own behaviour and spoke feelingly about this.

Contact between children in the study and their fathers or father figures varied widely. Direct contact could be frequent or occasional, regular or irregular, informally organized or based on court orders. Sometimes it worked and sometimes it had broken down in renewed abuse or broken promises. Where safety could not be assured or the children were adamant they did not want to see their father, there tended to be no contact at all or only phone calls or accidental meetings. Where the danger appeared to be past, the most successful examples included instances of the man visiting the home frequently to see the children and take them out and of regular stays for the children in their father's home. Where the man lived in a different city, there might be intermittent meetings, often backed up by more or less frequent telephone calls. Much of this contact was voluntary, flowing from the children's wishes and the mothers' concern that the children should be in touch with their fathers and the fathers not be deprived of seeing their children. However, even here, there seemed often to be differences between the way in which mothers and fathers wanted matters to be organized. Women, from the mothers' accounts, were more likely to want regular and orderly arrangements, while their ex-partners, the women said, were more likely to go for 'spontaneity' and sometimes resented any limitations on times or types of contact. This was far more difficult for children to cope with and could also feel as if the man was continuing to attempt to exert control on the rest of the family. Some men also used contact to put pressure on children to convey information or to try and persuade their mothers to reunite. In all circumstances, the history of violence and the justified fears it aroused were inescapable complications in attempts to set up contact that was physically safe for both the children and their mothers and not too distressing in other ways. Indeed, what was remarkable in our study was the extent to which mothers were willing to maintain a variety of forms of contact between the children and their fathers. This was often done despite enormous difficulties and dangers, and mainly without legal intervention or any help from outside the family, belying assumptions about women's supposed hostility to contact or about the courts' need to enforce it.

Whatever the circumstances, and whether they were or wished to be in touch with their fathers, whether they felt they still loved them or hated and feared them, the lives of all of these children had been deeply marked by having lived with violent, authoritarian men. The clearest thing to emerge was that, with very few exceptions, the children who expressed an opinion on the subject felt that it was no longer possible or desirable for them all to live together as a family.

As with much of the information from this study, the most powerful messages for policy and practice were the children's need for sympathetic friends or adults to go to, especially when the situation became acute, whether these were members of their own families or teachers or other professionals. The cogency of some of the children's thinking about the situations they had come from, and the question of ongoing contact with fathers, also emphasizes the importance of recognizing that children, even quite young children, are capable of forming their own views and assessing their own needs in ways that adults often fail to understand. It points to the need for practitioners to understand that when children voice opinions conflicting with received professional wisdom they are not necessarily acting as mouthpieces for their mothers but may well be expressing thoughts and feelings they have pondered over for a long period of time as they have worked to make sense of difficult and often very frightening situations. We have to make a reality of listening to children, especially about their safety and happiness rather than thinking we know what is best for them.

9 Listening to the Children: The Way Ahead

We conclude this book by drawing out its major themes and, in particular, the key messages for policy and practice. Listening to children who have lived with domestic violence has meant not only hearing voices that were previously silenced, including those from a range of ethnic backgrounds, but seeing familiar problems from a new, child-centred perspective. It has highlighted children's understandings and coping strategies in the face of protracted abuse of their mothers and often themselves. It has moved us on from seeing domestic violence as primarily a child protection issue to seeing it as an educational, health, welfare, civil and criminal justice issue of some complexity. Consequently we are able, below, to draw out a range of lessons that should be applied across the inter-agency spectrum. In this chapter we will first summarize what children have had to tell us in this research study about their experiences of living with abuse, supplemented at times with insights from their mothers, and will then move on to what can be learnt from children about improving services and policy responses.

WHAT CHILDREN AND THEIR MOTHERS TOLD US ABOUT LIVING WITH ABUSE

Many children live with patterns of abuse of their mothers over many years, sometimes from the moment they are born, occasionally with more than one violent man. Some children can remember a happy time before this. Others, especially the younger ones in the family, have known nothing but fear and insecurity, with mothers by this time weakened and depleted by constant emotional undermining and physical abuse. Only a minority have mothers who leave as soon as the violence starts. The abuse that children witness or overhear may be physical – anything from slaps and punches to attempted murder – emotional, sexual and/or financial and it frequently overlaps with direct child abuse against one or more of the children in the household. Once violence has a presence in the home, it does not need to be constantly repeated in order to engender fear and distress in children and their mothers. There is often a pervasive atmosphere of threats and intimidation that mean life is lived in constant dread.

Children respond as unique individuals to what they are experiencing. Mothers describe them as becoming clingy and withdrawn, or aggressive and disturbed. Problems with sleeping are commonly mentioned by children of all ages, not surprisingly given that violence often happens late at night, but also because some lie awake worrying or trying to remain vigilant in case of a recurrence.

Developmental delays are common, with many, markedly amongst South Asian children, developing speech problems. Educational progress may suffer, including through having to move schools, although some children experience school as a respite from the violence at home and do well there. There is no one syndrome. Even siblings within the same family react differently from one another to what they see and hear of identical events, depending on where they are at the time, their own personalities and resilience, the support available to them, their age and understanding, and how aware they are of what is taking place and what it means. The eldest one in the family may make themselves scarce, for example, whenever trouble is brewing. A middle one may witness much more while trying to protect other family members. The youngest may hide or even be relatively unaware of what is going on, picking up mainly on a distressing and frightening atmosphere. There can be a wide range of adverse reactions in children's health, development and well-being, not dependent on understanding all of what is happening but resulting, perhaps, from seeing their main carer hurt and unhappy yet apparently powerless to do anything about it. We found little evidence that boys 'grow up like it', more typically seeing boys who were thoughtful, sensitive and protective of their mothers and siblings. We were concerned, though, that children and their mothers who have lived with abuse are haunted by this spectre of intergenerational transmission of violent behaviour. It is such a widespread idea that young people in schools volunteered it in our survey as a possible impact on younger children living with abuse, while not seeing it as something they thought would happen to their own age group.

At the same time as living with so much unpleasantness, children talk about using a variety of coping strategies, both in the immediate situation and over the longer term. They may block out the violence and pretend it is not happening, keeping themselves busy with distracting and often noisy activities or, alternatively, keeping totally still. Some run and hide, or leave the house if old enough. Taking action such as shouting, or less often intervening physically, to try and protect siblings or their mothers or to summon help, is a common response. Over time, children vary as to whether they turn to a trusted adult to help them cope, and perhaps try and find ways to get adults to take responsibility for ending the violence, or retreat into their own private world and conceal the abuse from others. Many children and young people survive even the direst circumstances with resilience. An example was two boys who could easily have ended up in care but who, instead, moved between family members and were eventually reunited with their mother after she separated from her drug-using partner. Together they and she were later able to reflect openly and honestly on all that had happened. Those families that cope least well appear to experience frequent and protracted violence and multiple moves, with the woman being severely physically and emotionally drained over the period when all this is taking place. Perhaps earlier intervention could help women and children in these circumstances to survive more successfully.

Mothers typically have no idea that the children have seen and heard so much. They think the children are asleep when they are lying awake upstairs listening to shouting and crying downstairs, for example. Women go to great lengths to hide or disguise what is going on, often demeaning or diminishing themselves in the process by complying with unreasonable demands, burying their own personality beneath their partner's dominance, or pretending to be clumsy and accident-prone in order to explain away the injuries they sustain. Children, though, do witness and overhear a great deal. While initially confused about what is going on (except where they witness an overt physical assault) and tending to see it as mutual fighting, they develop a clearer understanding over time and come to recognize the abuser's behaviour as unreasonable, unchanging, and as his own responsibility, typically wishing that their mothers had left sooner. Women often say that the trigger for leaving is when they eventually recognize the effect the abuse is having on their children, or perceive a direct threat to them, and realize that their attempts to hold the home together for the sake of the children have been misguided.

Once children reach safety, they continue to talk with great poignancy about the losses they have sustained. With a child's sense of natural justice, and without losing sight of preferring being safe, they talk about the unfairness of having lost their home, their belongings, toys and precious collections of valued objects, their friends, their school, their pets, their contact with family and community, through no fault of their own. The man who has abused their mother has damaged them also, even where there has been no direct abuse. The overwhelming sense of multiple losses that emerges from the accounts of children who have had to move away to escape the violence is starker than adults might realize. It is also multi-layered. The losses link with coping strategies (people to talk to, familiar local havens), with personal identity (not least through family and community for South Asian children, but in other ways for all), with quality of life, with learning and developing, with richness of experience, with the ability to make choices; indeed, with the whole fabric of children's daily life. Children are resentful, angry and sad about their losses. They may also be damaged by them in ways no one has previously fully considered.

That we put children through all this as our routine response to protracted or escalating violence, expecting or demanding that women should leave instead of removing abusers, is an indictment of our present system of justice and welfare. Predicated as this is on women and children escaping violence, the problem is compounded by families having to move on from a refuge if the abuser pursues them and traces their whereabouts. Any roots the children have started to put down are torn up yet again. Children see all this as intensely unjust and they are surely right. For their sakes, if for no other reason, it is surely time to develop far more effective sanctions and interventions with perpetrators so that it is they who leave or are removed and they who pay the price for their conduct. There may be other ways, too, of networks of formal agencies and informal networks helping women with safety planning so as to throw an effective cordon around them and allow them and their children to remain safely in their own homes. (We are thinking here of any appropriate combination of injunctions, alarms, mobile phones, changed locks, vigilance by neighbours and friends, involvement of workplaces, churches, clubs and other organizations in blocking the abuser's access to the woman, interventions of a range of agencies to ensure that the woman and children remain safe, and so on.) Meanwhile, it makes a difference to children if they can be helped to retain some of their friends, belongings and pets, and to stay at the same school if they are doing well there and this is at all practicable.

Once they get to safety, many children feel instantly happier and show marked improvement in any problems they previously exhibited. For some, though, psychological, developmental or behavioural problems persist. One child we heard about (now a young adult) had been institutionalized since babyhood, as a result of severe direct abuse that had co-existed with the abuse of her mother, and will never recover. Others were still in need of professional help. Children also continue to resent the loss of their home and the fact that their mothers have no money, sometimes while the perpetrator continues to enjoy his former lifestyle. They may still feel confused, with strong and conflicting emotions that they need to make sense of. Relationships with their mothers have not always been conducive to open communication while the violence has been going on and there may be an unresolved need to talk. Those who have planned or accidental contact with the abuser may still be afraid. Overall, children have much to tell us about the aftermath of domestic violence, as well as about the phenomenon itself.

TALKING TO CHILDREN ABOUT DOMESTIC VIOLENCE

The first and overarching message from this book is, as we hoped, that children and young people are able to talk in a research context about the abuse they have witnessed and overheard, about its effect on their household and on themselves. It is not always easy for them to find the right words to express what they want to convey, but they speak with passion and conviction, and sometimes in an alarmingly matter of fact way, about distressing, even traumatising events which no rational adult would want any child to have to experience. At least a third can remember, when asked directly, specific incidents of violence to their mothers. More bring events to mind over the course of an interview. Fewer than 10 per cent of our sample said they had not really been aware at all of what was happening at home. Those who remember clearly are also more likely to have been attacked or threatened themselves or to have seen this happen to brothers or sisters.

Children told us that the violence and abuse made them feel sad and angry as well as frightened. (Children in schools also predicted sadness in others who live with violence, more readily than adults might perhaps do.) Younger children try to continue loving and respecting their fathers but, where men manifest their fatherhood only through punishment and power, their unreasonable and intolerable behaviour gradually kills children's feelings for them. It is a sad comment that only one child in our sample expressed genuine sorrow at having left her father. South Asian children do not regard respect for fathers, as for elders in general, as something that can be won or lost – it is given – but are just as vehement as others in condemning their fathers' behaviour and considering that they and their mothers are well out of it once they leave the violence.

Talking to children and their mothers casts some fresh light on why men behave in these unacceptable and criminal ways. A pattern of power and control is undoubtedly evident, as has been recognized for some years (Pence and Paymar, 1990). However, within this, a child's-eye view of abusive men's behaviour brings to the fore the petty jealousies and selfishness that loom large for children. Violent men appear to need always to be the centre of attention. Though children's and mothers' accounts do also contain evidence of sexual jealousy, which perhaps adults are more aware of, it is everyday tantrums over games, hobbies or birthday presents that children remember, together with the cruelty and brutality with which abusive men vent their rages at such times, regardless of who else is present, be they adult or child.

HEADLINE MESSAGES

The headline message from what children tell us they need is, first, to be safe and, second, to have someone to talk to. This was conveyed clearly and consistently by the qualitative sample, on the basis of having lived with danger and fear, often for long periods of time, and of having encountered communication blocks in many different directions. Things were uniformly happier when children and their mothers were free of the violence and when friends, family or professionals had helped the children to open up and talk about what had happened. We will explore in more detail below who had been able to do this.

There is a wider lesson here, too, about children. Not only were they perfectly well able to talk to us in an interview situation, but they generally want far more opportunities to talk to other people about what is going on at home. They also want others to discuss things with them, giving them information and seeking their opinions. This applies to their mothers and also to helping agencies. Many are not told what is happening or given any clear explanation as to why they have to leave home. Some find another adult to talk to (a family friend or close relative, the latter especially amongst South Asian children). Other children – friends, peers, siblings – play an important role, too. Only a very few place their trust in a professional such as a teacher, social worker or counsellor. A small but worrying group talk to no one. Once they get into a refuge, as half the sample had done, the workers there, and especially the children's workers, get a great vote of thanks from children for the way they enable them to open up and talk about the past, present and future. Mothers remain most important to their children, however, and the minority of women who pursue their own interests (notably another abusive relationship) to the detriment of their children consequently pose particular dilemmas for practitioners in refuges and elsewhere who are trying to help.

INFORMAL HELP: AN UNDERVALUED RESOURCE

In the literature on domestic violence, informal responses (Kelly, 1996) generally play second fiddle to the statutory services. Yet, in the lives of children, as of women survivors, they are often paramount.

RELATIONSHIPS WITH MOTHERS

Mothers are cited more frequently by children who have lived with domestic violence as their most important source of help than anyone else in their lives. It would only be necessary to count the number of times the word 'mother' has already been used in this chapter to know that this is the case. Their relationship with their mother is most children's major support in coping and it is vitally important that policy and practice should recognize this and not cut across this one element of continuity and hope:

> My mum has helped me the most. No one else really talked about it very much apart from my mum. I can't really think of anyone else who has really helped me apart from my mum. All the help was from my mum, she explained everything. (13-year-old South Asian boy)

Women may need positive reinforcement in this role which, at present, they rarely receive. They have been encouraged by their abusers to see themselves as having failed as mothers. This is all too easy to succumb to, given not only a context in which being a 'good mother' is socially constructed as impossible to achieve for any woman who is not superhuman but also one in which the constant intimidation and violence force all women to fall below their own standards of parenting. They see their children dragged into the abuse in various ways and turned against them, they may smack in order to pre-empt worse punishment from the violent man, the children may even be removed from them by the perpetrator. Many women, however loving and however good their care has been in the past, are simply too injured, exhausted and dazed to give their children the attention they need. Some become compliant to the man's demands and demean themselves in order to try and reduce the amount of violence their children have to see. Even so, it is not uncommon for children to blame their mothers for not leaving sooner, even when they can appreciate that they stayed for the children's sake. Children tend to regard staying put as faulty logic because they would prefer to be out of the violence.

One major finding from the research was that a conspiracy of silence often builds up as mothers try and shield children from further knowledge of the abuse, not realizing how much they are already aware of. Children, meanwhile, sensing that their mothers do not want them to know or to talk about the violence, keep quiet and do not ask their mothers for explanations, even after they are safe. Ironically, each is trying to protect the other. Where communication does open up between mothers and their children, children are able to make far more sense of the situation, to move on emotionally and, also, to support their mothers in carrying forward their plans for a new life together. Helping agencies could encourage this openness to develop by assisting women and children to start talking to one another, confronting misconceptions, and showing that honest discussion is healthier than continued secrecy and concealment.

THE ROLE OF SIBLINGS

Brothers and sisters offer one another reassurance and support (Mullender, 1999):

> You stick together. We did ... We're a team! We help each other. (9-year-old white boy with a younger brother and sister)

They may cuddle together while an assault is taking place, or attempt to distract each other with computer games or music. Older ones may try to protect younger siblings, or those with learning disabilities, from knowing too much of what is happening and, overall, children value the fact that there is someone there, even if they do not talk directly about the violence in any detail. Almost half report not discussing it at the time, although they may do so much more later. This may perhaps link with the fact that mothers and children are often not as open as they might be. Perhaps this atmosphere of secrecy carries over to the children themselves. Some children are more likely to go somewhere else in the house and distract themselves. Abusive men may cut across this support network by scapegoating a particular child or by having a favourite. Where the latter is the case, the child who is not being abused or who is being protected from exposure to abuse may have less awareness of what is going on and be a less good ally, therefore, to the other siblings.

Adults tend to assume that children obtain all their support from their relationships with adults and completely underestimate the role of child–child links. They may separate siblings or allow them to lose touch with one another, or fail to understand the closeness that can develop through sharing adverse and frightening experiences. Parents and others miss a great deal of what goes on between siblings at such times. Children can be there for one another when no adult is available to them – even if it means climbing out of the window to do so. This is a strength that can be built on by mothers and by those who work with children. Fostering close links between siblings means that adults do not have to provide all the succour and support at a time when their emotional resources may be very stretched.

THE ROLE OF FRIENDS

Whether or not children can talk to the adults in their lives, but more poignantly when they cannot, they talk to trusted friends. Older girls, in particular, do this and it might make life easier for boys if they could learn to do it more. The most likely person a child will tell about the violence, as opposed to those who know anyway, is a friend. At the same time, children choose very carefully whom they tell because they fear their confidentiality may be breached and that they may be stigmatized if everybody gets to know. Finding someone trustworthy, for example a friend who has had a similar experience and so will truly understand, is special. Perhaps an ability to understand better the role of friends in children's lives might make us more sensitive to the importance of the loss of such a friendship when the behaviour of the abusive man and/or the need to flee to a refuge breaks it up. (Indeed, friendship generally is undervalued in research and practice; see Pahl, 2001.) Children put a lot of attention into making and keeping their friends and are upset when the ties are broken by time, distance or circumstance. Where a family has to move in secrecy in order to be safe, even the ubiquitous mobile phones and text-messaging may not be usable to keep children in touch with one another, added to which money is often lacking for necessities, let alone gadgets, when a woman has to leave her home and everything behind.

Teenage respondents to the schools survey, especially girls, saw friends as the most likely confidants for young people experiencing violence at home or in a dating relationship. The survey, as well as what children told us in interview, reveals that many children know there is violence in the lives of their friends, either between parents or in teenage dating relationships, even when they do not live with it themselves. This provides added support to the argument for educating children more about domestic violence and what they can do about it, in school and youth settings, which we will consider below.

Classes in school about non-violent relationships and conflict resolution, where they are offered (notably in the USA and Canada), often stress peer support and may be linked with peer counselling schemes. As we noted with siblings, above, there is a tendency in professional thinking to regard child-to-adult relationships as the only important ones, particularly when the child needs help. This is very far from the case. Children's links with their friends and peers (Horrocks and Milner, 1999) can be crucially important to them. Children may be able to voice things to one another that adults would never be willing to hear (or not without censure). In refuges, children value their contact with their peers, again because they have undergone a similar experience and so can understand what it is like. Those refuges that foster this kind of interaction and openness, as opposed to allowing conflict and jealousy to build up, are particularly valued. Refuge childworkers can facilitate a rich and helpful interchange between children but children also make it happen themselves, as a natural part of living in a collective environment, unless the atmosphere restricts them. Workers need to be aware that some children who have had experiences that most others do not share, such as direct sexual abuse, will need additional support if they are not to feel even more 'different' than before in a context where everyone else now seems to have found a shared understanding. Teenagers, too, can be thin on the ground in refuges and may need other ways to build networks, for example, through youthwork or other services.

THE ROLE OF FAMILY MEMBERS
AND OTHER ADULTS IN THE COMMUNITY

Not surprisingly, South Asian children talk the most about the role of other family members in their lives. They have a traditional expectation of practical help from their father's family and comment on it when this is not forthcoming. Aunts, uncles and cousins are all named as sources of support.

> My mum's brother ... would sometimes talk to me and try to explain to me what was happening ... He would tell me not to worry and that everything will be all right ... it did help a little bit. It helped to hear that everything will be all right again. (13-year-old South Asian boy)

Amongst children more generally, too, there are mentions of grandparents, in particular, as people who either provide support or are seen in retrospect as people who could have done so if asked:

> When I am with *Nani* [maternal grandmother] I can talk to her about how I feel, what is happening. (16-year-old Asian girl).

> Thinking about it, I could have told Grandma more. But I didn't do it then. I thought he might bully her [mother] even worse if I said anything. (11-year-old white boy)

Where the perpetrator is not the child's father, their own father may be an important source of help, including somewhere safe to stay for a time. Adult friends of the family occasionally play a similar role where an abused woman has been able to retain a supportive network, though less so in South Asian communities where it is important to keep matters within the family in order to prevent gossip and preserve family honour and pride. Two children were particularly grateful to friends of their mothers who had helped foster the courage to leave.

Children do not always expect any direct intervention from the relative or other adult concerned. What they value may be a respite – a sanctuary from the violence and from the atmosphere at home. They may stay over for a night or a few days, or they may just pop in for a chat. Family members and friends who know something of what is going on can help by giving the child permission to talk, reassuring them that they are no less lovable as a result of what is happening at home, and involving them in any decisions about what to do. Adults, on the other hand, who side with the abuser or who do not believe what children tell them about their home lives, let children down very badly.

THE VOLUNTARY SECTOR: GETTING IT RIGHT FOR CHILDREN

MESSAGES FOR REFUGES, INCLUDING CHILDWORKERS, AND FOR OTHER SPECIALIST PROJECTS

The first and most powerful message here is 'keep up the good work'. While refuges are far from perfect, and children have their share of criticisms to make, specialist staff in refuges and community domestic violence projects come a close second to mothers and siblings as people who children living with domestic violence say have given them most help. This is because children's workers, in particular, pay specific attention to children's own perspectives and needs. Children can talk to the workers and they find them supportive. It matters a great deal to children that they can tell their story at their own pace and voice their fears. They appreciate being believed, valued and listened to by someone with an understanding of domestic violence and the dynamics involved. They gain from being able to talk about their feelings, what they have been through, and how to make sense of it:

> The child care worker – she was great. If I was upset, she's ask why and make it OK. She'd talk about it with me. The childworker was the best. (12-year-old white girl)

Being in a safe place is also an important part of the equation because it helps to break out of the trap of secrecy and fear that has controlled everything up to this point. Children like being able to relax and enjoy playing and going on outings – being taken out of themselves instead of thinking constantly about the violence. They notice whether staffing levels in refuges mean that there is someone available for them whom they can trust when they want to talk. They want to see their mothers being given similar support and an opportunity to talk.

Children's criticisms of refuges were typically made where the above had not been possible – where staff had not talked to them, had spent time with the women to the exclusion of the children or had not been consistently available when promised, or where there was nothing for children to do. Since there are more children than women in refuges, it is right that most refuges have now recognized that children have needs in their own right and, indeed, overall, refuge childworkers constitute the major national resource for specialist work with children who have lived with domestic violence. Nevertheless, work with children is not included within the Supporting People resourcing strategy (Department of the Environment, Transport and the Regions et al., 1998). Where funding shortages or lack of awareness restrict play opportunities, direct work or aftercare, children are very alert to this – especially where they have been through more than one refuge and have a point of comparison. One mother insightfully pointed out that seeing her children unhappy in a refuge might be enough to make a woman go back to her abuser, so providing sensitive help to children, separately from their mothers, might have an impact beyond meeting their immediate needs. Another stressed that refuges need to ensure they empower residents, with a minimum of rules and regulations and a maximum of involvement in determining these, if women are to come out from under their partners' control and rebuild their lives with their children. Women who have developed alcohol or drug problems, or eating disorders, perhaps as a result of the abuse or exacerbated by it, will find these especially difficult to control while making the break for freedom and are likely to need specialist services either instead of, or in addition to, what an ordinary refuge can offer.

Another important message for refuges is to continue being vigilant about racism. A constantly changing mix of women and children is bound to include some with attitudes that need to be challenged and there is a need for continual input on inclusion to ensure that they learn to co-exist with others without harming other residents – women and children. At the same time, it is clear from this research that specialist refuges for different minority ethnic groups need continuing support since they provide a service which some South Asian women and children simply find more appropriate to their needs. Currently, funding for such provision appears particularly vulnerable.

MESSAGES FOR THOSE UNDERTAKING SAFETY PLANNING WITH CHILDREN

Virtually all abused women remember at least one of their children doing something courageous and supportive in naming and condemning the abuse while it was actually happening. Shouting at the abuser, to distract his attention and tell him to stop, appears to be particularly common, though children themselves may not count this as intervening. Older children, those of twelve and above, are more likely to do something physically to stop the abuse. Half overall (of all ages) say they have done this. Current professional practice, notably in safety planning with children, regards this as dangerous and teaches children to keep themselves and their siblings safe instead, summoning the police or other help if possible without endangering themselves. Obviously, we would not advocate children placing themselves in danger. However, our study is the first to analyse children's decision-making processes about their interventions. Children are clearly aware of the threat to their mothers and may sense when this is becoming potentially lethal. They learn over time what strategies they can use that may be effective in standing up to the abuser and in stopping or lessening an assault, as well as times when this would be hopeless. A small number of teenage boys try physically to fight the abuser, to protect their mother, if they think they are strong enough to make any impact.

Like adults, children and young people make rapid and complex decisions about an incident in context; it is patronizing and an oversimplification to assume that they react unthinkingly. Advice adults may give needs to allow for and build on this. If we merely instruct children not to do what they judge is right, or to hide where they cannot see whether their mother might even be being killed, we may cause them more distress. In fact, safety planning does typically build on an awareness of children as social actors in a situation of danger who want to do something to help. It encourages them to follow a plan designed to keep themselves and younger siblings safe, and to summon help where possible. It is not a 'do nothing' approach but it could be reframed in a less negative way, building not just on children's knowledge of their own situation but also on their desire to help, rather than being presented as adults knowing best, abstracted from the real contexts in which children have to construct their own survival strategies.

MESSAGES FOR COUNSELLING SERVICES

More women and children recognize the need for counselling services than actually have access to them. Children who mentioned it understand counselling as meaning someone who can talk to them and understand how they feel without being judgemental, and who can make them feel good about themselves and that the violence was not their fault. The few children who access it find counselling helpful:

> I talked to her about everything. That made me feel better. (12-year-old white girl)

> The counselling helped. I've talked about it [the domestic violence] a lot. Now I just want to get on with my life. (15-year-old white girl)

The young woman just quoted said her mother had also received considerable counselling help. Another woman felt that in order to be non-judgemental (one of the bedrocks of counselling) those offering help needed a good understanding of domestic violence that was best acquired by having been through it themselves:

> I think [they] must be like me – must have been through it ... to know that you're going to be talking to someone who's going to reassure you that it wasn't your fault and to

understand because, well, personally, I know, all throughout it, you do blame yourself, and I still do now. That's why I'm really for counselling because you doubt yourself. (White mother)

In the UK, unlike the USA, it is regarded as exceptional to seek therapeutic or other professional help with one's problems so any suggestion that this might be needed can make a young person feel negatively labelled:

> I thought they would think I was mad. I thought, 'I'm not crazy, I know what I'm doing.' But then, later on, I felt that it was good, actually talking to someone. I got a lot off my chest. Originally, I thought … 'I can deal with his myself' … [but] I talked to her about what was going on. It sort of made me feel better. Every time I left, I felt good. She's a really good listener and she gives advice and she does help – like, contact people. (13-year-old African girl)

This young woman's counsellor was accessed through a community domestic violence service and had not only been able to reassure her, but also to give practical help such as getting her involved in activities that drew on her artistic skills. A 9-year-old white girl, similarly receiving help through a specialist domestic violence aftercare service, had been asked to keep a feelings diary and was having one-to-one sessions that had succeeded in bringing her nightmares to an end. She was also attending a group for children who had lived with abuse, with a parallel group for mothers, that was helping her understand and come to terms with what had happened using a range of techniques such as drawing and discussion (see Mullender, 1994a; Loosley et al., 1997). Another, a 12-year-old white girl, had seen a school counsellor. A 14-year-old east Asian boy was aware that he needed counselling and was upset that an attempt to refer him for help had been diverted into a child protection referral to social services (see Chapter 6). These appeared to be the only young people who had been even potentially linked with such services.

Children do not always wait for adults to give them the help they need but may, for example, telephone a helpline:

> I phoned ChildLine twice, just to talk to them really. It's just nice to have someone you don't know who you can put all your bits and pieces on to and, even if they don't take it in, as long as they are listening. It's easier to talk to a stranger sometimes because you can let all your real feelings out. You don't have to worry about what they may think of you. You don't have to be afraid of saying something. (16-year-old white boy)

He had seen the poster in the refuge and had found the number easy to memorize. It had felt better, he said, to get things off his chest but, of course, it had not solved the underlying problem of the abuse of his mother. The other young people mentioned above had been referred for help after leaving the violence.

Only one young person, a 12-year-old white girl, made reference to the need for services to help men change their behaviour.

THE STATUTORY SECTOR: COULD DO BETTER

It will be noticed in this chapter, and throughout this book, that more has been said about informal support from family and friends, and about the role of the specialist voluntary sector, than about the statutory agencies that often appear to place themselves at the centre of interagency responses to domestic violence. In the lives of children whose mothers are abused, statutory professionals play a very small part and typically, it would seem, not a very helpful one. Children may not understand or remember which agency has tried to help them, they may well not trust the individual practitioner, and they may fear an unwanted consequence, such as being forced to see their father again. Those who are working to help children need to understand far more about the role of friends, family and the local community in their lives and about which other children, as well as which adults, are significant in children's help-seeking endeavours. Nevertheless, this does not exempt them from making improvements to their own services, along the lines that children say would help.

MESSAGES FOR SCHOOLS

Children who live with domestic violence may move schools several times. They need teachers and senior staff with an awareness of domestic violence who will be sensitive to what they are going through while preserving confidentiality. Information should only be shared on a 'need to know' basis. A 12-year-old white girl was relieved that only her form tutor and deputy head-teacher had known when she was in a refuge and they were 'nice about it'. Not all children whose mothers are being abused exhibit problems in their schoolwork – some had never had a problem, one used to love school as an escape from the violence at home, and at least two were doing better in new schools they had moved to. For those who do, however, or whose other psychological, behavioural or developmental problems (such as speech and language difficulties) impinge there, sensitive understanding is again vital. Referral to mainstream (i.e. other than specialist domestic violence) provision, such as the schools psychological service, does not necessarily lead to anyone asking what is wrong at home. Both teachers and the back-up services they rely on need a greater awareness of domestic violence so that they can confidentially find out what is wrong at home and take appropriate steps.

Disruption of schooling can be a real problem, even for able pupils. One mixed-race girl found home tuition useful until her family had to move yet again. At the time of the interview, she was again settled into a new school and was anxiously trying to catch up with her 'A' level work. Her 15-year-old brother said he had been to about seven different schools. He had also been using a home education course and was attending an extra tuition centre. And when children are at school, they may find that lack of sleep, headaches (mentioned by at least four children) and poor concentration impede their ability to study. One or two mentioned overcoming shyness as an issue for them at school, especially when they had moved and had to make new friends.

Teachers are not often trusted with revelations of what is happening by children who are themselves living with violence and even children in the schools survey, who were asked to hypothesize about sources of help, were more likely to mention the police. Given the amount of their waking time that children spend with their teachers, these are sad findings and suggest that teachers could do far more to offer a listening ear and emotional support to the children and young people in their charge. This is not the same as becoming social workers, which teachers understandably fear in an already over-stretched working life and without the necessary training. Rather, it means being an effective channel for children to gain access to welfare services outside of school, by opening up an early opportunity for them to confide that something is wrong. Children would like to be able to go to their teachers as a route to getting help for themselves and their mothers. One or two had done so: for example, a 16-year-old Asian girl said she had had to talk to teachers when things became serious at home, despite constraints on taking such matters outside the family, because no one there was doing anything about it. A 16-year-old white boy had found a teacher 'quite helpful', in at least giving him some attention. There had also been some bad experiences of lack of sympathy or trust, however:

> The teacher wouldn't have believed me anyway even if I tried to tell her. The teacher didn't like me and if I had told her she would probably have said that I made it all up. The teacher was always nasty to me so I wouldn't tell her. (8-year-old Asian girl)

> I had headaches all the time. At school, the teachers just thought I was complaining all the time but I wasn't. I really did have the headaches. (12-year-old mixed-race girl)

Demonstrating to children that you are listening and that you believe what they are telling you is an important starting-point for children. The staff concerned also need to know what to ask and how to ask it (Children's Subcommittee of the London Coordinating Committee to End Woman Abuse, London, Ontario, 1994), so as to help children confide what they are longing to be able to tell someone. Then teachers need to know how to make links with outside services through the necessary procedures.

Arguably, the strongest message of the whole study is one for schools and for those who make educational policy. The quantitative phase of the research, the survey of 8- to 16-year-olds in schools, found widespread lack of knowledge about domestic violence, together with worryingly high levels of tolerance of abuse. As many as a third of teenage boys and a fifth of teenage girls agree with a statement that some women deserve to be hit and, while girls appear to grow in their appreciation of the dangers and complexities as they get older, boys' attitudes seem to harden throughout secondary school. This leads us to conclude that educational work in school and youth settings needs to start early – at least from the age of 11 and preferably in primary school – if it is to influence the attitudes of a rising generation of young people. Nor are boys very good at naming a perpetrator as responsible for his own behaviour, even in a starkly over-simplified scenario. Furthermore, boys under-rate the likelihood of violence in a range of scenarios, even though three-quarters of them consider it possible or likely that they might themselves use violence if a partner had sex with another man. Once again, we can realistically look only to preventative work in schools to teach boys that this is illegal, unacceptable and outmoded and that it is possible to learn alternatives based on mutual respect and self-control. Whilst it is good that girls already have a better understanding than boys of the risks of violence, it is also saddening that they emerge as considering sexual jealousy as almost inevitably related to violence. In different ways, then, both boys and girls regard abuse in relationships as a fact of life and far too many of them appear willing to tolerate it.

The good news is that a large majority of pupils of secondary age realize that they do not know enough and would welcome lessons in school to learn more about what domestic violence is, why it happens, and what to do if it should occur. Older children in particular also want to know how to stop it. We know from other work in the field (Reid-Howie Associates, 1996) that they would prefer discussion-based classes in which they can explore the issues involved although, of course, these could usefully be underpinned with basic information to rectify misconceptions we uncovered, such as the assumption, common amongst older boys, that women do not get hit during pregnancy and that women can easily leave a violent partner. Our findings show that anti-violence work needs to be gendered, not diluted or subsumed under more general anti-bullying/conflict resolution work as has happened with some North American programmes (Hague et al., 2001). Very few boys or girls in the schools survey showed an awareness of problematic attitudes towards women or a desire to control a partner as underlying men's violence in relationships, though girls were more likely than boys to see discussion as a potential solution to an abusive situation between teenagers. Again, it would be highly valuable to see these issues explored in schools.

Further support for our call for mainstream educational work on domestic violence comes from the survey's revelation that almost a third of children know someone who has experienced domestic violence, the more so as they get older, and from the interview finding that children are most likely to tell a friend when violence is happening in their household. This is heavy stuff for a child to have in their life and it is arguably unfair to leave young people carrying this burden without some attempt in school to give them a greater understanding of what domestic violence is and to equip them to know what can be done about it. At present, preventative work in schools is localized and patchy. Little of it has been evaluated, although interest is growing in establishing 'what works' (Parsons, forthcoming). Coming full circle between the qualitative and quantitative aspects of our research, we would suggest that the experts on what children need to understand about domestic violence include other children who have lived with it. They could usefully be asked to work (ethically and sensitively, of course) with those who design manuals and packs of materials for use in schools to ensure that these are accurate, useful and designed in child-centred ways.

MESSAGES FOR THE POLICE AND THE CIVIL AND CRIMINAL JUSTICE SYSTEM

Children who live with domestic violence are very aware of the police and have often summoned them to the house or asked an adult to do so. They are not slow to criticize, however. Their chief complaints are that, though the police may be quick to arrive, their intervention is rarely effective, because the man is not removed or is soon allowed to return, and that the police do not talk to them, even when the children are present at the incident or at the police station or even when it is a child who has dialled 999. Children get frightened if they do not know what is happening. They know the police have powers to take them or their mother away and they may need considerable reassurance, as well as someone to sit with them and ensure that they are all right. This is all pretty basic stuff but it appears not to be happening in all cases. Police officers who deal with domestic violence need to take on board that children are often present and that this means they need skills in listening and talking to children.

Children consider it intensely unfair when their lives are disrupted and made miserable by having to move around from refuge to refuge and then live in poverty (for many) while the perpetrator appears to get away with his behaviour and to continue with his former life. Might there not be wisdom here? We need far more progress in making men accountable for their criminal actions in abusing their partners and for the impact this has on the children. This has implications at every stage of the criminal justice process, from arrest, through charging and successful prosecution, to sentencing. Perhaps keeping the effect on children in mind could spur professionals on to redoubled efforts at all these stages and end any collusion with perpetrators that may still persist. If children can tell us that these men have not learnt their lesson over many years but, rather, have got worse, then maybe we will understand that we need tougher responses and sanctions in the courts. The Crown Prosecution Service announcement that it will be creating a national network of co-ordinators to facilitate domestic violence prosecutions and using supporting evidence to pursue cases where charges are dropped is to be welcomed in this regard.

We also need to make greater use of options that avoid uprooting women and children, such as removing the man from the scene. One child had seen his family tracked down by the perpetrator who now had an injunction against him and was awaiting a criminal case after breaking in and destroying property. A 'court order saying he couldn't come within one hundred yards of my mum', a distance that was later substantially extended, resulted in this boy being the only one to describe the police as 'very helpful'. His mother used the existence of this injunction with power of arrest to reassure both her teenaged sons that they were now safe. Two children with points of comparison overseas considered the English legal system to give greater protection than that in other parts of the world where they had lived.

Women, too, have criticisms of the police. It can be very hard to explain that you have a greater fear of being killed if you leave than if you stay in the violence. While women see some signs of increased awareness in policing practices, there also continues to be examples of officers who blame women for dropping charges against their abusers or whose intervention is sufficient to place the woman in danger of being blamed by the abuser for calling in the police, but not enough to prevent her being re-abused.

MESSAGES FOR THE FAMILY COURT
AND THE LEGAL PROFESSION

The selfishness and self-centredness of abusers, as well as the fear they engender, recur as themes running through children's and women's accounts of contact. Some of those children who do retain contact experience their fathers pumping them for information or pressuring them into trying to effect a reconciliation between their parents. One man arguably perverted the course of justice by persuading his daughter not to give evidence against him after she witnessed a life-threatening attack on her mother. Another snatched his young daughter in the street. Even where contact is less dangerous or problematic, women say that men typically want it to suit their own convenience or whims, rather than fitting in with children's needs or routines. Some men fight for contact, only to let the children down and not turn up at appointed times, whether these are regulated by the court or agreed informally between the estranged couple. Neither contact orders nor contact centres (Harrison et al., forthcoming) are any guarantee against such eventualities.

Whilst it is recognized that women and children sometimes have conflicting interests – for example, not all children are as scared of the abusive man as their mothers are, perhaps being unaware of the full scale of what has gone on at home – women often go to great lengths to persist with contact so that their children can see their fathers. We found no evidence of women's hostility to contact, or of their pursuing agendas against ex-partners that impeded contact, or of contact needing to be enforced in the face of women's objections or intransigence. Rather, we can offer stark examples where women have continued with, or reinstated, direct contact at considerable danger to themselves and it tends only to be when this threatens their children's safety or well-being that they call a halt or go back to court. Men's pro-fatherhood lobbying groups may have an apparently sympathetic cause to pursue, and may win sympathy from a largely male judiciary and legislature, but they cast a veil over much of what abusive fathers and abused mothers actually do in relation to contact. Studies such as ours can provide a crucial insight into the dangers for women and children if society fails to place safety at the centre of contact decisions.

While most separated families manage contact without legal intervention, there are important lessons in this study for the courts and for all those practitioners associated with them, including the staff of CAFCASS (the Children and Family Court Advisory and Support Service). It is essential that any history of domestic violence be taken into account when deciding residence and contact issues and that current risks to both the woman and the children be assessed. Not only is their mother typically their main carer but any harm threatened to her is likely to be highly traumatic for children also. A child was present when one woman in our small sample was threatened with a knife during a sustained two-hour attack on a contact visit, for example. There also needs to be the opportunity for rapid reaction if danger becomes evident at a later stage. Men may revert to previous patterns of behaviour or may convince professionals that they have reformed when this is far from the case. Indirect forms of contact, such as letters and phone calls, may provide a safe alternative to visits and meetings, and may be substituted for direct contact, but even these can be exploited by abusive men and should ideally be monitored in contested cases. Certainly, they may need to be controlled by the woman and the children, for example by their initiating all the calls and withholding their own number so that their whereabouts cannot be traced, or by refusing to engage in some topics of conversation such as who the woman is seeing or whether she can be persuaded to return.

The issue of contact in the context of domestic violence is currently under debate. While Northern Ireland has seen legislative change, England and Wales has, to date, had guidance to the courts as an alternative. Whether this will be a sufficiently strong measure remains to be seen. Some are still calling for the law to contain a rebuttable presumption against contact unless it can be guaranteed to be safe for both the woman and the children (Saunders, 2001). This whole matter is certainly urgent and needs to be kept under review. By giving children a voice in research, we have learnt that some children are terrified of ever seeing their fathers again and that they only feel well and happy when they know that this cannot happen. Others are reluctant or ambivalent and need adults to listen to their fears and concerns. Some, for example, still have feelings for their father but need to know that they will be safe if they have direct contact with him. Children resent pressure from courts, creeds and adults in general to make them have contact when they do not want it and they object to not being believed when they have reached a decision, for example about not having contact, on the basis of years of experience of living with violence and very careful reflection as to how they feel and what they can cope with. Today's young people are educated to think for themselves and, for those who live with domestic violence, life is a stern but effective teacher.

For all that it may be a contemporary social problem that men in general do not feature more in their children's lives, children who have lived with every form of violence and abuse are not the ones who should be made the subject of a social experiment in reinforcing fatherhood. Men need to change first. Attempts in work with perpetrators of domestic violence, itself still patchy and of unproven efficacy, to teach them how to be good parents need to make considerably more progress before contact ceases to be a highly dangerous test-bed for children and their mothers. It is a long step from seeing fathering as being about discipline and control, as violent men tend to do, to seeing it as focusing on affection and sharing, with loving boundaries gently imposed and with age-appropriate responses to children's enthusiasms and energies. The law says that contact must be in the interests of children's welfare but practice falls short of this aim.

MESSAGES FOR SOCIAL SERVICES

Few children who live with domestic violence obtain any help from social workers. Where social services does become involved with a family, this tends to be as a result of child protection concerns which may be taken out of context in ways that fail to provide any help or support to the non-abusing carer – herself often in fear of her life.

Mothers who are abused for protracted periods of time typically feel that they have failed as mothers and are encouraged in this view by their abusers who commonly threaten to report them to social services. This does not necessarily give an accurate reflection of the quality of care the woman gave before the violence started or of the type of parent she would be if she could be helped to feel safe as the head of a lone parent family. Assessments need to look beyond current circumstances and to be conducted by professionals with a good understanding of the dynamics of abuse. Training is key to this. Anti-racist and anti-oppressive awareness are also essential, together with adequate interpretation services and networking with specialist minority ethnic services, if culturally inappropriate responses and wrong conclusions about levels of danger and safety are to be avoided.

It is a potentially fatal error to assume that children will always be safer if their mothers leave the abuser. Post-separation violence can be more lethal than anything that went before, posing grave risks both to women and children. Intervention needs to take the whole family into account and multi-agency working designed to hold the perpetrator to account while helping the woman and children to be safe may be most effective overall. Nor is it fair, or without cost, always to expect women and children to leave their home. There is already provision[1], in an amendment to the Children Act 1989, to remove the abuser in conjunction with an emergency protection order or interim care order that could be used far more widely than is currently the case.

Children value firm action that stops the violence. They also typically rely on their mothers as their main source of help and emotional support. Interventions that combine awareness of these two key aspects of an abusive situation, by helping children and their mothers to be safe together, should be aimed for whenever possible. There are a small number of women who pursue their own interests to the detriment of their children's safety or well-being but they are in the minority. Whilst alert to this possibility, practice should not be generalized from an assumption that abused women are typically making simplistic choices between their partners and their children.

Above all, children want to feel safe and to have someone to talk to. Categorizing children who live with domestic violence as children in need under the Children Act 1989, and recognizing that a proportion of them have disabilities as a result of the abuse, can release funding for one-to-one and groupwork services that give children the chance to talk about what has happened and to feel better about themselves and their lives. One white woman described the battles she had had to convince social workers that children who had lived with domestic violence have support needs as great, or greater, than their mother's. She had attended a case conference at which she felt blamed for having stayed in the situation but was able to throw back at the professionals all the times when they had failed to ask her the right questions or to give her any effective help. It is ironic that this awareness was not the other way round. A narrow child protection response on its own will not meet children's needs. It also obscures the fact that abused women and their children may ask for help from, or come to the attention of, any area of social services provision (Mullender, 1996). We wonder whether, for example, those caring for the young woman who had been institutionalized as a result of abuse had ever really asked about the cause of her injuries. Were the family to have received adequate help at that early stage, it might have prevented many more years of violence towards the girl's mother and distress for her younger sister.

MESSAGES FOR HOUSING AND HOMELESSNESS SERVICES

Housing and homelessness services appear to suffer both from a lack of understanding and a lack of resources. Mothers criticize housing departments that have caused them inordinate amounts of running between departments and excessively long stays in refuge accommodation, waiting to be rehoused. Even respect and understanding are sometimes missing. One woman said she had been made to feel 'like the dirt on their feet' by council housing officials who had shown no understanding whatsoever of how daunting it had been to leave her marriage with her two children.

One child remembered having been moved around when the perpetrator had traced the family's whereabouts. The last time they had ended up in a refuge because their housing offer had been completely unacceptable on health grounds:

'[T]hey offered us a new place but it was on the fifth floor and I'm scared of heights and my mum's got asthma' (10-year-old black British girl).

The complexities of living with domestic violence require training and experience to understand, as well as particular treatment in law and policy, because women who are escaping abuse may not be able to conform to neat expectations. One mixed-race family had moved at least ten times, according to the teenage children, for example, and needed to live near a hospital because one of their brothers had a condition that sometimes went into crisis. Another family had had to be rehoused a second time when the perpetrator and his adult son had come to the house, broken the door down and destroyed all the furniture. There were accounts of living here, there and everywhere – for example, staying with friends, family and in rented rooms – before ending up in a refuge and then applying for rehousing.

To children, the need is perfectly straightforward:

Interviewer: What did you need?
Young Person: Another house. (12-year-old Asian boy)

... a good home, a nice clean home. (8-year-old Asian girl)

OTHER AGENCIES

In a small sample that was not recruited through statutory agencies and where children often could not remember which professionals they had encountered, there were only isolated examples of policy and practice in other settings, such as one child who had seen a child psychologist. Taking these together, we can say that children are more impressed with professionals who are aware of domestic violence as an issue and who attempt to do something constructive about it. They are dismissive, or actively negative, about those who get involved in their lives because of health, educational or developmental problems but who do not even get as far as finding out what is actually wrong in their home life. If they sense that practitioners do not understand about domestic violence, then they do not fully confide in them. They cannot understand if others, who know what is happening, do not talk to them about it. The warmest praise was reserved for the isolated examples of professionals, such as a splendid teacher, who took the child's fears seriously and kept the child informed and appropriately involved while taking effective action.

As with other services, considered above, anti-racist awareness is also crucial. Bad practice includes a readiness to jump to conclusions that minority ethnic children have learning difficulties when they temporarily lose an earlier fluency in English.

MESSAGES FOR ALL PROFESSIONALS WORKING WITH CHILDREN AND YOUNG PEOPLE IN THE STATUTORY AND VOLUNTARY SECTORS

Children may exhibit their emotional distress in a range of physical symptoms and behavioural changes. Their development may be delayed and speech problems appear particularly common. This can lead to a range of professionals in educational and health, therapeutic and counselling settings misinterpreting what is presented to them as illness, learning difficulties or a child protection concern when it may, in fact, result from living with domestic violence. There need to be routine procedures – protocols, as they are called in North America – in place in all child health, child protection, family support, youth offending, educational and youth settings for routine questioning of children and their parents or carers to find out whether there is anything wrong at home. If we are going to move in this direction, the professionals concerned need awareness and intervention training so that they do not inadvertently increase the dangers through unsafe practices or breaches of confidentiality.

At the same time, professionals need not to pathologize children but to recognize that they are resilient and that many recover from their problems as soon as they are away from the violence:

> Once he'd left that, to be honest, I didn't really need any help after that – once he'd left. From the first day, I actually did feel a lot better. (15-year-old mixed-race girl)

Many, though not all, talk about difficulties they had in sleeping or in concentrating at school ending when they feel safe. They feel more relaxed, they can see their friends again, and they are happier.

While children are living with domestic violence, their two key needs, they tell us, are safety and someone to talk to. Professionals could do far more than at present to offer help and a listening ear. For minority ethnic children, safety involves freedom from racial harassment and abuse, as well as from violence in the home.

Children are easily silenced by adults placing moral strictures on them, threatening them or simply ignoring them. They can maintain a family secret in the face of considerable anxiety and isolation. If questioned by professionals who show no awareness of domestic violence and who do not ask the right questions, or who are condescending or patronizing, they are likely to clam up or to go into mental overdrive to think of something to say that will not betray the true situation. South Asian children bear a particular burden of upholding family honour and pride by not talking about the abuse. They look to adult family members to condemn the abuser and support their mothers, thus creating conditions within which the abuse can be acknowledged without disloyalty. Where this does not happen, they feel caught in a trap that some abusers are well able to exploit so as to avoid taking the responsibility for the problems they have caused within the family. Minority ethnic workers who understand the additional cultural concerns are particularly well placed to help them and can be useful intermediaries for white workers in other settings. One mother reminded us that even specialist services have to ensure they extend appropriate help to all the ethnicities, religions and cultures represented in the local area.

What children and their mothers experience as appropriate forms of help to children focus around having someone to talk to who goes at the child's pace and who creates an environment, in a safe place, where the child can speak openly and confidentially about how they feel. While their mother needs to know that this work is being done, it is often helpful for a child to have their own space with the childworker, counsellor or other professional who is helping them, so that they can speak frankly without feeling disloyal or fearing that they will upset their mother by reopening old wounds.

Women also need to be able to confide in someone in confidence. One mother told us that she had had social workers, health visitors, community psychiatric nurses and others to her home, asking her questions about her partner, but always while he was present in the house so that she could not speak freely. Because he would not allow her out of the house, neither could she go elsewhere to ask for help. Professionals need to find ways to talk to women in confidence if they and their children are not to remain in danger and a great deal of public money wasted on ineffective interventions. A mixed-race family had been traced by the perpetrator, even after changing their name, in a way that could only have happened through a professional breach of confidentiality. This should perhaps lead to some caution in the current enthusiasm for 'sharing information' between agencies. A Bangladeshi mother had experienced similar breaches between professionals talking about her, as well as a patchy availability of interpreters, inadequate, inappropriate and insensitive services, and a tendency by professionals, throughout all this, to label her as the problem. The one or two workers she trusted were not in positions that were given respect by more senior colleagues.

There is a common belief amongst professionals that the overwhelming reason for intervening in domestic violence (as if ending present torment were not enough) is that children who live with domestic violence will 'grow up like it'. This is widely accepted in the North American literature, though UK social scientists are more sceptical (Morley and Mullender, 1994). It is particularly sad in our interview accounts to find both boys and their mothers worrying that they will turn out like their fathers: 'I'm frightened I'll be like that when I grow up ... I might grow up to be mean and nasty like my dad' (8-year-old mixed-race boy). Arguably, in our view, a child who is already reflecting at the age of 8 or 10 about what he will be like as a husband and father, and talking to his mother about it, is using his free will to ensure that he makes responsible and rational choices in his later conduct. Some were adamant that they would not become violent – 'It's one thing I ain't going to do when I get older' – and anxious to tell others not to: 'Don't be like that when you're older' (both quotes from a 13-year-old mixed-race boy). Also, the older boys in our in-depth sample, of all social and ethnic and backgrounds, were often highly protective of their mothers and siblings, and more than usually sensitive to the danger and unhappiness that abuse can inflict. They were determined not to repeat the same behaviour. One young man had been for help with anger management to ensure that he could take control of his own behaviour (not an ideal response for perpetrators – see Mullender and Burton, 2001 – but quite appropriate for this boy's circumstances). A 12-year-old girl saw looking forward to a family of their own as a chance for young people to know that 'One day, everything will be fine'. South Asian boys and girls were thinking carefully about how to have sufficient in common with their future spouses, within a preferential marriage system. The most worrying group of young men we encountered was not those who had lived with abuse but the general population of young men in schools, who appeared to get worse rather than better as they got older at understanding that men must take responsibility for their own behaviour and attitudes. It is here that we would want to see preventative efforts concentrated, and with all the young women who, not surprisingly, are growing up with low expectations of their future partners in this regard.

A WIDER DEBATE? FURTHER INFORMATION FOR THE GENERAL PUBLIC

Interestingly, we are able to pull out of the research some broader issues which would be worthy of debate beyond the normal policy and practice arenas. These include thought-provoking findings about young children's attitudes towards arguments, about talking to children, and about what children can do and want others to do when there is violence at home.

MESSAGES FOR ALL PARENTS

Younger children, we learn from the schools survey, find even non-violent arguments distressing, with younger girls in particular finding them emotionally upsetting. It might well help if parents explain what is wrong and that there are safe ways of disagreeing and clearing the air. Perhaps children know others whose parents have separated and think it might happen to them, or perhaps they simply find anger confusing and frightening. It is easy to think that anger is always destructive until you learn otherwise.

Indeed, there are messages throughout this research about the value of talking to children, including when things are going badly wrong at home, so as to help them understand and give them a voice in decision-making wherever possible. This is not the same as saying that children always know what is best for them – sometimes their inexperience and naïvety is all too apparent – but it does at least prevent the kinds of misunderstandings where parents think they are acting in children's best interests by hiding things that children already know, perpetuating situations that they cannot cope with, or leaving them in an ignorance that is more frightening than a sensitively explained truth.

MESSAGES FOR MOTHERS WHO ARE LIVING WITH ABUSE

Though women who leave as soon as violence starts are in a minority, we may perhaps hope that, if the message about the damage to children of staying in the abuse could be spread more widely and if effective help to women could be better funded and publicized, this number might grow. A wide-scale public debate, including in the social issues and women's media, might be of great assistance in helping mothers, families and communities to realize that early action is often best. Tied in with firmer intervention to challenge perpetrators to change their behaviour and more effective sanctions against them, this might provide a useful way forward. To the extent that they can do so safely and without causing renewed problems in their own lives, it can help if women who have been abused are willing to talk about it, both within their own circles of acquaintance (not least because this can make it easier for children to have other adults to talk to about what is happening at home) and more widely. The greater the public awareness and condemnation of domestic violence, the more other women will know they are not the only ones and that it is not their fault, so they need not feel ashamed, and most importantly that they deserve something better (Kelly, 1999).

There is also a key message to mothers who are living with domestic violence in the need children have to talk about what is happening, to understand it better, and to be consulted about major decisions such as whether to leave or stay. It is completely understandable that women want to protect their children from the truth but we are able to state that many children already know far more than their parents realize and that they are only keeping quiet about it because they sense this is what is expected. Children told us they were not too young to understand, as adults seemed to think, and that they had a great many unanswered questions that 'niggled' their minds, such as why their mother had become bad-tempered and seemed to lash out at everything. Children and young people can benefit greatly from a more open and honest discussion, with age-appropriate explanations at their own pace in answer to questions they pose. Many children are already doing what they can to protect, help and support their mothers. Opening up a dialogue with them would bring this to the fore, and would often facilitate a combined effort to find safety and a new happiness together.

MESSAGES FOR ALL CHILDREN

Children are important to one another as well as to their families and communities. They can provide each other, at school and at home, with emotional support and sometimes with practical help. We know that children may also want to help their mothers when they are being hurt and there may well be safe ways of doing this, as well as of helping brothers and sisters.

It is good to talk to concerned adults who can help make sense of difficult and troubling events. Sometimes this has to be done carefully, and to someone you can really trust, so as to avoid spreading gossip – for example in South Asian families. It is especially difficult if you think something should be done but your mother is not ready to take that step. Can you talk to her about this?

Schools could do more to help children learn how to avoid conflict with their peers and in family relationships, now and in the future. This is something that you and other children might want to ask for. Other professionals are there, in a range of settings, to try and help children who are feeling unhappy and frightened but they do not always ask the right questions. It may be worth finding out whether they can be trusted with information they do not necessarily know how to ask for. You know more about your own life than they do, though they owe it to you to learn more about domestic violence. Once other people start to know what has been happening at home, talk to them about the help you need.

It is understandable to have 'gone a bit off men' (12-year-old white girl) after living with domestic violence. However, vowing never to get married is not enough to avoid problems in your own life, as some young people appear to think, because violence can also happen between people who live together. As a 14-year-old South Asian boy explained in his interview, a successful relationship is about having something in common, trust and friendship. This is possible whoever finds your partner, you or your family, provided there is love and care involved in choosing the right person. Marriage also involves respecting the other person and finding non-violent ways to resolve disagreements.

CONCLUSION

Children do not think that they or other children should have to live with domestic violence. Yet at least six children in our small qualitative survey still did not feel safe and a third of the majority who did only felt safe so long as they were not found. This is a shocking indictment of our continuing failure to tackle the behaviour of perpetrators, despite a decade of rhetoric. It is a dreadful thing not to be able to guarantee a child safety, not from a context of war or unrest but from just one man who has held sway in a household where he has typically committed repeated criminal acts and has thus given the authorities ample opportunity to intervene and control him. Children are waiting for us to catch up with their generally very clear understanding that men who abuse are selfish and unreasonable, that they are responsible for their own behaviour, and that it is unfair when others are made to pay with their health, happiness and quality of life – and sometimes with everything they own or hold dear.

Whilst policy and practice in the UK have begun to be aware of the frequently adverse impact of domestic violence on children, our research reveals that we are still not listening to children sufficiently or ensuring that they have someone to talk to who can understand and help them. For many this will be their mothers and there is much that could be done quite quickly to help mothers better meet their children's needs by feeling confident about opening up communication with them at an earlier stage rather than trying to protect them through silence.

There are messages in the research, too, for every voluntary and statutory agency that works with children and their mothers during, and in the aftermath of, domestic violence. Some of these are lessons we should already have learnt from other areas of practice, such as the need to listen to children, to hear what they are saying, to ask sensitive questions that will help them tell us what is really wrong, and to go at their own pace. Where children receive this kind of help, they value it highly. Family, friends and specialist domestic violence services remain the main sources of such assistance at present. Statutory agencies are not yet getting it right for children but there is no magical unknown preventing them from doing so. A little child-centredness can go a long way, as can understanding the key role in a child's life of his or her non-abusing parent and of the help that she may need in ensuring that both she and her children can be safe. Above all, we need to recognize the life-threatening danger that abusive men pose, before and after separation, and to do more to end the damage they cause in children's lives.

After a decade of raising awareness of the impact of domestic violence on children, let us hope that the next era can be one of listening to children more effectively in deciding what to do about it. May there never be another 17-year-old girl who can say to us of their whole childhood: 'I had no one to talk to.' And if an 11-year-old boy trustingly says to us: 'Adults can sort it out', we owe it to him to make sure his words come true.

NOTE

1. The Family Law Act 1996 s.52 and Schedule 6 amended s.38 and s.44 of the Children Act 1989. Where an emergency protection order or interim care order is being applied for, or is in place, the local authority may also apply for an order to remove the suspected abuser from the family home where the child lives, to prevent him from entering the home, and/or to exclude him from the area round about (with a power of arrest if required). This interim arrangement (pending other civil or criminal justice remedies being used to exclude or deal with the abuser) is designed to prevent significant harm to the child, as an alternative to removing the child from the home. It can only be used if someone living in the family home consents to the exclusion and is available to care for the child.

Appendix   Children's Advice to Other Children about Coping with Domestic Violence

Start making friends. Children need friends and need each other. If it hurts you, you have to change again. (8-year-old mixed-race boy)

All the interviewees in the qualitative stage of our research had experienced domestic violence, although in almost all cases they were no longer living with the violence and had been able to reflect upon their experiences. Thus their views may be particularly helpful to other young people still living in abusive situations. During the study we specifically asked children and young people what advice they would like us to pass on to other children as a result of their experiences and expertise on the issue. The children and young people we interviewed took on board the question in a committed way and offered passionately felt advice for us to pass on to other children. With a sense of solidarity, they often expressed themselves strongly, maintaining an urgent eye contact. They frequently prefaced their advice with such statements as 'You must tell the other children', 'Make sure that they know' and 'It's really important that you tell them'. While many of the points raised repeat issues that have already been discussed as coping strategies in Chapter 5, we have tried to respect the views of our informants by conveying as much as possible of the advice they have offered in their own words, as an example of children's expertise in their own issues. Points are also repeated here from other chapters in order that the list can 'stand alone' in its own right, independent of other parts of the book on how children cope.

ADVICE FROM CHILDREN TO OTHER CHILDREN ABOUT USEFUL FRAMES OF MIND TO ADOPT

Children and young people had useful general advice to offer on how to deal with their experiences on an overall, psychological level:

- Sit down, think about what's going on, keep a level head. Try and compose yourself because, once you stop and think, your mind arranges itself and you know what to do.
- Write down your thoughts and feelings.

- Try to ignore it and keep yourself busy, play with toys or watch TV, occupy yourself.
- Try and think happy thoughts.
- Stick together, help each other. You can get help from your mum or relatives. I suppose to try and get on with your life and not let it dominate everything.
- Be brave.
- Stay calm.
- Don't get hysterical.
- Tell the children to just calm down, try to relax and cuddle their toys.

SUPPORTING YOUR MOTHER AND SIBLINGS

One of the major areas of advice that children had for other children concerned their mothers – the need to offer them support and assistance and also to value their support and love; similarly, advice often featured supporting and helping siblings:

- Help your mother be strong.
- Give your mum advice because sometimes she can't think straight.
- Have lots of cuddles with your mum and brothers and sisters.
- Talk to your brothers and sisters.
- Get lots of reassurance and love from your mother.
- If you are a child, think what your mum is going through.
- Stick to your mum.

GETTING ADULTS OR OLDER CHILDREN TO TAKE RESPONSIBILITY

Additionally, some of the strongest advice to emerge from the interviews was for children to tell someone and to get an adult to take responsibility. As discussed previously, many of the children were clear that adults, not children, should sort the problem out:

- Tell a grown-up. Find someone and tell them.
- Tell your grandma or family.
- Get older brothers and sisters and your relations to help.
- Children need to tell an adult. Adults can sort it out.
- Younger children – try and tell an older sister, your mother. Always be with someone.
- If you have older sisters and brothers, talk to them about it so they can help sort it out.

WHO TO ASK FOR HELP?

As regards who to tell, the children interviewed had much useful advice for other children. The best person to tell, apart from adults in the family, was generally thought to be the police or someone in authority. As noted previously, however, children recognized that it could be difficult to call the police and it would sometimes be better to get another adult to do it. Also, some minority ethnic children warned about possible racism from agencies and the need to be careful about involving the 'white' authorities.

AGENCIES THAT ARE TRUSTED AND CULTURALLY SENSITIVE

- Teenagers – tell teachers, social services, adults whom you can trust in case something happens.
- Phone an agency. Tell someone. Agencies need to make sure they understand about our family and religion and they don't take things the wrong way.

THE POLICE

- Get an adult to go to the police on your behalf.
- Phone the police and then they'll come in a couple of days and take him away.

EDUCATION

- Talk to teachers and get them to help you.

CHILDLINE

- Phone outside agencies, or ChildLine.
- I phoned ChildLine twice, just to talk to them really. It's just nice to have someone you don't know who you can put all your bits and pieces to ... It's easier to talk to a stranger sometimes because you can let your real feelings out. You don't have to worry what they may think of you.

HAVING PLANS FOR KEEPING SAFE

Another piece of essential advice that children wished to pass on was to plan to be safe and to stay safe:

- Don't hesitate to get out of the house.
- Run out into the street or the garden.
- You need a safe place to hide yourself until the shouting and fighting stops.
- Put the light on to see what is going on at night and to feel safe.
- Put a bed against the door.
- Round up the other children and take them off into another room.
- Have plans for where to go and how to get away. (This interviewee had undertaken safety planning with a children's worker in a refuge).
- Get help to get away.

HAVING SOMEWHERE SAFE TO GO

- Someone to go and stay with until it's sorted out.
- Get out as soon as there's an argument. Even just go to the park or to the nearest relative so that things don't escalate.
- Make sure you are safe, have safe places to go to or other places to stay at, preferably with people you trust.
- Move somewhere safe so you know it's not going to happen again.
- Leave home with your mum and brothers and sisters and go to a refuge.

A refuge was generally regarded positively as a helpful place to go, and one where there might be supportive child workers. Some Asian children felt that general refuges were unsuitable and that specialist Asian refuges would be better places for Asian children and young people to escape to.

- The children will need a refuge or place of safety.
- Someone to trust, a nice environment – homely – that will raise their confidence.
- More refuges, not English refuges, they are not suitable for Asian children. They don't understand the Asian way of life so they are not helpful.
- The child care workers in the refuge will help you and believe in you.

NOT INTERVENING DIRECTLY

Almost all the children and young people advised other children not to intervene as it might result in getting hurt:

- Stay out of the argument, keep safe.
- You need a room to be where you can't see or hear as much. You will know about it [the violence] but this will make it easier.
- If you are in the house, STAY OUT OF THE WAY.

THE NEED TO TELL YOUR PARENTS HOW YOU FEEL

- Tell your parents about it and how it makes you feel, don't keep it bottled up.
- Tell them they should be looking after you instead of fighting with each other. Tell your parents you should be the most important things to them in the world rather than fighting.
- Tell those who are shouting to stop it and tell you they are sorry.

THE NEED TO TALK WITH AND CONFIDE IN SOMEONE

On a general level, apart from asking an adult to take responsibility for the situation, or asking agencies to help, almost all the children advised others to confide in someone informally in order to share and lessen the load, rather than keeping it inside them. This piece of advice to other children was repeated often in the interviews:

- Talk to people. Don't take it too seriously. Don't think that the world is going to end. Don't just think of all the bad things all the time.
- Stick together with your mum and your brothers and sisters. Be a team! You can help each other.

THE NEED TO BUILD SELF-ESTEEM AND CONFIDENCE AND TO SPEAK ABOUT FEELINGS

Children also had good advice to offer about the emotional needs of children experiencing domestic violence and the need to build self-esteem, confidence and self-respect:

- Someone to make them feel good about themselves and make them feel it wasn't their fault.
- Take them out somewhere and that would make them feel easier and better about it.
- Say their feelings.

THE NEED TO HAVE CUDDLY TOYS FOR YOUNGER CHILDREN AND TO TAKE POSSESSIONS IF YOU LEAVE

Many children brought up the importance of and need for cuddly toys as reassurance. The very good advice was offered that if you are going to leave home to go to a refuge or other alternative accommodation it is a good idea to have a familiar and loved toy or possession with you and also to try to take your own clothes:

- You need cuddly toys and possessions.
- Have cuddly toys and start cuddling them.
- Have your own toys and belongings if you have to leave home to make the change easier.
- Children need clothes so they can move quickly.
- Keep books and read them [to occupy yourself].

WHAT CHILDREN WHO ARE NOW SAFE SAY TO OTHER CHILDREN WHO ARE STILL LIVING WITH DOMESTIC VIOLENCE

These points are derived from a group interview with children of varying ages, ethnic and cultural backgrounds and of both sexes:

- Hide when it's happening.
- Cuddle up with your brothers and sisters.
- Try not to listen.
- Get support from someone if you can, someone you trust. Tell someone if you can.
- Go to friends' houses or to relatives.
- Your nan might be able to help.
- Tell your teacher.
- If there is no one to help, try not to get in too much of a state about it.
- Keep going.
- Some children like to keep it a secret and hide it.
- It's OK to hide it but you need to be sure you feel OK about that and not torn apart with worry.
- Tell them not to argue and hit each other.
- Don't try and intervene to stop it.
- Remember that it is not because of you.
- It's not children's fault.
- Try the police if it gets really bad. Get a grown-up to phone them if you don't feel able to. But remember, the police can be more trouble than they are worth. If you are going to call the police, good to have talked about it with your mum first (another time beforehand).
- Social workers might help sometimes.
- Refuges are OK. The child workers are good for helping. Consult the child workers – don't be shy, that is their job and they know about what children feel.
- Give your mum advice because sometimes she can't think straight.
- Help your mum and your brothers and sisters.
- Get a big dog!!
- Try not to turn out the same way.
- When you're bigger, you can read books and stuff.

- When you're bigger, you can watch things on TV about it.
- Programmes like *EastEnders* already have it on.
- Talk with other children who know about it – like in a refuge.

WHAT THEY SAY TO MOTHERS EXPERIENCING ABUSE

- Go to the police. Don't put up with it.
- It won't get any better, even though you think it will.
- Get out as soon as you can.
- Don't wait.
- Go to a refuge. They'll help you there.
- Try and make a new life — you can do it.
- Don't see him again.
- Don't go back to him.
- Try and be strong.
- If you have a relationship, have your own house because you can be safe then.
- Talk to us more about it.

A FINAL WORD

The evidence of our study was that children who have witnessed domestic violence want to be listened to, taken seriously and involved in the decision-making process. They want support, understanding and reassurance, to be in safety with their mothers, and to have their own belongings, friends and support structures around them. Wide-ranging coping strategies used by children and young people include helping their mothers deal with the practical and emotional impacts of the violence, intervening directly or getting help, calling the police, and taking responsibility for looking after younger siblings, protecting them and keeping them away from the violence. There seemed to be little variation as regards ways of coping, either in terms of age or sex. Nor were there clear differences on the basis of ethnicity, although children from many minority ethnic families were more likely to seek help from other members of the family, and their coping was adversely affected where there were fears that their communities would be rejecting and official agencies might be racist or non-comprehending.

Notable, also, was the way in which several older children (both boys and girls) described how they had chosen to support their mothers and had taken on sometimes greatly increased responsibility for helping and advising them and their siblings and for seeking help and advice. Freedom from fear and the opportunity to form better relationships with their mothers were notable gains for many of the children who had previously lived with violence and abuse, and such relationships facilitated effective coping strategies. Children who have lived with domestic violence were shown in the study to be able to talk about and cope with their experiences and understandings if the context is right. Their tenacity and resilience are key resources for agencies to work with and their comprehensive advice to other children is a rich source of assistance and help.

The final word of advice lies perhaps with the moving words of a young boy who had established a successful new life with his mother and brother after many years of extreme abuse and trauma:

> This is what you must tell the children. Tell them this. This is really important. If you can, persuade your mum to leave. If you're in a difficult situation and you feel you can't get out of it, this is what you need to do. *Tell someone.* Doesn't matter what's happening. *Tell someone.* The adults should deal with it, not you. Get it sorted out and get out if you can. We've gained so much strength by being far away. If you do leave, tell yourself you're safe now. You're safe. Keep telling yourself this. Build your confidence. Hopefully you can become stronger and more confident in such situations. Get stronger. You can do it.
>
> That's really important and that's what I want you to tell other young people. (14-year-old white boy)

Bibliography

Abraham, M. (1999) 'Sexual abuse in South Asian immigrant marriages', *Violence Against Women*, 5 (6): 591–618.

Abrahams, C. (1994) *The Hidden Victims: Children and Domestic Violence*. London: NCH Action for Children.

Advisory Board on Family Law, Children Act Sub-committee (2001a) *Guidelines for Good Practice on Parental Contact in Cases where there is Domestic Violence*. London: Family Policy Division, Lord Chancellor's Department.

Advisory Board on Family Law, Children Act Sub-committee (2001b) *Making Contact Work*. London: Family Policy Division, Lord Chancellor's Department.

Ahmad, B. (1990) *Black Perspectives on Social Work*. Birmingham: Venture.

Ahmed, S. (1986) 'Cultural racism in work with Asian women and girls', in S. Ahmed, J. Cheetham and J. Small (eds), *Social Work with Black Children and their Families*. London: Batsford.

Alcott, A. and Potter, E. (eds) (1993) *Feminist Epistemologies*. London: Routledge.

Alderson, P. (1995) *Listening to Children: Children, Ethics and Social Research*. Barkingside: Barnardo's.

Alderson, P. (2000) 'Children as researchers: the effects of participation rights on research methodology', in P. Christensen and A. James, *Research with Children: Perspectives and Practices*. London: Falmer.

Alderson, P. and Montgomery, J. (1996) *Health Care Choices: Making Decisions with Children*. London: Institute for Public Policy Research.

Amos, V. and Parmar, P. (1984) 'Challenging imperial feminisms', *Feminist Review*, 17: 3–20.

Anderson, K.L. and Umberson, D. (2001) 'Gendering violence: masculinity and power in men's accounts of domestic violence', *Gender and Society*, 15 (3): 358–80.

Anthias, F. and Yuval-Davis, N. (1992) *Racialised Boundaries: Race, Nation, Gender and Class and the Anti-Racist Struggle*. London: Routledge.

Anwar, M. (1998) *Between Cultures: Continuity and Change in the Lives of Young Asians*, London: Routledge.

Archard, D. (1993) *Children, Rights and Childhood*. London: Routledge.

Ariès, P. (1979) *Centuries of Childhood*. Harmondsworth: Peregrine.

Azmi, S. (1997) 'Professionalism and social diversity', in R. Hugman, M. Peelo and K. Soothill (eds), *Concepts of Care: Developments in Health and Social Welfare*. London: Edward Arnold.

Backett, K. (1987) 'The negotiation of fatherhood', in C. Lewis and M. O'Brien, *Reassessing Fatherhood*. London: Sage.

Baldry, S. and Kemmis, J. (1998) 'What is it like to be looked after by a local authority?' (research note), *British Journal of Social Work*. 28: 129–36.

Ball, M. (1990) *Children's Workers in Women's Aid Refuges: a Report on the Experience of Nine Refuges in England*. London: National Council of Voluntary Child Care Organisations.

Barford, R. (1993) *Children's Views of Child Protection Social Work*. Norwich: University of East Anglia, Social Work Monograph 120.

Berens, H. (2000) 'Children's experiences with violence in the family brought into the open', paper presented at Violence in the Family: Plan of Action for the 21st Century, Nicosia, Cyprus, 26–30 November.

Beresford, B. (1997) *Personal Accounts: Involving Disabled Children in Research.* London: The Stationery Office.

Bertoia, C.E. and Drakich, J. (1995) 'The fathers' rights movement: contradictions in rhetoric and practice', in W. Marsiglio, (ed.), *Fatherhood: Contemporary Theory, Research and Social Policy.* Beverley Hills, CA: Sage.

Bewley, S., Friend, J. and Mezey, G. (eds) (1997) *Violence against Women.* Royal College of Obstetricians and Gynaecologists Press.

Bhachu, P. (1996) 'The multiple landscapes of transnational Asian women in the diaspora', in V. Amit-Talai and C. Knowles (eds), *Resituating Identities: the Politics of Race, Ethnicity and Culture.* Toronto: Broadview Press.

Bhopal, K. (1997) *Gender, Race and Patriarchy: a Study of South Asian Women.* Aldershot: Ashgate.

Bilinkoff, J. (1995) 'Empowering battered women as mothers', in E. Peled, P.G. Jaffe and J.L. Edleson (1995), *Ending the Cycle of Violence: Community Responses to Children of Battered Women.* Thousand Oaks, CA: Sage.

BMA (British Medical Association) (1998) *Domestic Violence: a Health Care Issue?* London: BMA.

Borland, M., Laybourn, A., Hill, M. and Brown, J. (1998) *Middle Childhood: the Perspectives of Children and Parents.* London: Jessica Kingsley.

Boushel, M., Fawcett, M. and Selwyn, J. (2000) *Focus on Early Childhood: Principles and Realities.* Oxford: Blackwell.

Brah, A.S. (1992a) 'Diversity, difference and differentiation', in J. Donald and A. Rattansi (eds), *'Race', Culture and Difference.* London: Sage.

Brah, A. (1992b) 'Women of South Asian Origin in Britain', in A. Rattansi and R. Skellington (eds), *Racism and Anti-Racism: Inequalities, Opportunities and Policies.* London: Sage.

Bray, M. (1997) *Sexual Abuse – The Child's Voice: Poppies on the Rubbish Heap.* London: Jessica Kingsley. (First published in 1991 by Canongate Press.)

Bridge Child Care Consultancy Service (1991) *Sukina: An Evaluation of the Circumstances Leading to her Death.* London: Bridge Child Care Consultancy Service.

Broad, B. (1997) *Young People Leaving Care: Life after the Children Act 1989.* London: Jessica Kingsley.

Bronstein, P. and Cowan, C. (eds) (1998) *Fatherhood Today: Men's Changing Role in the Family.* New York: John Wiley and Sons.

Bruckner, M. (2001) 'Reflections on the reproduction and transformation of gender differences among women in the shelter movement in Germany', *Violence Against Women,* 7 (7), 760–78.

Burgess, A. (1997) *Fatherhood Reclaimed.* London: Verso.

Burgess, A. and Ruxton, S. (undated) *Men and Their Children: Proposals for Public Policy.* London: Institute for Public Policy Research.

Burghes, L., Clarke, L. and Cronin, N. (1997) *Fathers and Fatherhood in Britain.* London: Family Policy Studies Centre.

Burton, S. and Kitzinger, J. with Kelly, L. and Regan, L. (1998) *Young People's Attitudes Towards Violence, Sex and Relationships: A Survey and Focus Group Study.* Edinburgh: Zero Tolerance Charitable Trust.

Burton, S., Regan, L. and Kelly, L. (1999) *Supporting Women and Challenging Men.* Bristol: Policy Press.

Butler, I. and Williamson, H. (1994) *Children Speak: Children, Trauma and Social Work.* Harlow: Longman.

Buunk, B. (1986) 'Husbands' jealousy', in R.A. Lewis and R.E. Salt (eds), *Men in Families.* Beverley Hills, CA: Sage.

Cambridge, A. (1996) 'The beauty of valuing black cultures', in V. Amit-Talai and C. Knowles (eds), *Resituating Identities: the Politics of Race, Ethnicity and Culture.* Toronto: Broadview Press.

ChildLine (1996) *Talking with Children about Child Abuse: ChildLine's First Ten Years.* London: ChildLine.

ChildLine (undated) *Unhappy Families: Unhappy Children.* London: ChildLine.

Children's Subcommittee of the London Coordinating Committee to End Woman Abuse, London, Ontario (1994) 'Make a difference: how to respond to child witnesses of woman abuse', in A. Mullender and R. Morley (eds), *Children Living with Domestic Violence: Putting Men's Abuse of Women on the Child Care Agenda.* London: Whiting and Birch.

Choudry, S. (1996) *Pakistani Women's Experience of Domestic Violence in Great Britain.* Home Office Research Study No.43. London: HMSO.

Cicchetti, D., Rogosch, F., Lynch, M. and Hot, D. (1993) 'Resilience in maltreated children: processes leading to adaptive outcomes', *Development and Psychopathology*, 5: 629–47.

Connor, M.E. (1986) 'Some parenting attitudes of young black fathers', in R.A. Lewis and R.E. Salt (eds), (1986) *Men in Families.* Beverly Hills, CA: Sage.

Costley, D. (2000) 'Collecting the views of young people with moderate learning difficulties' in A. Lewis and G. Lindsay (eds), *Researching Children's Perspectives.* Buckingham: Open University Press.

Culp, R., Watkins, R., Lawrence, H., Letts, D., Kelly, H. and Rice, M. (1991) 'Maltreated children's language and speech development: abused, neglected and abused and neglected', *First Language*, 11: 377–89.

Daly, K.J. (1995) 'Reshaping fatherhood: finding the models', in W. Marsiglio (ed.), *Fatherhood: Contemporary Theory, Research and Social Policy.* Beverley Hills, CA: Sage.

Daniel, B. and Taylor, J. (2001) *Engaging with Fathers: Practice Issues for Health and Social Care.* London: Jessica Kingsley.

Davies, G., Lyon, E. and Monti-Catania, E. (1998) *Safety Planning with Battered Women: Complex Lives/Difficult Choices.* Thousand Oaks, CA: Sage.

Davis, J., Watson, N. and Cunningham-Burley, S. (2000) 'Learning the lives of disabled children', in P. Christensen and A. James (eds), *Research with Children: Perspectives and Practices.* London: Falmer.

Debbonaire, T. (1994) 'Work with children in Women's Aid refuges and after', in A. Mullender and R. Morley (eds), *Children Living with Domestic Violence: Putting Men's Abuse of Women on the Child Care Agenda.* London: Whiting and Birch.

Department of the Environment, Transport and the Regions, Department of Health, Department of Social Security, HM Treasury, Home Office, Scottish Office, Welsh Office and Women's Unit (1998) *Supporting People: A New Policy and Funding Framework for Support Services. Produced for the Inter-Departmental Review of Funding for Supported Accomodation.* London: Department of Social Security.

Department of Health, Home Office and Department for Education and Employment (1999) *Working Together to Safeguard Children: a Guide to Interagency Working to Safeguard and Promote the Welfare of Children.* London: The Stationery Office.

Dobash, R.E., Dobash, R.P., Cavanagh, K. and Lewis, R. (2000) *Changing Violent Men.* London: Sage.

Dullea, K. and Mullender, A. (1999) 'Evaluation and empowerment', in I. Shaw and J. Lishman (eds), *Evaluation and Social Work Practice.* London: Sage.

Dunn, J. and Deater-Deckard, K. (2001) *Children's Views of their Changing Families.* York: York Publishing Services.

Dupont-Smith, C. (1995) 'Aboriginal Canadian children who witness and live with violence', in E. Peled, P.G. Jaffe and J.L. Edleson (1995), *Ending the Cycle of Violence: Community Responses to Children of Battered Women.* Thousand Oaks, CA: Sage.

Edleson, J. (1999) 'Children's witnessing of adult domestic violence', *Journal of Interpersonal Violence*, 14: 839–70.

Edwards, S.S.M. (1989) *Policing 'Domestic' Violence: Women, the Law and the State.* London: Sage.

Emery, R. (1982) 'Interparental conflict and children of discord and divorce', *Psychological Bulletin*, 92: 310–30.

Epstein, C. and Keep, G. (1995) 'What children tell ChildLine about domestic violence' in A. Saunders with C. Epstein, G. Keep and T. Debbonaire, *'It Hurts Me Too':*

Children's Experiences of Domestic Violence and Refuge Life. Bristol: Women's Aid Federation of England /ChildLine /NISW.

Eriksson, M. and Hester, M. (2001) 'Violent men as "good enough" fathers: a look at England and Sweden', *Violence Against Women,* 7 (7): 779–98.

Fantuzzo, J.W. and Lindquist, C.U. (1989) 'The effects of observing conjugal violence on children: a review and analysis of research methodology', *Journal of Family Violence,* 4 (1): 77–94.

Farmer, E. and Owen, M. (1995) *Child Protection Practice: Private Risks and Public Remedies.* London: HMSO.

Farmer, E. and Owen, M. (1996) 'Child protection practice: private risks and public remedies: decision making, intervention and outcome', in Department of Health, *Child Protection: Messages from Research.* London, HMSO.

Farmer, E. and Owen, M. (1998) 'Gender and the child protection process', *British Journal of Social Work,* 28 (4): 545–64.

Fawcett, B., Featherstone, B., Hearn, J. and Tofts, C. (1996) *Violence and Gender Relations: Theories and Interventions.* London: Sage.

Fonagy, P., Steele, M., Steele, H., Higgitt, A. and Mayer, L. (1994) 'The theory and practice of resilience (Emmanual Miller Memorial Lecture 1992)', *Journal of Child Psychology and Psychiatry,* 35 (2): 231–58.

France, A., Bendelow, G. and Williams, S. (2000) 'A "risky" business: researching the health beliefs of children and young people', in A. Lewis and G. Lindsay (eds), *Researching Children's Perspectives.* Buckingham: Open University Press.

Franklin, B. (ed.) (1995) *The Handbook of Children's Rights: Comparative Policy and Practice.* London: Routledge.

Furstenberg, F.F. (1988) 'Good dads, bad dads: two faces of fatherhood', in A.J. Cherlin (ed.), *The Changing American Family and Public Policy.* Washington D.C.: Urban Institute.

Garmezy, N. (1983) 'Stressors of childhood' in N. Garmezy and M. Rutter (eds), *Stress, Coping and Development in Children.* New York: McGraw-Hill.

Garmezy, N. and Rutter, M. (1983) *Stress, Coping and Development in Children.* New York: McGraw-Hill.

Ghate, D. and Daniels, A. (1997) *Talking About My Generation: a Survey of 8–15-Year Olds Growing Up in the 1990s.* London: NSPCC.

Ghuman, P.A.S. (1994) *Coping with Two Cultures: a Study of British-Asian and Indo-Canadian Adolescents.* Clevedon: Multilingual Matters.

Ghuman, P.A.S (1999) *Asian Adolescents in the West.* Leicester: BPS Books.

Glaser, B. and Strauss, A. (1967) *The Discovery of Grounded Theory.* New York: Aldine de Gruyter.

Goddard, C. and Hiller, P. (1993) 'Child sexual abuse: assault in a violent context', *Australian Journal of Social Issues,* 28 (1): 20–33.

Gondolf, E. (1988) 'The effects of batterer counselling on shelter outcome', *Journal of Interpersonal Violence,* 3: 275–89.

Gordon, D., Loughran, F. and Parker, R. (2000) *Disabled Children in Britain: a Reanalysis of the OPCS Disability Surveys.* London: The Stationery Office.

Green, M. (1976) *Goodbye Father.* London: Routledge and Kegan Paul.

Grotberg, E. (1997) 'The International Resilience Project', in M. John (ed.), *A Charge against Society: the Child's Right to Protection.* London: Jessica Kingsley.

Gupta, S.R. (1999) 'Forged by fire: Indian-American women reflect on their marriages, divorces and on rebuilding lives', in S.R. Gupta (ed.), *Emerging Voices: South Asian American Women Redefine Self, Family and Community.* London: Sage.

Guru, S. (1986) 'An Asian women's refuge', in S. Ahmed, J. Cheetham and J. Small (eds), *Social Work with Black Children and their Families.* London: Batsford.

Hagemann-White, C. (2001) 'European research on the prevalence of violence against women', *Violence Against Women,* 7 (7): 732–59.

Hague, G., Aris, R. and Mullender, A. (forthcoming) *Women Survivors of Domestic Violence: User Views, Accountability and Involvement.* London: Routledge.

Hague, G., Kelly, L., Malos, E. and Mullender, A. with Debonnaire, T. (1996) *Children, Domestic Violence and Refuges: a Study of Needs and Responses.* Bristol: Women's Aid Federation of England.

Hague, G., Kelly, L. and Mullender, A. (2001) *Challenging Violence Against Women: The Canadian Experience.* Bristol: Policy Press.

Hague, G. and Malos, E. (1998) *Domestic Violence: Action for Change*, 2nd edn. Cheltenham: New Clarion Press.

Hague, G., Mullender, A., Kelly, L., Malos, E. with Debbonaire, T. (2000) 'Unsung innovations: the history of work with children in UK domestic violence refuges', in J. Hanmer and C. Itzen (eds), *Home Truths about Domestic Violence.* London: Routledge.

Hague, G. and Wilson, C. (1996) *The Silenced Pain: Domestic Violence, 1945–1970.* Bristol: Policy Press.

Hall, L. and Lloyd, S. (1993) *Surviving Childhood Sexual Abuse.* 2nd edn. London: Falmer Press.

Hall, S. (1992) 'New ethnicities', in J. Donald and A. Rattansi (eds), *'Race', Culture and Difference.* London: Sage.

Hanmer, J. and Maynard, M. (eds), (1987) *Women, Violence and Social Control.* Basingstoke: Macmillan.

Harding, S. (ed.) (1987) *Feminism and Methodology*, Milton Keynes: Open University Press.

Harne, L. (forthcoming) 'Violence, power and the meaning of fatherhood in issues of child contact'. Bristol: School for Policy Studies, University of Bristol. Unpublished PhD thesis.

Harrison, C., Humphreys, C. and Aris, R. (forthcoming) *Thresholds to Safety? Identifying Thresholds for Arrangements for Child Contact in the Context of Domestic Violence and Child Welfare Concerns.* London: Lord Chancellor's Department.

Healey, K. and Smith, C. with O'Sullivan, C. (1998) *Batterer Intervention Program Approaches and Criminal Justice Strategies.* Washington, DC: National Institute of Justice. (*http://www.ncjrs.org/txtfiles/168638.txt*)

Hearn, J. (1996) 'Men's violence to known women – men's accounts and men's policy developments', in B. Fawcett, B. Featherstone, J. Hearn, J. and C. Tofts, *Violence and Gender Relations: Theories and Interventions.* London: Sage.

Hearn, J. (1998) *The Violences of Men.* London: Sage.

Hendessi, M. (1997) *Voices of Children Witnessing Domestic Violence: A Form of Child Abuse.* Coventry, Coventry City Council Domestic Violence Focus Group.

Hester, M. and Pearson, C. (1998) *From Periphery to Centre: Domestic Violence in Work with Abused Children.* Bristol: The Policy Press.

Hester, M., Pearson, C. and Harwin, N. (2000) *Making an Impact: Children and Domestic Violence – a Reader.* London: Jessica Kingsley.

Hester, M. and Radford, L. (1996) *Domestic Violence and Child Contact in England and Denmark.* Bristol: Policy Press.

Higgins, G. (1994) 'Children's accounts', in A. Mullender and R. Morley (eds), *Children Living with Domestic Violence: Putting Men's Abuse of Women on the Child Care Agenda.* London: Whiting and Birch.

Hill, M. (1997a) 'Participatory research with children', *Child and Family Social Work*, 2 (3): 171–83.

Hill, M. (1997b) 'What children and young people say they want from social services', *Research, Policy and Planning.* 15 (3): 17–27.

Hood, S., Kelley, P. and Mayall, B. (1996) 'Children as research subjects: a risky enterprise', *Children in Society,* 10 (2): 117–28.

hooks, b. (1991) *Yearning: Race, Gender and Cultural Politics.* London: Turnaround.

Hooper, C.-A. (1992) *Mothers Surviving Child Sexual Abuse.* London: Routledge.

Horrocks, C. and Milner, J. (1999) 'The residential home as serial step-family: acknowledging quasi-sibling relationships in local authority residential care', in A. Mullender (ed.), *We Are Family: Sibling Relationships in Placement and Beyond.* London: British Agencies for Adoption and Fostering.

Humphreys, C. (1999) 'The judicial alienation syndrome: failures to respond to post-separation violence', *Family Law*, 313: 513–15.

Humphreys, C. (2000a) *Social Work, Domestic Violence and Child Protection: Challenging Practice.* Bristol: The Policy Press.

Humphreys, C. (2000b) *Starting Over: a Consultation with Women and Children from Milton Keynes Women's Aid Outreach Project.* Bristol: Women's Aid Publications.

Humphreys, C., Atkar, S. and Baldwin, N. (1999) 'Discrimination in child protection work: recurring themes in work with Asian families', *Child and Family Social Work*, 4: 283–91.

Humphreys, C., Hester, M., Hague, G., Mullender, A., Abrahams, H. and Lowe, P. (2000) *From Good Intentions to Good Practice: Working with Families where there is Domestic Violence.* Bristol, Policy Press.

Humphreys, C. and Mullender, A. (2000) *Children and Domestic Violence: a Research Overview of the Impact on Children.* Dartington, Totnes: Research in Practice.

Imam, U.F. (1994) 'Asian children and domestic violence', in A. Mullender and R. Morley (eds), *Children Living with Domestic Violence: Putting Men's Abuse of Women on the Child Care Agenda.* London, Whiting and Birch.

Imam, U.F. (1999a) 'Black workers as mediators and interpreters', in S. Banks (ed.), *Ethical Issues in Youth Work.* London: Routledge.

Imam, U.F. (1999b) 'South Asian young women's experiences of violence and abuse', in J. Pritchard and H. Kemshall (eds), *Good Practice in Working with Violence.* London: Jessica Kingsley.

Jaffe, P.G., Wolfe, D.A. and Wilson, S.K. (1990) *Children of Battered Women.* Newbury Park, CA: Sage.

Jaffe, P., Wolfe, D., Wilson, S. and Zak, L. (1985) 'Critical issues in the assessment of children's adjustment to witnessing family violence', *Canada's Mental Health*, 33 (4): 14–19.

James, A., Jenks, C. and Prout, A. (1998) *Theorizing Childhood.* Cambridge: Polity Press.

James, A. and Prout, A. (1997) 'Introduction', in A. James and A. Prout, (eds), *Constructing and Reconstructing Childhood: Contemporary Issues in the Sociological Study of Childhood.* London: Falmer.

Jenks, C. (1982) *The Sociology of Childhood.* London: Batsford.

Joseph Rowntree Foundation Findings (1996a) SP 99, *Exploring Variations in Men's Family Roles.* York: Joseph Rowntree Foundation. (Also at http//www.jrf.org.uk)

Joseph Rowntree Foundation Findings (1996b) SP 106, *Parenting in the 1990s.* York: Joseph Rowntree Foundation. (Also at <http//www.jrf.org.uk>)

Joseph Rowntree Foundation Findings (1997) SP 120, *Fathers and Fatherhood in Britain.* York: Joseph Rowntree Foundation. (Also at <http//www.jrf.org.uk>)

Joseph Rowntree Foundation Findings (1999) REF 659, *Fathers, Work and Family Life.* York: Joseph Rowntree Foundation. (Also at <http//www.jrf.org.uk>)

Jouriles, E., Murphy, C. and O'Leary, K. (1989) 'Interspousal marital discord and child problems', *Journal of Consulting and Clinical Psychiatry*, 57: 453–5.

Kashani, J. and Allan, W. (1998) *The Impact of Family Violence on Children and Adolescents.* London: Sage.

Katsikas, S., Petretic-Jackson, P. and Knowles, E. (1996) 'Long-term sequelae of childhood maltreatment: an attachment theory perspective', paper presented at the Annual Meeting of the Association for the Advancement of Behaviour Therapy, New York. November.

Kelly, L. (1988) *Surviving Sexual Violence.* Cambridge: Polity Press.

Kelly, L. (1994a) *Evaluation of Hammersmith and Fulham Women's Aid Childwork Project, June 1993 – June 1994*, London: University of North London, Child Abuse Studies Unit.

Kelly, L. (1994b) 'The interconnectedness of domestic violence and child abuse: challenges for research, policy and practice', in A. Mullender and R. Morley (eds), *Children Living with Domestic Violence: Putting Men's Abuse of Women on the Child Care Agenda*. London: Whiting and Birch.

Kelly, L. (1996) 'Tensions and possibilities: enhancing informal responses to domestic violence', in J.L. Edleson and Z.C. Eisikovits (eds), *Future Interventions with Battered Women and their Families*. Thousand Oaks, CA: Sage.

Kelly, L. (1998) *Violence Against Women: a Briefing Document*. London: British Council.

Kelly, L. (1999) *Domestic Violence Matters: an Evaluation of a Development Project*. Home Office Research Study no. 193. London: Home Office.

Kelly, L. (2000) 'Ending the silence: challenging the tolerance: developing community responses in the prevention of domestic violence', keynote paper presented at Violence in the Family: Plan of Action for the 21st Century, Nicosia, Cyprus, 26–30 November.

Kelly, L. and Mullender, A. (2000) 'Complexities and contradictions: living with domestic violence and the UN Convention on Children's Rights', *The International Journal of Children's Rights*, 8: 229–41.

Kelly, L. and Radford, J. (1998) 'Sexual violence against women and girls: an approach to an international overview', in R.E. Dobash and R.P. Dobash (eds), *Rethinking Violence against Women*. London: Sage.

Kelly, L., Regan, L. and Burton, S. (1991) *An Exploratory Study of the Prevalence of Sexual Abuse in a Sample of 1244 16–21-Year-Olds. Final report to the ESRC*. London: Child Abuse Studies Unit, Polytechnic of North London.

Kirby, P. (1999) *Involving Young Researchers: How to Enable Young People to Design and Conduct Research*. York: YPS for Joseph Rowntree Foundation in association with Save the Children.

Knowles, C. and Mercer, S. (1990) 'Feminism and anti-racism', in A. Cambridge and S. Feuchtwang (eds), *Anti-Racist Strategies*. Aldershot: Avebury.

Koss, M. and Burkhart, B. (1989) 'A conceptual analysis of rape victimization: long-term effects and implications for treatment', *Psychology of Women Quarterly*, 13: 27–40.

Lansdown, G. (1994) 'Children's rights', in B. Mayall (ed.), *Children's Childhoods Observed and Experienced*. London: Falmer.

Levendosky, A., Lynch, S. and Graham-Bermann, S. (2000) 'Mothers perceptions of the impact of woman abuse on their parenting', *Violence Against Women*, 6 (3): 238–47.

Lewis, C. and O'Brien, M. (1987) *Reassessing Fatherhood*. London: Sage.

Lewis, R.A. and Salt, R.E. (eds), (1986) *Men in Families*. Beverly Hills, CA: Sage.

Loosley, S. (1994) 'Women's Community House children's program: a model in perspective', in A. Mullender and R. Morley (eds), *Children Living with Domestic Violence: Putting Men's Abuse of Women on the Child Care Agenda*. London: Whiting and Birch.

Loosley, S., Bentley, L., Lehmann, P., Marshall, L., Rabenstein, S. and Sudermann, M. (1997) *Group Treatment for Children who Witness Woman Abuse: a Manual for Practitioners*. London, Ontario: Community Group Treatment Program for Child Witnesses of Woman Abuse, Children's Aid Society of London and Middlesex.

Lupton, D. and Barclay, L. (1997) *Constructing Fatherhood: Discourses and Experiences*. London: Sage.

MacInnes, E. (2001) 'Public policy and private lives: single mothers, social policy and gendered violence', unpublished PhD thesis, Flinders University, Adelaide, Australia.

MacLeod, M. (1996) *Talking with Children about Child Abuse*. London: ChildLine.

Mahon, A., Glendinning, C., Clarke, K. and Craig, G. (1996) 'Researching children: methods and ethics', *Children and Society*. 10 (2): 145–54.

Mama, A. (1989) *The Hidden Struggle: Statutory and Voluntary Sector Responses to Violence against Black Women*. London: London Race and Housing Unit/Runnymede Trust. (Reissued by Whiting and Birch in 1996)

Marchant, R., Jones, M., Julyan, A. and Giles, A. (1999) *'Listening on all Channels': Consulting with Disabled Children and Young People*. Brighton: Triangle (Unit 310, 91

Western Road, Brighton BN1 2NW) and East Sussex County Council Social Services Department.

Marchant, R., Jones, M. and Martyn, M. (1999) *'Tomorrow I Go': What You Told Us about Dorset Road.* Brighton: Triangle and East Sussex County Council Social Services Department.

Marsiglio, W. (ed.) (1995) *Fatherhood: Contemporary Theory, Research and Social Policy.* Beverley Hills, CA: Sage.

Mathews, D.J. (1995) 'Parenting groups for men who batter', in E. Peled, P.G. Jaffe and J.L. Edleson, *Ending the Cycle of Violence: Community Responses to Children of Battered Women.* Thousand Oaks, CA: Sage.

Mauthner, M. (1997) 'Methodological aspects of collecting data from children: lessons from three research projects', *Children and Society,* 11: 16–28.

Mayall, B. (1994) 'Introduction', in B. Mayall (ed.), *Children's Childhoods Observed and Experienced.* London: Falmer.

Mayall, B. (1996) *Children, Health and the Social Order.* Buckingham: Open University Press.

Maynard, M. and Purvis, J. (1994) *Researching Women's Lives from a Feminist Perspective.* London: Taylor and Francis.

McAdoo, J.L. (1986) 'Black fathers' relationships with their preschool children and the children's development of ethnic identity', in R.A. Lewis and R.E. Salt (eds) (1986) *Men in Families.* Beverly Hills, CA: Sage.

McAdoo, J.L. (1988) 'Changing perspectives on the role of black fathers', in P. Bronstein and C.P. Cowan, *Fatherhood Today: Men's Changing Role in the Family.* New York: John Wiley and Sons.

McGee, C. (1997) 'Children's experiences of domestic violence', *Child and Family Social Work,* 2 (1): 13–23.

McGee, C. (2000) *Childhood Experiences of Domestic Violence.* London: Jessica Kingsley.

McGregor, R., Pullar, A. and Cundall, D. (1994) 'Silent at school: selective mutism and abuse', *Archives of Disease in Childhood,* 70: 540–1.

McIntosh, I. and Griffin, A. (undated) *Teenage Tolerance: The Hidden Lives of Young Irish People.* Dublin, Ireland: Women's Aid.

McWilliams, M. and McKiernan, J. (1993) *Bringing It Out in the Open: Domestic Violence in Northern Ireland.* Belfast: HMSO.

Mezey, G.C. (1997) 'Domestic violence and pregnancy', *British Journal of Obstetrics and Gynaaecology.* 104, May: 528–31.

Ministerial Implementation Advisory Committee (1997) *It's My Choice – A Focus on Women and Children: Implementation Plan for Reform of SAAP-funded Domestic Violence Services in South Australiaa.* Adelaide, Australia: Ministerial Implementation Advisory Committee.

Mirande, A. (1988) 'Chicano fathers: traditional perceptions and current realities', in P. Bronstein and C.P. Cowan, *Fatherhood Today: Men's Changing Role in the Family.* New York: John Wiley and Sons.

Mirrlees-Black, C. (1999) *Domestic Violence: Findings from a New British Crime Survey Self-Complete Questionnaire.* Home Office Research Study no. 191. London: Home Office.

Modood, T., Berthoud, R., Lakey, J., Nazroo, J., Smith, P., Virdee, S. and Beishon, S. (1997) *Ethnic Minorities in Britain: Diversity and Disadvantage: the Fourth National Survey of Ethnic Minorities.* London: Policy Studies Institute.

Mooney, J. (1994) *The Hidden Figure: Domestic Violence in North London.* London: London Borough of Islington, Police and Crime Prevention Unit (or from Middlesex University, Centre for Criminology).

Mooney, J. (2000) *Gender, Violence and the Social Order.* Basingstoke: Macmillan.

Morgan, D. (1987) 'Masculinity and violence', in J. Hanmer and M. Maynard, *Women, Violence and Social Control.* Basingstoke: Macmillan.

Morgan, P. (1995) *Farewell to the Family? Public Policy and Family Breakdown.* London: IEA, Health and Welfare Unit.

Morley, R. and Mullender, A. (1994) 'Domestic violence and children: what do we know from research?', in A. Mullender and R. Morley (eds), *Children Living with Domestic Violence: Putting Men's Abuse of Women on the Child Care Agenda.* London: Whiting and Birch.

Morran, D. and Wilson, M. (1997) *Men who are Violent to Women: a Groupwork Practice Manual.* Lyme Regis: Russell House Publishing.

Morris, J. (1998) *Don't Leave Us Out: Involving Disabled Children and Young People with Communication Impairments.* York: Joseph Rowntree Foundation.

Morrow, V. (1998) *Understanding Families: Children's Perspectives.* London: National Children's Bureau in association with the Joseph Rowntree Foundation.

Morrow, V. and Richards, M. (1996) 'The ethics of social research with children: an overview', *Children in Society,* 10 (2): 90–105.

Mullender, A. (1994a) 'Groups for child witnesses of woman abuse: learning from North America', in A. Mullender and R. Morley (eds), *Children Living with Domestic Violence: Putting Men's Abuse of Women on the Child Care Agenda.* London: Whiting and Birch.

Mullender, A. (1994b) 'School-based work: education for prevention', in A. Mullender and R. Morley (eds), *Children Living with Domestic Violence: Putting Men's Abuse of Women on the Child Care Agenda,* London: Whiting and Birch.

Mullender, A. (1996) *Rethinking Domestic Violence: the Social Work and Probation Response.* London: Routledge.

Mullender, A. (ed.) (1999) *We Are Family: Sibling Relationships in Placement and Beyond.* London: British Agencies for Adoption and Fostering.

Mullender, A. (2001) 'Meeting the needs of children', in J. Taylor Browne (ed.), '*What Works in Reducing Domestic Violence? A Comprehensive Guide for Professionals.* London: Whiting and Birch.

Mullender, A. and Burton, S. (2001) 'Dealing with perpetrators', in J. Taylor Browne (ed.), *What Works in Reducing Domestic Violence? A Comprehensive Guide for Professionals.* London: Whiting and Birch.

Mullender, A., Debbonaire, T., Hague, G., Kelly, L. and Malos, E. (1998) 'Working with children in women's refuges', *Child and Family Social Work,* 3: 87–98.

Mullender, A. and Humphreys, C. with Saunders, H. (1998) *Domestic Violence and Child Abuse: Policy and Practice Issues for Local Authorities and Other Agencies. Briefing Paper from the Task Group on Domestic Violence and Child Abuse.* London: Local Government Association.

Mullender, A., Kelly, L., Hague, G., Malos, E. and Imam, U. (2000) *Children's Needs, Coping Strategies and Understanding of Woman Abuse: End of Award Report Submitted to the ESRC (Award no: L 129 25 1037).* Coventry: University of Warwick, Department of Social Policy and Social Work. (Now obtainable from: School of Health and Social Studies, University of Warwick, Coventry CV4 7AL.)

Mullender, A. and Morley, R. (1993) *Preventing Domestic Violence to Women.* Policy Research Group, Crime Prevention Unit Series, Paper 48, London: HMSO.

Mullender, A. and Morley, R. (eds) (1994) *Children Living with Domestic Violence: Putting Men's Abuse of Women on the Child Care Agenda.* London: Whiting and Birch.

National Crime Prevention (2000) *Young People and Domestic Violence: National Research on Young People's Attitudes and Experiences of Domestic Violence. Fact Sheet.* Canberra, ACT, Australia: Attorney General's Office.

National Family and Parenting Institute (2000) *Teenagers' Attitudes to Parenting: a Survey of Young People's Experiences of Being Parented, and their Views on How to Bring up Children.* London: NFPI.

NCH Action for Children (undated) *NCH Action for Children Family Forum Findings: a Briefing and Discussion Paper.* London: NCH Action for Children.

NCH Action for Children in partnership with the Newcomen Centre and the Bloomfield Clinic at Guy's Hospital (1994) *Children's Evaluations of the Professional Response to Child Sexual Abuse*. London: NCH Action for Children.

Neighbors, B., Forehand, R. and McVicar, D. (1993) 'Resilient adolescents and inter-parental conflict', *American Journal. of Orthopsychiatry*, 63: 462–71.

Nicolson, P. (1993) 'Motherhood and women's lives', in D. Richardson and V. Robinson (eds), *Introducing Women's Studies*. Basingstoke: Macmillan.

Nielsen, J. (ed.) (1990) *Feminist Research Methods: Exemplary Readings in the Social Sciences*. Boulder: Westview Press.

NUD*IST Version 4. Quality Solutions and Research Pty Ltd.

OPCS (Office of Population Censuses and Surveys) (1993) *1991 Census: Ethnic Group and Country of Birth (Great Britain)*, London: HMSO.

O'Hagan, K. and Dillenburger, K. (1995) *The Abuse of Women within Child care Work*. Buckingham: Open University Press.

O'Hara, M. (1994) 'Child deaths in contexts of domestic violence', in A. Mullender and R. Morley (eds), *Children Living with Domestic Violence: Putting Men's Abuse of Women on the Child Care Agenda*. London: Whiting and Birch.

O'Kane, C. (2000) 'The development of participatory techniques', in P. Christensen and A. James (eds), *Research with Children: Perspectives and Practices*. London: Falmer.

Owen, D. (1993) *Ethnic Minorities in Britain: Age and Gender Structure*. NEMDA 1991 Census Statistical Paper no. 2. Coventry: University of Warwick, Centre for Research in Ethnic Relations.

Pahl, R. (2001) *On Friendship*. Cambridge: Polity.

Parkinson, P. and Humphreys, C. (1998) 'Children who witness domestic violence: the implications for child protection', *Child and Family Law Quarterly*, 10 (2): 147–60.

Parmar, P. (1982) 'Gender, race and class: Asian women in resistance', in Centre for Contemporary Cultural Studies, *The Empire Strikes Back*. London: Hutchinson.

Parsons, C. (forthcoming) *Violence Against Women Programme: Evaluation of the Education and Awareness Projects. Final Report*. London: Home Office.

Peach, C. (1992) 'Estimating the growth of the Bangladeshi community', *New Community*, 16 (7): 481–93.

Peled, E. and Edleson, J. (1995) 'Process and outcome in small groups for children of battered women', in E. Peled, P.G. Jaffe and J.L. Edleson (eds), *Ending the Cycle of Violence: Community Responses to Children of Battered Women*. Thousand Oaks, CA: Sage.

Peled, E. and Edleson, J. (1999) 'Barriers to children's domestic violence counselling', *Families in Society*, 80: 578–86.

Peled, E., Jaffe, P.G. and Edleson, J.L. (1995) *Ending the Cycle of Violence: Community Responses to Children of Battered Women*. Thousand Oaks, CA: Sage.

Pence, E. and Paymar, M. (1990) *Power and Control: Tactics of Men who Batter. An Educational Curriculum*. Revised edition. Duluth, MN: Minnesota Program Development Inc. (206 West Fourth Street, Duluth, MN 55806, USA).

Pence, E. and Paymar, M. (1996) *Education Groups for Men who Batter: the Duluth Model*. 2nd edn, New York: Springer. (1st edn, 1993)

Price, E.L., Byers, E.S., Sears, H.A., Whelan, J. and Saint-Pierre, M. (2000) *Dating Violence among New Brunswick Adolescents: a Summary of two Studies*. Fredericton, New Brunswick, Canada: University of New Brunswick Department of Psychology and Muriel Fergusson Centre for Family Violence Research. Research Paper Series, no. 2.

Pryke, J. and Thomas, M. (1998) *Domestic Violence and Social Work*. Aldershot: Ashgate.

Qureshi, T., Berridge, D., Wenman, H. (2000) *Where to Turn? Family Support for South Asian Communities: a Case Study*, London: National Children's Bureau and Joseph Rowntree Foundation.

Qvortrup, J. (1994) 'Childhood matters: an introduction', in J. Qvortrup, M. Bardy, G. Sgritta and H. Wintersberger (eds), *Childhood Matters: Social Theory, Practice and Politics*. Aldershot: Avebury.

Qvortrup, J., Bardy, M., Sgritta, G. and Wintersberger, H. (eds), (1994) *Childhood Matters: Social Theory, Practice and Politics*. Aldershot: Avebury.

Radford, L. and Hester, M. (2001) 'Overcoming mother blaming? Future directions for research on mothering and domestic violence', in S. Graham-Bermann and J.L. Edleson (eds), *Intimate Violence in the Lives of Children: the Future of Research, Intervention and Social Policy*. Washington, DC: American Psychological Association.

Radford, L., Sayer, S. and AMICA (1999) *Unreasonable Fears? Child Contact in the Context of Domestic Violence: a Survey of Mothers' Perceptions of Harm*. Bristol: Women's Aid Publications.

Rai, D. and Thiara, R. (1997) *Re-defining Spaces: the Needs of Black Women and Children in Refuge Support Services and Black Workers in Women's Aid*. Bristol: Women's Aid.

Regan, L. and Kelly, L. (2001) *Teenage Tolerance: Exploring Young People's Experience and Responses to Violence and Abuse*. Dublin: Dublin Women's Aid.

Reid-Howie Associates (1996) *The Zero Tolerance Campaign in Fife: Post Campaign Research, September-November 1996*. Edinburgh: Reid-Howie Associates.

Respect (The National Association for Domestic Violence Perpetrator Programmes and Associated Support Services) (2000) 'Statement of Principles and Minimum Standards of Practice', revised version. Master [*sic*] copy held by DVIP, PO Box 2838, London W6 9ZE.

Rich, A. (1985) *Of Woman Born*. London: Virago.

Richardson, D. (1993) 'Sexuality and male dominance', in D. Richardson and V. Robinson (eds), Introducing Women's Studies. Basingstoke: Macmillan.

Roberts, H. and Sachdev, D. (eds) (1996) *Young People's Social Attitudes. Having Their Say: the Views of 12–19-Year-Olds*. Barkingside: Barnardo's.

Robinson, L. (1995) *Psychology for Social Workers: Black Perspectives*. London: Routledge.

Rubin, A. (2000) 'Standards for rigor in qualitative enquiry', *Research on Social Work Practice*. 10 (2): 173–8.

Rutter, M. (1983) 'Stress, coping and development in children: some issues and some questions', in N. Garmezy and M. Rutter (eds), *Stress, Coping and Development in Children*. New York: McGraw-Hill.

Rutter, M. (1985) 'Resilience in the face of adversity: protective factors and resistance to psychiatric disorder', *British Journal of Psychiatry*, 147: 598–611.

Ryan, W. (1971) *Blaming the Victim*. London: Orbach and Chambers.

Saunders, A. with Epstein, C., Keep, G. and Debbonaire, T. (1995) *'It Hurts Me Too': Children's Experiences of Domestic Violence and Refuge Life*. Bristol: Women's Aid Federation of England/London: ChildLine/London: NISW.

Saunders, H. (2001) *Making Contact Worse? Report of a National Survey of Domestic Violence Refuge Services into the Enforcement of Contact Orders*. Bristol: Women's Aid Federation of England.

Schwartz, M.D. (2000) 'Methodological issues in the use of survey data for measuring and characterising violence against women', *Violence Against Women*, 6 (8): 815–38.

Scott, J. (2000) 'Children as respondents: the challenge for quantitative methods', in P. Christensen and A. James (eds), *Research with Children: Perspectives and Practices*. London: Falmer.

Scottish Women's Aid (1999) *Young People Say. Volume One: Young People Speak Out about Domestic Violence*. Edinburgh: Scottish Women's Aid.

Seith, C. (2001) 'Security matters: domestic violence and public social services', *Violence Against Women*, 7 (7): 799–820.

Shah, R. (1995) *The Silent Minority: Children with Disabilities in Asian Families*. London: National Children's Bureau.

Shemmings, D. (1996) *Involving Children in Child Protection Conferences*. Norwich: University of East Anglia, Social Work Monographs no. 152.

Shepard, M. and Pence, E. (1999) *Coordinating Community Responses to Domestic Violence*. Thousand Oaks, CA: Sage.

Silva, E.B. and Smart, C. (eds), (1999) *The New Family?* London: Sage.

Simpson, B., McCarthy, P., Walker, J. (1995) *Being There. Fathers After Divorce: an Exploration of Post-Divorce Fathering*. Newcastle upon Tyne: University of Newcastle upon Tyne, Relate Centre for Family Studies.

Smith, P.B. and Bond, M.H. (1993) *Social Psychology across Cultures: Analysis and Perspectives*. London: Harvester Wheatsheaf.

Smith, P.B. and Schwartz, S.H. (1997) 'Values', in J.W. Berry, M.H. Segall and C. Kagitcibasi (eds), *Handbook of Cross-Cultural Psychology: Social Behaviour and Applications*. Boston: Allyn and Bacon.

SNAP (Scottish Needs Assessment Programme) Women's Health Network (1997) *Domestic Violence*. Glasgow: Scottish Forum for Public Health Medicine.

Solberg, A. (1996) 'The challenge in child research: from "being" to "doing"', in J. Brannen and M. O'Brien (eds), *Children in Families: Research and Policy*. London: Falmer.

Somerville, J. (2000) *Feminism and the Family: Politics and Society in the UK and the USA*. Basingstoke: Macmillan.

Southall Black Sisters (1993) *Domestic Violence and Asian Women. A Collection of Reports and Briefings*. London: Southall Black Sisters.

Stagg, V., Willis, G.D. and Howell, M. (1989) 'Psychopathology in early childhood witnesses of family violence', *Topics in Early Childhood Special Education*, 9: 73–87.

Stanko, E., Crisp, D., Hale, C. and Lucraft, H. (1998) *Counting the Costs: Estimating the Impact of Domestic Violence in the London Borough of Hackney*. Swindon: Crime Concern.

Stanley, L. and Wise, S. (1993) *Breaking Out Again: Feminist Ontology and Epistemology*. London: Routledge.

Stopes-Roe, M. and Cochrane, R. (1990) *Citizens of this Country: the Asian British*. Clevedon: Multilingual Matters.

Students from Sarah Bonnell and Brampton Manor Schools facilitated by Anne Crisp and others (1997) *'Challenging Newham – Young Power': Views Expressed by Young People at the Conference*. London: London Borough of Newham.

Sturge, C. and Glaser, D. (2000) 'Contact and domestic violence: the experts' court report', *Family Law*, September: 615–29.

Thomas, C. and Beckford, V. with Lowe, N. and Murch, M. (1999) *Adopted Children Speaking*. London: British Agencies for Adoption and Fostering.

Thomas, M. and Lebacq, M. (2000) *Beyond Fear: Social Work Practice and Domestic Violence*. Sheffield: University of Sheffield, Joint Unit for Social Services Research.

Thomas, N. and O'Kane, C. (1998) 'The ethics of participatory research with children', *Children and Society*. 12: 336–48.

Thomas, N. and O'Kane, C. (2000) 'Discovering what children think: connections between research and practice', *British Journal of Social Work*, 30: 819–35.

Thompson, A. (2000) 'A police/mental health collaboration for children who witness violence', paper presented at Violence in the Family: Plan of Action for the 21st Century, Nicosia, Cyprus, 26–30 November.

Thompson, N. (1993) *Anti-Discriminatory Practice*. Basingstoke: Macmillan.

Thorne-Finch, R. (1992) *Ending the Silence: the Origins and Treatment of Male Violence Against Women*. Toronto, Canada: University of Toronto Press.

Triandis, H.C. (1995) *Individualism and Collectivism*. Boulder, CO: Westview.

Utting, D. (1995) *Family and Parenthood: Supporting Families, Preventing Breakdown*. York: Joseph Rowntree Foundation.

Valentine, L. and Feinauer, L. (1993) 'Resilience factors associated with female survivors of child sexual abuse', *American Journal of Family Therapy*, 21: 216–24.

Walby, S. and Myhill, A. (2001) 'New survey methodologies in researching violence against women', *British Journal of Criminology*, 41: 502–22.

Wallerstein, J.S. (1980) *Surviving the Breakup: How Children and Parents Cope with Divorce*. London: Grant McIntyre.

Wallerstein, J.S. (1989) *Second Chances*. London: Bantam.

Ward, L. (1997) *Seen and Heard: Involving Disabled Children and Young People in Research and Development Projects*. York: YPS for Joseph Rowntree Foundation.

Warin, J., Solomon, Y., Lewis, C. and Langford, W. (1999) *Fathers, Work and Family Life*. London: Family Policy Studies Centre.

Watt, N., David, J., Ladd, K. and Shames, S. (1995) 'The life course of psychological resilience: a phenomenological perspective on deflecting life's slings and arrows', *Journal of Primary Prevention*, 15: 209–46.

Westcott, H.L. and Davies, G.M. (1996) 'Sexually abused children's and young people's perspectives on investigative interviews', *British Journal of Social Work*, 26: 451–74.

Westra, B.L. and Martin, H.P. (1981) 'Children of battered women', *Maternal Child-Nursing Journal*. 7: 41–51.

Williams, O. (1994) 'Group work with African American men who batter: toward more ethnically sensitive practice', *Journal of Comparative Family Studies*, 25: 91–103.

Williams, O. (1999) 'African American men who batter: treatment considerations and community action', in J. Staples (ed.), *Black Family: Essays and Studies*, Boston: Wadsworth Press.

Williamson, H. and Butler, I. (1997) 'No one ever listens to us: interviewing children and young people', in C. Cloke and M. Davies, *Participation and Empowerment in Child Protection*. Chichester: John Wiley and Sons.

Willow, C. and Hyder, T. (1998) *'It Hurts You Inside': Children Talking about Smacking*. London: National Children's Bureau in association with Save the Children.

Wilson, A. (1978) *Finding a Voice*. London: Virago.

Wilson, M. and Daly, M. (1992) *Homicide*. New York: Aldine de Gruyter.

Wilson, M. and Daly, M. (1998) 'Lethal and nonlethal violence against wives and the evolutionary psychology of male sexual proprietariness', in R.E. Dobash and R.P. Dobash (eds), *Rethinking Violence against Women*. Thousand Oaks, CA: Sage.

Winnicott, D.W. (1964) *The Child, the Family and the Outside World*. Harmondsworth: Penguin.

Wolfe, D.A., Zak, L., Wilson, S. and Jaffe, P. (1986) 'Child witnesses to violence between parents: critical issues in behavioural and social adjustment', *Journal of Abnormal Child Psychology*, 14 (1): 95–104.

Women's Aid Federation of England (WAFE) (1997) *Women's Aid Federation Briefing Paper on Child Contact and Domestic Violence*. Bristol: WAFE.

Woolett, A., Marshall, H., Nicolson, P. and Dosanjh, N. (1994) 'Asian women's ethnic identity: the impact of gender and context in the accounts of women bringing up children in east London', in K. Bhavnani and A. Phoenix (eds), *Shifting Identities, Shifting Racisms: a Feminist and Psychology Reader*. London: Sage.

Worrall, S. (2000) *Young People as Researchers: a Learning Resource Pack*. London: Save the Children.

Young Researchers, The (Tolley, E., Girma, M., Stanton-Wharmby, A., Spate, A. and Milburn, J.) (1998) *Young Opinions: Great Ideas*. London: National Children's Bureau.

Index